Grains, Pasta & Pulses

by
THE EDITORS OF TIME-LIFE BOOKS

TIME-LIFE BOOKS·AMSTERDAM

TIME-LIFE BOOKS
EUROPEAN EDITOR: Kit van Tulleken
Design Director: Louis Klein
Photography Director: Pamela Marke
Chief of Research: Vanessa Kramer
Chief Sub-Editor: Ilse Gray

THE GOOD COOK
Series Editor: Alan Lothian
Series Co-ordinator: Liz Timothy
Head Designer: Rick Bowring

Editorial Staff for *Grains, Pasta & Pulses*
Text Editor: Gillian Boucher
Anthology Editors: Josephine Bacon, Liz Clasen
Writer: Thom Henvey
Researcher: Krystyna Davidson
Sub-Editors: Katie Lloyd, Sally Rowland
Permissions Researcher: Deborah Litton
Anthology Researcher: Margaret Hall
Design Assistants: Cherry Doyle, Adrian Saunders
Editorial Assistant: Molly Sutherland

EDITORIAL PRODUCTION FOR THE SERIES
Chief: Ellen Brush
Quality Control: Douglas Whitworth
Traffic Co-ordinators: Pat Boag, Helen Whitehorn
Picture Co-ordinators: Kate Cann, Philip Garner
Art Department: Julia West
Editorial Department: Debra Dick, Beverley Doe

THE EPIC OF FLIGHT
THE SEAFARERS
WORLD WAR II
THE GOOD COOK
THE TIME-LIFE ENCYCLOPAEDIA OF GARDENING
HUMAN BEHAVIOUR
THE GREAT CITIES
THE ART OF SEWING
THE OLD WEST
THE WORLD'S WILD PLACES
THE EMERGENCE OF MAN
LIFE LIBRARY OF PHOTOGRAPHY
THIS FABULOUS CENTURY
TIME-LIFE LIBRARY OF ART
FOODS OF THE WORLD
GREAT AGES OF MAN
LIFE SCIENCE LIBRARY
LIFE NATURE LIBRARY
YOUNG READERS LIBRARY
LIFE WORLD LIBRARY
THE TIME-LIFE BOOK OF BOATING
TECHNIQUES OF PHOTOGRAPHY
LIFE AT WAR
LIFE GOES TO THE MOVIES
BEST OF LIFE

Cover: A forkful of pasta is lifted from a generous helping of home-made noodles and meat sauce. Pressed against the bowl of a spoon to keep the pasta from slipping off, the fork is swivelled to wind the pasta round its prongs. The noodles were prepared from a flour and egg dough, kneaded, rolled out thinly and cut into ribbons with a pasta machine (*page 46*).

THE CHIEF CONSULTANT:
Richard Olney, an American, has lived and worked since 1951 in France, where he is a highly regarded authority on food and wine. He is the author of *The French Menu Cookbook* and the award-winning *Simple French Food,* and has contributed to numerous gastronomic magazines in France and the United States, including the influential journals *Cuisine et Vins de France* and *La Revue du Vin de France.* He has directed cooking courses in France and the United States and is a member of several distinguished gastronomic and oenological societies, including *L'Académie Internationale du Vin, La Confrérie des Chevaliers du Tastevin* and *La Commanderie du Bontemps de Médoc et des Graves.*

THE PHOTOGRAPHER:
Tom Belshaw was born near London and started his working career in films. He now has his own studio in London. He specializes in food and still-life photography, undertaking both editorial and advertising assignments.

THE INTERNATIONAL CONSULTANTS:
Great Britain: *Jane Grigson* was born in Gloucester and brought up in the north of England. She is a graduate of Cambridge University. Her first book on food, *Charcuterie and French Pork Cookery,* was published in 1967; since then, she has published a number of cookery books, including *Good Things, English Food* and *Jane Grigson Vegetable Book.* She became cookery correspondent for the colour magazine of the London *Observer* in 1968. *Alan Davidson* is the author of *Fish and Fish Dishes of Laos, Mediterranean Seafood* and *North Atlantic Seafood.* He is the founder of Prospect Books, which specializes in scholarly publications on food and cookery. *Jean Reynolds,* who prepared many of the dishes for the photographs in this volume, is an American from San Francisco. She trained as a cook in the kitchens of several of France's great restaurants. **France:** *Michel Lemonnier* was born in Normandy. He began contributing to the magazine *Cuisine et Vins de France* in 1960, and also writes for several other important French food and wine periodicals. The co-founder and vice president of the society *Les Amitiés Gastronomiques Internationales,* he is a frequent lecturer on wine, and a member of most of the vinicultural confraternities and academies in France. **Germany:** *Jochen Kuchenbecker* trained as a chef, but worked for 10 years as a food photographer in many European countries before opening his own restaurant in Hamburg. *Anne Brakemeier,* who also lives in Hamburg, has published articles on food and cooking in many German periodicals. She is the co-author of three cookery books. **Italy:** *Massimo Alberini* divides his time between Milan and Venice. He is a well-known food writer and journalist, with a particular interest in culinary history. Among his 14 books are *Storia del Pranzo all'Italiana, 4000 Anni a Tavola* and *100 Ricette Storiche.* **The Netherlands:** *Hugh Jans,* a resident of Amsterdam, has been translating cookery books and articles for more than 25 years. He has also published several books of his own, including *Bistro Koken* and *Sla, Slaatjes, Snacks,* and his recipes are published in many Dutch magazines. **The United States:** *Carol Cutler,* resident of Washington, DC, is the author of *Haute Cuisine for Your Heart's Delight* and the award-winning *The Six-Minute Soufflé and Other Culinary Delights.* A contributing editor of both *International Food and Wine* and *Working Woman* magazines, she frequently lectures about food and gives demonstrations of cooking techniques. *Julie Dannenbaum* has directed a cooking school in Philadelphia, Pa. for many years and is the author of two cookery books and numerous magazine articles. The late *José Wilson* was food editor of *House and Garden* magazine for 15 years and wrote many books on food and interior decoration.

Valuable help was given in the preparation of this volume by the following members of TIME-LIFE Books: *Maria Vincenza Aloisi, Joséphine du Brusle* (Paris); *Janny Hovinga* (Amsterdam); *Elisabeth Kraemer* (Bonn); *Ann Natanson* (Rome); *Bona Schmid, Maria Teresa Marenco* (Milan).

CONTENTS

Sustenance from the Store Cupboard

As humanity's basic foodstuff, the role of grains is undisputed. One need only contemplate a world without wheat or rice to be awed by our profound dependence on them. Yet, in the kitchen, grains are often treated with less care and imagination than other foods, simply because many people are unaware of their creative possibilities. Pulses too—the family of lentils, peas and beans that share grains' attribute of easy drying for storage—offer far more than many cooks realize. First, there are the many forms in which grains are available, from pearly whole rice to pasta, cornmeal and couscous; as for pulses, there are hundreds of varieties. Then, although boiling is fundamental to the cooking of grains, grain products and pulses, there are many variations in technique, with strikingly different results. Above all, these foods are bases for dishes of all sorts, combining gracefully with many other ingredients and supporting their character.

The first half of this book is designed to teach the principles behind the cooking of grains, pasta and pulses. The second half is an Anthology of recipes from 36 nations; in themselves, they provide ample variety but, as you gain confidence, you can use them as starting points from which to improvise your own dishes.

The most ancient of crops

The grasses that yield grains were almost certainly the first plants that mankind learned to cultivate. Before men became farmers, they had gathered wild grains along with berries and roots. About 10,000 years ago, men learned to return some of the grains to the earth to provide a future supply of food, instead of eating all the grains they had collected.

It may seem strange that such humble, weed-like plants as grasses should have ushered in the era of agriculture. In fact, the explanation probably lies precisely in the grasses' weed-like qualities: their ability to spring up from any odd patch of bare ground on which a grain has happened to fall. Men must have gathered wild grains, carried them home, accidentally dropped some near their dwellings—and later found, to their delight, that no longer need they journey to their source of nourishment: it had come to them. From that great discovery, it was only a small innovation for men deliberately to scatter grains on the ground.

The first farmers were fortunate that it was grass, rather than some other plant, which was thus domesticated. Grasses combine many qualities that were—and still are—extremely desirable in a crop. They take up little room, sending up stems ending in a crowded spike of nutrition-packed seeds. They mature in a few short months, and all of the grains ripen simultaneously. They are easily gathered and prepared for cooking, even using primitive equipment—a sickle to cut the ears from the stalks, a stick to loosen the individual grains and some sort of pestle and mortar to separate the inedible chaff from the grains. Best of all, grains are often dry enough when fully ripe or after brief parching in the sun to be stored for months without becoming mouldy; a good harvest ensures a year-round supply of food.

In spite of all these valuable properties, grains were demanding crops for the early farmers to produce. Success depended on weeding and irrigating the soil, choosing the best seed, timing the sowing and reaping, and designing the most efficient equipment. By contrast, roots such as yams—almost as ancient a crop as grains—are far less trouble: the farmer need only return broken sections of root to the ground to grow, and nature takes care of the rest. Yet perhaps the most valuable aspect of grain cultivation was, paradoxically, the very demands it made on human ingenuity: all the great early civilizations—in the Middle East, China and Central and South America—developed from communities that had responded intelligently to the problems, and become successful grain farmers.

The wealth of grains

Wheat and barley grew wild in great abundance in the Middle East 100 centuries ago, as they still do today. They were the first grains to be cultivated, and later became the staples of ancient Egyptian, Indian and Chinese cooks. Although ideally suited to the warm Mediterranean lands, they did less well in chillier, wetter regions. But oats, rye and buckwheat—this last not a grass, but a plant with a similar starchy grain—could withstand a harsher climate. They had grown as weeds among the wheat and barley and were eventually cultivated for their own sakes where wheat and barley were less successful. Nowadays they are widespread, although rye and buckwheat are more prominent in eastern European cooking, and oats much favoured in Scotland.

Wheat and barley grow as reluctantly in very dry, hot climates as in cold, damp ones. But millet can withstand hot, even desert-like conditions, and is an important staple in arid parts of Asia and Africa. Rice also tolerates great heat but, unlike millet, requires a humid climate. Most kinds of rice grow half submerged in fields inundated with water—paddy fields. Rice cultivation began in Asia; the Arabs introduced it to Spain in the Middle Ages and the Spaniards later brought it to Italy. Rice was introduced to South Carolina in the United States as early as 1685; by the 18th century Carolina rice was being exported to Europe.

Rice was by no means the first grain to be cultivated in the New World. Maize had been grown in both North and South America for millennia; indeed, the wild plant probably died out thousands of years ago. Maize has come to be dependent on humans for its renewal: unlike the seeds of other grains, which scatter and take root when ripe, maize kernels remain tightly attached to the cobs unless they are picked off and planted.

The American Indians ate another grain, called wild rice by early English settlers because it is cooked like rice and, like rice, it grows in marshy land. The Indians gathered the wild rice from boats, by flailing it so that much of the grain fell into the boat. Attempts to cultivate the grain, by growing it in paddies like ordinary rice, met many obstacles. Not all the grains ripened at once and the plants often succumbed to insects and disease. Although attempts at cultivation are now having more success, wild rice still poses severe agricultural problems.

The difficulties in obtaining wild rice make it a rare and expensive product—sadly, since for many people it is the most delicious grain of all, with an unforgettable full, nutty flavour. The truffle of the grain world, it can be mixed with a milder grain such as ordinary rice and still dominate a dish. One of the best ways of serving it is with game—the flavours of the wild plant and the untamed creature complement each other superbly.

On a more everyday level, cultivated rice is the grain with the greatest culinary potential; writing in the early years of this century, the French chef Auguste Escoffier pronounced firmly that "Rice is the best, the most nutritive and unquestionably the most widespread staple in the whole world." It is far more often eaten in whole form than the other grains—although usually without its brown outer coating.

A list of the cooking methods for rice—boiling, simmering and steaming—hardly sounds inspiring. But there are countless variations on these basic methods, leading to very different results. One technique, for example, is to cook rice very slowly in approximately its own volume of water to produce tender but dry grains; a more usual method is to simmer rice in twice its volume of liquid for a shorter time, yielding fluffier results. The grains can be coated in fat before simmering to make a pilaff, or boiled more vigorously and stirred during cooking to produce a sticky risotto. Any number of ingredients can be simmered with the rice, or added to it when it is cooked, to transform the grain from an accompaniment or garnish into an independent dish.

Of course, rice is not the only grain to offer the cook a tempting range of possibilities. Although wheat and rye are most often ground to flour for bread-making, and barley's chief use is in beer-making, all these cereals can be cooked whole, like rice, to yield succulent, intact grains. Wheat exists in other appealing guises, from the little balls of meal known as couscous, cooked by steaming above a savoury broth *(page 36)*, to the irregular fragments known as *burghul*—prepared by parboiling, parching and cracking the whole grain. But the form of wheat that has kindled more enthusiasm than any other is undoubtedly pasta.

The origins of pasta

People feel the need to ascribe a date and hour to the invention of pasta: long strings of spaghetti and noodles are such bizarre foods that it is hard to imagine them being developed accidentally. Yet that is probably what happened. A basic way of cooking ground grains is to boil them with water to make porridge. Dumplings—made by shaping a grain and water dough into balls before boiling—are only a short step from porridge. Once somebody had decided to flatten out the dumpling for quicker cooking, pasta had been invented. Pasta shapes are still sometimes made by pressing small lumps of dough with the thumbs *(page 49)*, although the more usual method is to roll the dough into a thin sheet and cut it into ribbons or noodles.

Pasta has a long pedigree in many cuisines, but it figures most prominently in those of China—where it is made from a variety of grain and bean flours—and Italy, where it is always prepared from wheat. There has been much speculation over the possibility that knowledge of pasta was transmitted between these countries by some early traveller. One story is that Marco Polo—the Venetian who in the 13th century journeyed overland to China and spent many years there—brought the secret of pasta back to his native Italy. In all likelihood, pasta has a far older history in Italy; a painted relief in an Etruscan tomb near Rome, from the third century B.C., shows a rolling pin, a pastry wheel and a table apparently used for mixing and rolling out dough.

Pasta fresh and dried

The word pasta is of course Italian—it means paste or dough—and, together with such words as macaroni and spaghetti, it reinforces the idea that pasta is an especially Italian food. But although Italy is the source of much of the Western world's commercial pasta, and has supplied the names for the various dried forms, it does not have the monopoly of home-made pasta, which is common throughout Europe. Each nation has its own name for the home-made variety, although these are sometimes related. Noodles in England, *nouilles* in France and *Nudeln* in Germany, for example, all derive from the Latin *nodellus*, a knot, because the skeins of pasta tend to get tangled on the plate.

Fresh pasta can be made from any kind of wheat flour and is usually moistened with eggs. The number of formulae is large—from an economical mixture of flour and water supplemented with a whole egg or two, to the luxurious version cited in 1907 by the French gastronome Ali-Bab in his *Gastronomie Pratique*, where 18 egg yolks and a little butter are recommended to moisten 500 g (1 lb) of flour. Such proportions, Ali-Bab claimed with justice, give "an absolutely exquisite noodle pasta of incomparable finesse". But any fresh egg pasta is a delicious dish, whether merely tossed with butter or used as the framework for a more elaborate preparation.

Commercial pasta is prepared from a special type of hard wheat known as durum wheat, which gives a strong, resilient dough. The basic equipment for mass-producing pasta shapes is a metal cylinder closed at the end by a metal disc or die perforated with many uniformly sized holes. The dough is put in the cylinder and forced by a piston through the die; the pasta emerges as spaghetti, macaroni or whatever other form is dictated by the shape of the holes. The piston was originally worked by human energy; gradually pasta-making became fully mechanized. Nowadays, it is a continuous process: water and semolina are poured steadily into the machine, the pasta emerges and is carried by conveyer belt to air-conditioned drying chambers.

Commercial dried pasta that contains egg suffers from comparison with fresh, home-made egg noodles. Commercial pasta made simply from flour and water, however, is a very attractive food in its own right. It is often formed into shapes, such as spaghetti, that are beyond the domestic cook and the fact that it is dried makes for convenience; it will keep for months—a standby that is rapidly transformed into a delicious dish.

Making the most of pulses

Pulses—lentils, peas and beans—share with grains and pasta the immensely useful capacity to be dried and stored for long periods. Unlike grains, which are only rarely eaten when underripe and green, pulses such as peas, broad beans and haricot beans are often eaten when they are fresh and tender. However, the season

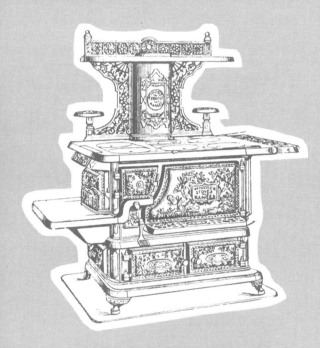

for fresh pulses is very short—only a few weeks—whereas dried pulses are available all year round. If a farmer intends his pulses for drying, he waits until the plant's leaves become yellow; by then, the peas or beans inside the pods will have lost water, and may be dry enough to be stored immediately without going mouldy; if not, a few days of exposure to sunshine or, in damper climates, a spell in a hopper where warm air is blown through them, will complete the drying process.

Pulses are usually stored and cooked in whole form; a few, such as chick peas and soya beans, may be available as a flour. Their diversity comes, not in the number of processed forms, but in the hundreds of varieties of pulse that exist. Those illustrated in this volume *(page 12)* are just a sample of what you may be able to buy. However, few pulses are native to Europe and many require a hot climate in order to flourish, so you will probably find that ethnic shops have the best selection.

Health-food shops are another good source of pulses. Although by no means the elixir of life, pulses are a very nourishing food, containing not only plenty of starch but also a high proportion of protein. Generally, pulses have been less important than grains as staples—partly because they are more demanding to farm, taking up more room than grains as they grow and requiring

more attention. In fact, a basic diet of grains supplemented with pulses makes splendid nutritional sense: most grains supply some elements of proteins that humans need in their diet, pulses supply the rest. Anybody who eats such dishes as couscous with chick peas *(page 36)* or rice with beans *(recipe, page 88)* with or without meat—has the basis of a well-balanced diet.

The basic way of cooking pulses is by gentle simmering; the results are likely to be hearty rather than elegant. For example, the most celebrated of pulse dishes, the cassoulet of south-western France *(page 82)* is a heavy, satisfying, rustic creation whose charm lies in its robust flavours and textures.

A cassoulet is a combination of haricot beans and different meats, pre-cooked, then layered and baked for hours until the dish has acquired a rich, thick crust. In the dish's land of origin, the choice of meats displays much local variation. According to the great chef Prosper Montagné, compiler of the *Larousse Gastronomique*, the cassoulet from the town of Castelnaudary contains pork of various sorts and often some preserved goose; the version from Carcassonne adds lamb and sometimes game; the one from Toulouse has a good deal of preserved goose and less of the other meats. In reality, of course, the cassoulet varies as much from cook to cook as from town to town; and, whatever the details of the composition, the combination of moist beans and meats with the thick crust is so devastatingly good as to bring the dish a reputation far beyond its native province.

Placing grains, pasta and pulses in a meal

When a porridge or a soup thick with beans was the only course for supper, structuring the meal caused no problems. At the other extreme, on the loaded tables of the wealthy in the Renaissance, a pasta dish might be just one of many tempting offerings. But as Western meals began to take their present two or three course shape, different countries took different approaches to the placement of such items in the menu. In Italy, a dish of pasta with a sauce, or a risotto, constitutes a first course, to be followed by meat and dessert. In France, buttered rice or noodles often appear as garnishes to a meat dish. In Chinese cooking, rice is served as the background for other dishes, while filled pasta shapes, such as *won ton (recipe, page 139),* may be served as a between-meal snack, a soup garnish or a main course.

But the way a dish is prepared also determines whether it is served as a first course, a second course or a garnish to another dish. The macaroni timbale on page 68, for example, is traditionally a first course; yet, if made on a large enough scale, it can easily become a main course. And a garnish of buttered noodles can be elevated to a worthy first course by the addition of grated cheese and some chopped ham or a few herbs.

Grain, pasta and pulse dishes are equally versatile when it comes to choosing a wine. Few of the dishes in this book are rarified enough to demand the finest wines as accompaniments, and it is worth remembering that no wine tastes its best in the company of very spicy or garlicky foods (with these, beer may be a better choice). But most dishes in the demonstrations that follow and in the Anthology will go well with any full-flavoured dry white or red wine. In fact, there is as much scope for experiment with wines as there is with dishes; making your own judgments and discoveries is a large part of the enjoyment.

Grains in Their Many Guises

All grains are capsules of starch with a protein-rich embryo or germ, outer layers of bran and more protein, and an inedible husk enclosing the whole. Cultivated grains, the fruits of no more than a dozen grasses, supply the staple diet of most of the world. Dried grains, displayed below, can be obtained as groats—that is, complete except for the husks—or in a range of processed forms.

Some grains—notably rice and barley—are available "pearled", with the outer layers and the germ removed by friction. Treated thus, the grains have a smoother texture than whole grains and cook more quickly. Alternatively, whole grains may be cracked into pieces—which may in turn be ground coarsely to produce grits, or more finely to produce meals and various flours. When cracked grains are heated and pressed flat, the result is sold as flaked or rolled grain.

Wheat is available whole, cracked, flaked and ground—and, of course, as flour. The whole grains keep their shape well when cooked, and have an attractively robust flavour. Many wheat products have their own names. *Burghul* is a kind of cracked wheat made by boiling and baking whole grains before they are cracked. Semolina is the meal ground from a hard wheat known as durum wheat. Couscous is a processed semolina; at home, it is made by rubbing coarse and fine semolina into small balls, which are passed through coarse sieves to form pellets and a fine sieve to remove loose semolina. Couscous is made commercially by extruding semolina from a machine.

Darker in colour and stronger in flavour than wheat—although similar in

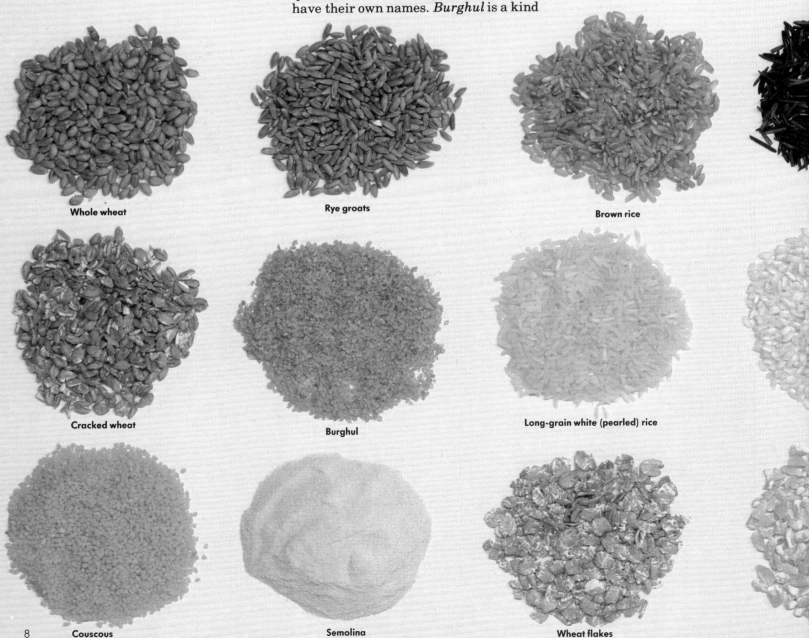

Whole wheat

Rye groats

Brown rice

Cracked wheat

Burghul

Long-grain white (pearled) rice

Couscous

Semolina

Wheat flakes

texture—rye is available in whole and processed forms. It can be used in recipes where wheat is called for.

Rice is grown in a continuum of shapes and sizes, each with a slightly different internal chemistry that affects its cooking qualities. Long-grain rice remains separate when cooked correctly; rice with shorter, rounded grains tends towards stickiness. Both long and round-grain rice are sold in whole (brown) and pearled (white) forms. Glutinous rice, a less common and quite separate variety, is available from Oriental delicatessens; it looks similar to ordinary round-grain rice, but when cooked it will form a sticky mass.

Wild rice, in spite of its name, is not related to rice. It is a rare grain harvested from a grass that grows wild in marshes in parts of North America. Much prized for its strong, nutty flavour, wild rice is always sold as a whole unpolished grain.

By contrast, white and yellow maize—also known as corn—are more often sold as a meal. Sometimes, however, dried maize kernels are soaked in lye, a powerful alkali that removes the tough outer layers. Maize treated in this way, then boiled to wash off the lye, is termed hominy. Dried hominy can be whole, cracked or coarsely ground into grits.

Barley is available both as a whole grain—pot barley—and in pearled form. It may also be cracked or ground to a meal.

Buckwheat is not a true grain, but the fruit of a plant related to rhubarb and sorrel; it is, however, cooked like grains. Whole or coarsely ground, buckwheat is often roasted to deepen its flavour.

Millet is a mild-flavoured, fragile grain which, even in whole form, quickly cooks to a porridge. Oats are another soft grain with a distinctive sweet flavour.

Wild rice

Pot barley

Buckwheat groats

Oat groats

Round-grain white rice

Pearl barley

Roasted buckwheat groats

Oatmeal

Cracked hominy

Cornmeal

Whole millet

Rolled oats

Classic Pasta Shapes

Pasta is prepared from flour or semolina, first moistened to make a dough, then formed into any one of a vast range of shapes. These pages illustrate a representative selection of what you may find in shops and markets. Although all the pasta shown is sold commercially, many of the shapes can be made at home (*page 48*). Home-made pasta is most often used immediately; commercial pasta is generally sold dried and can be kept for up to 6 months without its flavour deteriorating.

The semolina used in Western commercial pasta is milled from a particularly hard variety of wheat, called durum wheat, which yields an elastic, easily shaped dough. In Oriental food shops, however, you will find pasta made of other materials. The distinctively flavoured soba is prepared from buckwheat flour; rice noodles are soft and delicate in flavour and texture; cellophane noodles, made from soya or mung bean flour, are springy and slippery when cooked.

Spaghetti and macaroni are perhaps the most widely available pasta shapes, but there are hundreds of others, including numerous flat sheets, noodles and small shapes, that may resemble anything from wheels to butterflies. Most shapes can be obtained in a variety of sizes and many are sold with both smooth and ribbed surfaces.

The names for the various shapes can be confusing. Italy originated much of the Western world's pasta and most shapes are sold under their Italian names—but different regions of Italy use different names for the same or similar shapes. When buying pasta, look for the shape you want rather than concerning yourself too much with the name.

Common sense will tell you that some shapes are suited to particular purposes. To make a dish in which pasta is layered with a sauce (*page 62*), large flat shapes such as lasagne are an obvious choice. Long strands of macaroni can be coiled to make a casing (*page 68*) that could not be imitated with any other pasta. Otherwise, there are few constraints; even when recipes associate particular shapes with certain sauces, it is still up to you whether or not you follow the convention.

Capelli d'angeli ("angels' hair")

Tagliatelle verdi (green noodles)

Ruote ("wheels")

Taglierini (fine noodles)

Tagliatelle (noodles)

Ziti (broad macaroni)

Rice noodles

Soba (buckwheat noodles)

Cellophane noodles

Lasagne verdi (green lasagne)

Chinese egg noodles

usili ("spindles")

Gnocchi sardi ("Sardinian dumplings")

Farfalle ("butterflies")

Conchiglie ("shells")

Penne ("quills")

Spaghetti

Whole wheat spaghetti

Linguettine ("little tongues")

Elbow macaroni

nette (rippled noodles)

Narrow trenette

Mille righe ("a thousand ridges")

Cannelloni (large tubes)

Rigatoni (large ridged tubes)

Lasagne

Lasagne riccie un lato (lasagne with one side rippled)

The Multitudinous Pulses

Lentils, peas and beans, collectively known as pulses, are the seeds of leguminous plants—a group whose common feature is that the seeds are borne in pods. Strictly speaking, the word pulse covers both fresh and dried peas, beans and lentils; to cooks, however, pulses are invariably the dried vegetables.

Hundreds of types of pulses are sold dried, many of them available in several different colours. To add to the complexity, many pulses have several names. The pulses illustrated below are a good cross-section of those available in Europe—but you should not be deterred by an unfamiliar appearance or name from trying other pulses that you can buy.

All pulses consist of two sections encased in a strong skin. Some pulses are sold in split form—with the skin removed so that the two halves fall apart. Without its skin, a pulse may look quite different: split mung beans, for example, are yellow, although the whole beans are green. Split pulses cook more quickly than their whole counterparts, but will not retain their shape as well.

Dried pulses can be safely kept almost indefinitely. However, you should avoid using any that are more than a year old: pulses become harder with age and require longer cooking; eventually they dry out so much they fall to pieces in the water without becoming properly tender. Since it is impossible to tell a pulse's age from its appearance, the best safeguard is to buy small quantities at a time from a reputable shop which has a quick turnover.

The Latin name for lentil is *lens*—a word since borrowed to describe glass ground to a lentil's flattened form. The most widely available lentils are the split red variety, sometimes known as Egyptian lentils, and the larger beige lentils.

Red lentils

Green split peas

Soya beans

Chick peas

Puy lentils

Yellow split peas

Field beans

Beige lentils

Green whole peas

Broad beans

Black-eyed peas

Red lentils are bland-tasting; the beige ones have a more pronounced flavour. Puy lentils, a small mottled green or slate-coloured variety, are more rare but prized for their subtle flavour and ability to hold their shape when cooked.

Although all lentils belong to the same botanical grouping, the names pea and bean are both umbrella terms that cover a number of species. Round pulses are generally called peas, oval or kidney-shaped pulses are called beans. However, black-eyed peas are elongated—and are sometimes referred to as black-eyed beans.

Yellow and green peas are different types of common pea. Both are sweet but green peas have somewhat more flavour. Both are available whole and split.

The yellow soya beans illustrated here have a mild taste; a black variety of soya bean, however, is renowned for its sweet, full flavour. Chick peas have an almost nut-like taste and a crunchy texture. Mealy textured broad beans and field beans—also known as *foul medames*—are enveloped in leathery skin which you should remove after soaking or cooking. Pigeon peas and black-eyed peas are both succulent and have an earthy flavour.

The other pulses illustrated belong to the huge kidney bean family. Mung beans and aduki beans have a sweetish taste; butter beans are mild-flavoured and smooth. The remaining beans—black or turtle beans, Dutch brown, haricot, pinto, borlotti, flageolet, cannellini and red kidney beans—are all variants of the common kidney bean. They share a mealy texture, but their flavours range from robust to delicate. Red beans have the most full and meaty taste; pinto and borlotti beans a nut-like flavour. A relative of the pinto bean much used in Mexican cooking is the pink bean. Flageolets are the jewel of the kidney bean family, with a subtle, fresh and delicious flavour.

Mung beans

Black beans

Dutch brown beans

Haricot beans

Pigeon peas

Aduki beans

Pinto beans

Borlotti beans

Flageolet beans

Cannellini beans

Red kidney beans

Butter beans

A Trio of Versatile Sauces

The three sauces demonstrated here are among the most valuable in any cook's repertoire: a white sauce, a tomato sauce and a meat sauce (*recipes, pages 165-166*). None of them is made to a strict formula. The meat sauce, in particular, can be varied widely, according to your preference and the contents of your larder.

The first step in making a white sauce (*right*) is to heat butter and flour together to make a roux; milk is added to the roux, and the sauce is simmered for about 40 minutes until it has lost its floury taste. The result, enriched with cream if you like, is used in such baked dishes as lasagne (*page 62*) and macaroni cheese (*recipe, page 129*). Made extra thick by using less milk, it forms the basis of many soufflés (*page 74*).

The simplest tomato sauce (*opposite page, above*) is made by simmering quartered, unpeeled tomatoes in their own juice until they disintegrate, then sieving out the skins and seeds, and cooking the sauce until it has reduced to an appropriate consistency. You can add a little cream or herbs. If tomatoes are not in season, substitute canned tomatoes.

An alternative way of making a tomato sauce is to skin and seed the tomatoes before cooking them: immerse the tomatoes briefly in boiling water, pull off their skins, halve the tomatoes horizontally and scoop out the seeds. Thus prepared, the tomatoes do not need sieving. Sauté them rapidly to obtain a roughly textured, fresh-flavoured sauce. Either version can be served with boiled and baked dishes (*pages 40 and 71*).

A meat sauce (*right*) is simply a stew in which all the ingredients are finely chopped. Meat and vegetables are sautéed, then braised for an hour or two until they are tender. You can use any cooked leftover meat, and supplement it, if you wish, with raw meat. Aromatic vegetables—such as onions, leeks, celery and carrots—flavour the sauce; tomatoes are a particularly important ingredient, providing body and colour in addition to flavour. Here, dried mushrooms as well are added to the sauce for their special smoky taste. Like tomato sauce, a meat sauce can be used in both boiled (*page 61*) and baked (*page 62*) dishes.

Butter, Flour and Milk for Smoothness

1 Adding milk. Melt a chunk of butter in a saucepan over a low heat. Add an equal quantity of flour. With a whisk, stir the flour and butter together to make a roux. Cook the roux gently for 2 to 3 minutes, then pour in cold milk, whisking briskly at the same time (*above*).

2 Cooking the white sauce. Continue to whisk the sauce until it comes to the boil. Reduce the heat so that the sauce is barely simmering. Leave it to cook, uncovered, for about 40 minutes, stirring from time to time. The sauce will reduce considerably (*above*). Season it with salt and if you like, a little grated nutmeg.

Rich Flavouring from Mixed Meat

1 Sautéeing meat. Finely chop carrots and onions. Soften them in oil in a large pan over a low heat. Increase the heat and add finely chopped raw beef. Stir the beef to sear it on all sides, then add any cooked meat you wish to include—in this case, chopped ham and pork.

2 Pouring in wine. Cook the meat and vegetables together for a few minutes, until the meat is very well browned. Add a good splash of dry red or white wine (*above*) and scrape the saucepan vigorously to dissolve any savoury brown deposits into the liquid. Add a glass of stock (*page 21*) or water.

Quickly Prepared Tomato Purée

1 Seasoning tomatoes. Quarter some tomatoes and place them in a pan with herbs—here, a bay leaf, parsley and thyme—some coarse salt and, if you like, a sliced onion or a crushed garlic clove. Bring the tomatoes to the boil, crushing them lightly with a wooden spoon.

2 Sieving the tomatoes. After about 10 minutes of boiling, when the tomatoes are broken down to a mush, tip them into a sieve set over a bowl. Use a pestle to push the tomatoes through the sieve. Discard the seeds and skins that remain in the sieve. Return the pulp to the pan.

3 Reducing the sauce. Cook the sieved tomato pulp over a low heat until it has reduced to the consistency required. Season the sauce with salt and pepper and add herbs—here, basil and parsley.

3 Adding flavourings. Put some dried mushrooms—here, ceps—in a small bowl and cover them with cold water. Leave them to soften for about 30 minutes. Finely chop garlic and parsley. Add them, together with the mushrooms and a strip of lemon rind, to the sauce. Discard the mushrooms' soaking liquid.

4 Adding the tomatoes. Core some tomatoes and immerse them in boiling water for a second or two, to loosen their skins; slip off the skins. Halve the tomatoes crosswise, seed them and chop them coarsely. Add the tomatoes to the sauce and stir to mix the ingredients.

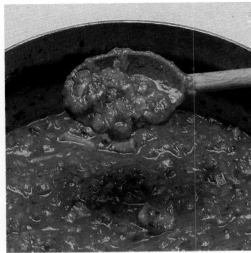

5 Testing the consistency. Cook the mixture at a bare simmer until the meat has become tender—at least 1½ hours. Leave the lid of the pan ajar to control the simmer and to allow the sauce to reduce to the consistency you want (*above*).

1
Cooking with Grains
Subtle Variations on Simple Techniques

Whether whole or cracked, flaked or ground, grains are parched when they are harvested and must absorb water to become plump and tender. Thus boiling and steaming loom large in the preparation of grains— although that hardly limits the inventive cook. Since the flavours of grains harmonize with almost any vegetable, fish or meat, endless dishes can be devised even with those basic cooking methods. Once the grains have absorbed enough water, new vistas open. Any grain meal, cooked to a prosaic porridge, for example, can be lifted to a higher culinary status when cooled, cut into shapes and fried or baked (*page 40*).

Rice is the grain that has inspired most culinary ingenuity: subtle variations in technique give strikingly different results even with similar added ingredients. To achieve the fluffy, separate grains typical of a pilaff, rice is heated in fat, then simmered undisturbed, as gently as possible, in precisely the amount of liquid it can absorb without overcooking (*page 20*). For a risotto (*page 22*), the stickiness of round-grain rice is exploited by boiling and stirring—and the creaminess of the end result is intensified with grated cheese and butter. In yet another rice dish, the parboiled grains are cooked in a saucepan containing a little water and butter; while the bottom layer of rice fries to a golden crust, the grains above are slowly steamed (*page 24*). And once rice has been boiled or steamed, it can be sautéed in oil (*page 32*), fashioned into balls and deep fried (*page 34*), or baked in the oven with fish such as salmon (*recipe, page 102*) or a rich meat stuffing (*recipe, page 104*).

All grains are an excellent basis for improvisation. With their satisfying bulk, they can stretch into a nourishing meal whatever foods you have available—leftover cooked meat, fresh and dried vegetables, stock or roasting juices, nuts and spices. Such well-loved dishes as paella and couscous are themselves essentially improvisations. Paella combines saffron-flavoured rice with virtually any fresh ingredient that is to hand; in particular, it has come to mean a dish that includes both meat or poultry and fish or shellfish (*page 28*). Couscous is a dish of poached meat and vegetables and a grain—usually a form of semolina—that has cooked in their steam. Lamb, chicken, game or fish may be included in the couscous together with pulses and half a dozen fresh vegetables (*page 36*).

Pearly round-grain rice, destined for a *risotto alla Milanese* (*page 23*), is strewn into a pan where flavourings—chopped onion and beef marrow—already stew in butter. To achieve the risotto's characteristic sticky consistency, hot stock will be added a little at a time, and the grains will be regularly stirred.

Three Basic Cooking Techniques

Cookery books abound with detailed—and contradictory—descriptions of the perfect technique for cooking grains. In fact there are many ways to achieve a good result: the three techniques demonstrated here are the most commonly used.

The simplest method is to boil the grains in an unlimited amount of water (*right*). To keep the grains from sticking to each other or the base of the pan, bring the water to the boil before adding the grains and give them a good stir at the start of cooking. Because more water is used than the grains can absorb, they will need to be drained after being cooked, then allowed to dry and swell in their own steam, either in the oven or over a very low heat. Approximate cooking times for each type of grain are shown on the chart (*box, opposite page, above*).

The chart also indicates the volume of water required by each type for the second method—boiling in a measured amount of liquid (*right, below*). With this method, all of the water is absorbed by the grains as they cook, leaving them ready to serve without drying. The wild rice used in the demonstration is soaked raw for a few hours in cold water—or, as here, for about an hour in hot water—to soften the grains. Soaking gives a fluffier, more tender result, but it does not affect either the volume of water required for cooking or the cooking time.

Steaming (*box, opposite page, below*) takes longer than other methods, and is thus less practical for long-cooking grains such as barley and brown rice. Indeed, this method is usually restricted to white rice. To ensure that the rice will be tender, soak it for about an hour beforehand. Most steamers have two sections: a lower one for the water and a perforated upper section—fitted with a lid—for the food. To prevent any grains from dropping into the water, line the upper section with muslin.

Whichever method you use, do not regard the times in the chart as immutable. Such imponderables as the variety and age of the grain affect the timing, and different people prefer different degrees of doneness. Try the grains—by pressing them between finger and thumb—about 5 minutes before the earlier time given on the chart and serve them when tender.

Boiling in Unlimited Water

1 **Boiling long-grain white rice.** Fill a large saucepan nearly full of salted water and bring it to the boil. Adjusting the heat to keep the water on the boil, gradually sprinkle in the rice (*above*). Stir once to separate the grains. To lessen the risk of the water boiling over, add a spoonful of oil and boil uncovered.

2 **Draining off the water.** To test if the rice is cooked, remove a few grains and try them between your teeth or pinch them with your fingertips. Drain the contents of the pan through a strainer (*above*) when the rice still has a slightly resilient core; it will finish cooking during the drying-out period in the oven.

A Measured Mode of Boiling

1 **Soaking wild rice.** Put a measured amount of dry wild rice in a large bowl. Pour hot or boiling water into the bowl (*above*) so that the rice is completely covered. Leave the rice to soak.

2 **Preparing to cook the grain.** After about an hour, drain the rice through a strainer set over a sink. Measure out a volume of water three times that of the rice before soaking (*chart, opposite page*) and pour it into a saucepan. Add salt and the drained rice (*above*).

3 **Drying and serving the rice.** Tip the rice into a large, flat, ovenproof dish and spread it out evenly. Cover the rice and put it in a preheated, 150°C (300°F or Mark 2) oven for 10 to 15 minutes, until it is sufficiently dry. Add a few small pieces of butter and toss the rice, using forks to avoid crushing the grains. Serve at once.□

Meeting Each Grain's Needs

The chart below gives the approximate amount of water that each type of grain absorbs when cooking, and the time each takes to cook. You may have to add more water as the grains cook, or extend the cooking time. But do not uncover the pan too often, or steam will escape and the grains will not cook properly.

Grain	Proportion of water to grain	Approximate cooking times (minutes)
Brown rice	2:1	50-60
Buckwheat	2:1	15-20
Millet	3:1	15-20
Oats	2:1	60-90
Pearl barley	2-2½:1	90
Pot barley	2-2½:1	90
Rye	2:1	60-90
Wheat	2:1	60-90
White rice	2:1	18-20
Wild rice	3:1	45

3 **Simmering the wild rice.** Bring the water to the boil, stir the rice once, then reduce the heat. Cover the pan and simmer the rice for about 45 minutes, or until all of the water has been absorbed (*inset*) and the grains feel soft when pinched. Take the pan off the heat; add small chunks of butter and toss the rice. Serve immediately.□

Soaking and Steaming Rice

Steaming rice in muslin. Soak rice in cold water for at least an hour, then drain it through a strainer. Half fill the bottom of a steamer with water and bring it to the boil. Put the top section of the steamer in place; lay a single piece of muslin in it. Tip the rice into the steamer; fold the muslin over the rice. Cover and steam the rice for 25 to 30 minutes, or until it is tender.

The Art of Creating Pilaffs

One of the easiest ways to obtain fluffy, separate grains is to heat them in a little oil or fat, then simmer them, tightly covered, in a measured amount of liquid. The fat, absorbed into the outer layers of the grains, helps to keep them from sticking together. Even so, gentle simmering—without stirring—is essential if the grains are to remain apart.

Grain dishes prepared by this technique are called pilaffs. In Western cookery, the term pilaff is often reserved for rice—usually, though not necessarily, long-grain rice, as demonstrated on the right. However, any whole or cracked grain can be cooked in this manner. Cracked wheat pilaffs are common in the Middle East, where the name originated; pearl barley is used in the demonstration on the right, below (*recipe, page 107*).

The simplest pilaff—the grains cooked gently in butter and then simmered in plain water—is an excellent accompaniment for any dish with a rich sauce. If you want to add more flavour to the grains, simmer them in stock (*box, opposite page*) or combine them with vegetables, either at the start or the end of cooking. Here, the rice pilaff receives a last-minute addition of tomatoes; the barley is prepared with mushrooms and onions in meat stock.

Grains take about the same time to cook by the pilaff method as by plain boiling (*box, page 19*). Rice will absorb roughly twice its own volume of liquid. Other grains may absorb liquid less predictably; if you are not sure how much liquid a grain will absorb, introduce the liquid in two or three stages, as for the barley pilaff here. Add approximately the grains' volume of liquid at the start of cooking, the same amount—or a little less, if not all of the first batch has been absorbed—midway through the cooking, and more later if the previous batches of liquid have all been absorbed.

Rice Garnished with Tomatoes

1 **Cooking the rice in butter.** Over a low heat, melt a little butter in a heavy pan. Measure out as much rice as you want and add it to the butter. Stir the rice gently but regularly with a wooden spoon for 2 to 3 minutes, until each grain is coated in butter and has turned opaque.

2 **Simmering the rice.** Pour over the grains twice the volume of boiling water as you used of rice. Salt the rice, and stir it once to ensure that no grains have stuck to the bottom of the pan. Turn down the heat so that the water just simmers, and cover.

A Barley Casserole

1 **Cooking the barley with onions.** In a casserole, melt some butter and add finely chopped onions. Stir the onions with a wooden spoon until they soften. Add a measured volume of pearl barley and stir until golden in colour.

2 **Adding the mushrooms.** Rinse and slice or quarter some mushrooms. Sauté them briefly over fairly high heat in butter or oil. Add the sautéed mushrooms to the pearl barley and onions (*above*).

3 **Mixing in the butter.** Simmer the rice, undisturbed, over very low heat for 18 to 20 minutes. When all the liquid has been absorbed, take the pan off the heat. Add butter, cut in small pieces; use two forks to incorporate the butter gently into the rice (*above*). You can serve the rice at this point, or mix it with a tomato flavouring before serving (*Step 4*).

4 **Adding tomatoes.** While the rice is still cooking, core some tomatoes and dunk them in boiling water; skin the tomatoes, halve them crosswise, remove the seeds and chop roughly. Heat the tomatoes in a frying pan with some butter; season with salt and pepper. Transfer them to the pan containing the rice, and toss them gently with the rice (*above*).☐

A Versatile Meat Stock

To make a hearty stock, suitable for cooking any kind of grain, combine aromatic vegetables—onions, carrots, leeks and celery, for example—with herbs and inexpensive cuts of meat. Here, beef provides rich flavour, while chicken and veal bring a slight sweetness and release their flavour rapidly (*recipe, page 165*). Cook the meat and vegetables in water until their essences are drawn out, then strain off the liquid.

1 **Adding the vegetables.** Place the meat on a rack in a large pan and cover with cold water. Bring the water slowly to the boil and remove the scum that rises. Add aromatic vegetables and herbs; skim again. Put the lid on the pan, slightly ajar.

3 **Pouring in the stock.** Ladle boiling stock or water over the barley (*above*); use about the same volume of liquid as of the barley. Cover the casserole and leave it for 30 minutes over a low heat or in a moderate oven, 180°C (350°F or Mark 4). Then add the same amount of liquid as before—or a little less, if some of the previous measure remains unabsorbed.

4 **The finished dish.** Simmer the barley, covered, for about 30 minutes, until it has absorbed all of the liquid. Check the seasoning and add salt if necessary. Mix the barley with a little finely chopped parsley and serve it.☐

2 **Straining the stock.** Adjust the heat so that the liquid barely simmers. Cook the stock for 4 to 5 hours. Strain it through a colander lined with muslin. Let the stock stand until fat rises to its surface; use paper towels to blot up the fat.

Risottos: Moist and Creamy

Although the aim in most preparations of rice is to produce separate grains, without a trace of stickiness, a risotto is an exception. A risotto should be moist enough to be poured; its final consistency depends on regular stirring, which agitates the surface starch of the rice so that the grains, still firm to the bite, are suspended in a creamy liquid.

The first requirement for a risotto is a round-grain rice, which is stickier than long-grain rice. Moreover, its grains withstand the stirring well; long-grain rice is more likely to break.

The cooking of a risotto starts like that of a pilaff (*page 20*): the grains are heated in fat, usually with a chopped onion for flavouring. But from then on, the cooking is almost the opposite of the pilaff technique. Boiling liquid is added a little at a time, and kept at a light boil; only after each addition has been almost completely absorbed is more added. Constant stirring is necessary to develop the rice's stickiness and also to prevent grains from adhering to the bottom of the pan. In all, the volume of liquid you will need is about two and a half times that of the rice; the precise amount depends on how much liquid is lost by evaporation.

The risotto's smoothness is enhanced by the addition of butter and grated Parmesan cheese; the butter and cheese should be added off the heat so the butter does not cook but stays thick and creamy.

A risotto can be as plain or elaborate as you please; the basic version (*recipe, page 93*) is shown on the right, and the demonstrations opposite show ways of combining the basic risotto with a flavouring.

A variety of vegetables, sautéed while the rice is cooking, makes a colourful last-minute addition (*opposite page, above*). Saffron, beef marrow and dry white wine give the traditional *risotto alla Milanese* its characteristic flavour (*opposite page, centre; recipe, page 92*). And for the dish known in the Venetian dialect as *risi e bisi*—"rice with peas"—peas and ham are cooked with rice from the start (*opposite page, below; recipe, page 94*). In order not to damage the peas, the risotto technique is modified: the rice is not sautéed and, to reduce the need for stirring, fewer and larger additions of stock are made.

Developing the Clinging Consistency

1 Adding the rice. Put a chunk of butter and a little olive oil in a large saucepan over a gentle heat. When the butter has melted, add a finely chopped onion and cook it until it softens. Pour in round-grain rice (*above*) and heat for 2 to 3 minutes, stirring constantly to ensure that all the grains are completely coated with fat.

2 Ladling in the stock. Add a ladleful of boiling stock (*page 21*); adjust the heat to maintain the stock at a light boil. Stir the rice occasionally while it cooks. When most of the stock has been absorbed by the rice, add another ladleful. Continue cooking the rice, stirring all the time and adding more stock as each ladleful is absorbed.

3 Sprinkling in the cheese. Towards the end of cooking, add the stock in smaller quantities, so that when the rice is cooked it will be moist but not swimming in the stock. Remove the pan from the heat when the grains are no longer brittle, but retain a chewy core—about 20 minutes. Add butter and sprinkle with grated Parmesan cheese.

4 Serving the risotto. Stir the risotto to incorporate the butter and cheese, add salt if necessary, and ladle the risotto into soup plates. Serve the risotto straight away, as hot as possible, with more grated Parmesan cheese on the side.□

Last-Minute Additions of Summer Vegetables

1 **Cooking the vegetables.** Chop leeks, carrots, beans and skinned, seeded tomatoes. Parboil the beans and carrots separately. Sauté the leeks; add the other vegetables and parsley.

2 **Adding the vegetables.** Cook all the vegetables and the parsley until they have heated through. Prepare a basic risotto (*Steps 1 to 3, left*) and add the vegetables before the butter and cheese.

3 **Mixing in the cheese.** Add butter and a handful of grated Parmesan cheese. Stir the risotto gently with a wooden spoon to incorporate the cheese and distribute the vegetables evenly.☐

Marrow and Saffron for Flavour and Hue

1 **Sautéing marrow.** Extract the marrow from a section of beef marrow bone and chop it. Cook it gently in butter with chopped onions, stirring occasionally, until the onions are golden. Add the rice.

2 **Pouring in the wine.** When the rice has turned opaque, add a pinch of powdered saffron and pour in some white wine (*above*). Simmer the mixture, stirring until the wine is almost absorbed.

3 **Completing the risotto.** Add stock, a little at a time, and cook the rice until it is just tender. Take the pan off the heat and stir in the butter and grated cheese.☐

Gentle Ways with Peas and Ham

1 **Ladling in the stock.** Finely chop onions and cook gently in butter until soft. Add chopped prosciutto and, after a minute, the peas. Stir gently to coat the peas with fat. Add a ladleful of hot stock.

2 **Adding the rice.** Bring the stock to the boil, then tip in the rice. Stir to mix the rice and peas. Pour in several ladlefuls of heated stock. Add more stock before the first batch is quite absorbed.

3 **Finishing the risotto.** Simmer the risotto gently, to avoid damaging the peas; do not stir. When the rice is tender, take the pan off the heat. Add butter and sprinkle with grated Parmesan cheese.☐

Steamed Rice Garnished with a Golden Crust

When parboiled rice is cooked gently in a deep pot with fat and a little water, the upper layers steam while the bottom layer of rice crisps and fries. Cooked plain, and served with a stew or sauce, this ingenious Iranian rice dish is called *chelo*. If meat or vegetables are cooked with the rice, as in the demonstration on the right (*recipe, page 98*), the dish is called *polo*.

Before being cooked, the rice is soaked in the Eastern fashion. Such pre-soaking, regarded as optional in the West, tenderizes the hard cores of the grains and helps the grains to cook evenly.

Although soaking partially rehydrates the rice, parboiling in plenty of water must precede the simultaneous steaming-frying process, because the amount of water used for the second stage of cooking is quite small. In this *polo*, broad beans are parboiled with the rice; other fresh vegetables, such as peas or sweet peppers, can be treated in the same way. But if you want to include leftover meat in the dish, mix it with the rice after parboiling—together with the flavourings, such as dill and saffron.

For the second cooking, melted butter is mixed with about half its volume of hot water. The butter is essential for the formation of the crust; the water prevents the rice from scorching and, as the water evaporates, it steams the upper layers of rice. Too much water, however, would keep the bottom layer of rice from frying. To form a good crust without danger of burning the rice, the best technique is to add the buttery mixture to the rice in two stages. Cook at a moderate heat after the first addition, so that the water evaporates and the crust forms, then more gently after the second addition, so that the crust does not burn (*Steps 6 and 7*).

The crust need not be formed of rice alone. For variety, you can mix a small portion of the parboiled rice with beaten eggs, thinly sliced raw potato or sautéed onion; cook this mixture in part of the buttery liquid before adding the rest of the rice and the remaining liquid.

1 **Shelling broad beans.** Put some long-grain rice in a bowl, add enough cold water to cover the rice generously, and leave it to soak for about 2 hours. While the rice is soaking, split open the pods of broad beans with your thumb-nail, take out the beans and discard the pods.

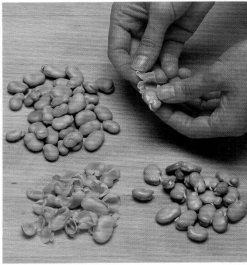

2 **Peeling the beans.** All but the smallest, bright green specimens of broad beans have a tough skin that should be removed before cooking. Pierce each skin with your nail and peel it away.

6 **Starting to form a crust.** In the saucepan used to boil the rice and beans, heat a few tablespoons of water with butter or oil and, if you like, a little saffron. Pour half of the buttery liquid into a bowl and set it aside. Add the rice, beans and dill to the pan and stir the mixture lightly with a fork (*above, left*). With the handle of a wooden spoon, make a deep hole in the mixture so that steam can circulate (*above, right*). Cover and cook the *polo* over a medium heat for 5 minutes.

3 **Chopping up dill.** Drain the soaked rice. Wash some fresh dill and shake it dry; remove the leaves from the stems and chop the leaves finely. If fresh dill is not available, substitute tender shoots of wild fennel, and treat in the same way.

4 **Boiling the rice and beans.** In a large saucepan, bring plenty of well-salted water to the boil. Add the rice and the beans (*above*). Boil them vigorously, uncovered, for 7 to 8 minutes, until the grains of rice are no longer brittle to the bite but are still firm.

5 **Mixing the dill.** Empty the rice and beans into a colander and rinse them with cold water to stop the cooking. When the water has drained away, empty the rice and beans into a bowl and add the chopped dill. Use your hands to mix the ingredients together and to separate the grains of rice (*above*).

7 **Adding the reserved liquid.** Pour the remainder of the buttery liquid evenly over the *polo*. Cover the pan and leave the *polo* to cook undisturbed over a low heat for about 40 minutes.

8 **Serving the polo.** Take the saucepan off the heat and let it cool for 5 minutes to loosen the crust. Fluff up the steamed part of the rice with a fork, then pile it up on a dish (*right*). Scrape the crust from the pan and lay it round the steamed rice. □

Meat and Spices in a Main-Course Pilaff

Hundreds of recipes from all over the world develop basic pilaffs (*page 20*) into elaborate, main-course dishes. The possible combinations of spices, vegetables, meats and fish are as varied as taste and imagination permit. Thus squid, tomatoes and rosemary feature in one Greek pilaff (*recipe, page 103*), while eel, juniper berries and curry powder are combined with rice in a Chilean dish (*recipe, page 92*). In the Indian pilaff demonstrated here (*recipe, page 89*), rice is cooked with cubes of lamb in a gelatinous mutton stock, made in the same way as the mixed stock shown on page 21.

The preparation begins by soaking the rice—a custom common to India and the Middle East (*page 24*). While the rice is soaking, the meat can be marinated with acidic liquids that tenderize it as they impart their flavour. In the demonstration here, lime juice, cream and yogurt are used to marinate the meat and subsequently are added to the cooking liquid; the juices of unripe mangoes and papayas may be used for a similar effect.

Varying blends of spices are another hallmark of Indian pilaffs. Whenever possible, spices should be bought and stored whole; in this form, they retain their freshness for long periods. Some dishes call for the spices to be used whole, others for them to be ground just before cooking, so that more of their flavour is released. Here, the mutton stock is infused with whole cloves; whole cardamoms and cinnamon are mixed with ground poppy seeds and included in the pilaff.

To intensify their aroma the spices are lightly fried with the drained rice. After frying, the rice and spices are simmered in the mutton stock enriched with the strained marinade. Meanwhile, the meat is briskly seared to seal in the flavour and drained of excess fat. Added finally to the rice for a few minutes of cooking in a gentle, basking heat, the meat exchanges flavours with the other ingredients.

1 Trimming the meat. Put long-grain rice in a bowl and cover it generously with cold water. Leave it to soak for about 1 hour. Using a sharp knife, trim boned shoulder of lamb of any excess fat (*above*), then cut the meat into large cubes.

2 Marinating the meat. Squeeze the juice from limes; pour the juice into a shallow dish. Use a mortar and pestle to grind fennel seeds to a coarse powder. Add the powder to the lime juice. Prick the cubes of meat with a fork (*above*) and rub them with the lime and fennel mixture.

6 Straining the marinade. Hold a sieve over the rice and tip the meat and marinade into the sieve. With the aid of a wooden spoon, force the marinade through the sieve (*above*). Leave the meat in the sieve and put it aside. Strain the hot stock into the rice from the small pan until the rice is well covered. Bring the ingredients to the boil.

7 Adding watercress. For contrasting texture, finely chop some watercress and add it to the pan (*above*). Place a sheet of greaseproof paper over the top of the pan to trap the steam and then position the lid. Place the pan in an oven preheated to 180°C (350°F or Mark 4) and cook for about 12 minutes.

3 **Adding cream and yogurt.** Whip double cream until it just holds its shape. Lightly beat in the same amount of yogurt. Coat the cubes of meat with the cream and yogurt mixture (*above*) and set it aside. Roast some poppy seeds on a flat baking sheet in a hot oven for about 15 minutes until they darken, indicating that they are brittle enough to grind easily.

4 **Preparing the spices.** Grind the poppy seeds to a fine powder in a mortar (*above*). Using the blade of a knife, press down firmly on whole cardamoms until the pods split. Use a mortar and pestle to bruise whole cloves and, separately, to splinter a cinnamon stick into large pieces. Set these four spices aside.

5 **Sautéing the rice.** In a small pan, heat mutton stock with the cloves. (If you have no mutton stock, substitute veal or mixed stock.) Set the hot stock aside. Melt butter in a heavy ovenproof pan over a medium heat. Put the remaining spices with two bay leaves and the drained rice into the pan (*above*) and stir until the rice grains have turned opaque.

8 **Sautéing the meat.** Melt a little butter in a frying pan. Add the cubes of lamb and brown them over a medium heat. Remove the pan of rice from the oven and, with a slotted spoon, transfer the meat from the frying pan to the rice and stir it in gently. Replace the greaseproof paper and lid on the pan and cook the pilaff in a slow oven, 170°C (325°F or Mark 3), for about 15 minutes.

9 **Garnishing the pilaff.** Sauté blanched, slivered almonds in butter. Serve the pilaff scattered with the almonds and, if you like, surrounded with raisins that have been soaked until plump, patted dry, and sautéed. Each diner should discard the bay leaves, cinnamon and cardamoms from his portion of pilaff. □

Paella: a Magnificent Assemblage

Paella is the apotheosis of the pilaff: a collection of meats, vegetables and seafood in such quantity that the rice recedes to an almost subordinate role. But although its presence is unobtrusive, the rice, with its bulk and mild flavour, provides the essential unifying background for the diversity of the other ingredients.

Paella can be made with long-grain rice, or with Spanish rice which has a large, plump grain and a slightly stickier texture. As in all pilaffs, the rice for paella is gently heated in fat and then simmered in double its volume of liquid. But the traditional vessel for cooking a paella—the shallow, two-handled earthenware or iron *paella* from which the dish takes its name—has no lid, so the rice, unlike that in a classic pilaff, cooks uncovered. Its surface becomes fairly dry—too dry in fact for many tastes. If you use a lidless pan, it is advisable to cover the pan with foil for part of the cooking time.

The paella demonstrated here includes artichokes, tomatoes, French beans, peppers, squid, clams, Dublin Bay prawns, rabbit, smoked sausage and pork. You could substitute peas for beans or mussels for clams, and chicken for rabbit (*recipes, pages 90-91*); you can add other ingredients, such as fish and snails; or you can omit any of the ingredients—except the rice—to make a less elaborate dish.

To ensure that each ingredient is properly cooked, all the ingredients—except the fresh prawns, which need only brief cooking—are partly cooked before being combined with the rice. You can add the raw ingredients sequentially to the paella pan, but for the best results, pre-cook each ingredient separately (*Steps 1 to 11*).

When the accompaniments to the rice are all but cooked, the assembly of the paella begins (*overleaf*). Rice is heated in oil and coloured with saffron, then most of the other ingredients are placed on top of the rice. The clam and squid liquor is then added, supplemented by water. While the rice cooks in the liquid, the other ingredients finish cooking and mingle flavours. The ingredients that need least extra cooking—the beans and clams—are added last and scattered on top of the dish to complete a colourful display.

1 **Preparing the vegetables.** Skin, seed and cut up some tomatoes. Top and tail some French beans: cut them into short lengths (*above*). Grill, skin and seed two or three red peppers—or a mixture of green and red ones—and cut or tear them into strips. Finally, chop some onions, a few cloves of garlic and some parsley.

5 **Preparing the squid.** Hold the body pouch of each squid in one hand. With the other hand, grasp the head just below the eyes. Pull the two sections gently apart. Most of the viscera will come away with the head (*above*). Pull the viscera free and discard it. Reserve the head and body pouch.

6 **Removing the pen.** Run your finger along the rim of the body pouch to locate the tip of the transparent bone, the "pen". Gently pull the pen free (*above*) and discard it. Rinse the pouch in water to remove the remaining viscera.

7 **Skinning the body pouches.** With your fingers, peel the skin off each squid's pouch. From each head, squeeze out the hard beak at the base of the tentacles, and discard it. Immerse the head in water; press out and discard the eyes.

2 **Trimming the artichokes.** Break off the stem from each artichoke. Pull away the tough dark outer leaves, snapping them off just above their fleshy bases (*above*). In order to prevent the exposed surfaces of the artichokes from turning black, rub them with half a lemon.

3 **Paring the artichokes.** Cut the top off each artichoke. With a sharp, stainless steel knife, cut spirally from the base (*above*) to pare away the hard, green outer part of the artichoke bottom and to reveal the pale, yellowish-green flesh. Cut the artichoke hearts into quarters. Cut the fibrous core from each quarter and rub the quarters with lemon.

4 **Cooking the hearts.** In a copper, earthenware or enamelled frying pan, heat about 1 tablespoon of olive oil. Gently cook the quartered artichoke hearts for 10 to 15 minutes, turning them from time to time with a wooden spoon. When they have coloured, remove them from the heat and set them aside.

8 **Stewing the squid.** In a sieve, drain the skinned body pouches and the heads of excess moisture. Heat a little butter or oil, sauté the squid briskly for a moment, then gently stew them until they are tender—about 20 minutes for small squid. Strain off the juices and reserve them separately from the squid.

9 **Cooking the clams.** Soak live clams in salted water for about 30 minutes, so they expel as much grit as possible. Scrub them thoroughly with a stiff brush. Put them into a saucepan with thyme, parsley, a bay leaf, garlic, onion and white wine (*above*). Cook, covered, over a high heat, shaking the pan regularly, until they open—5 to 10 minutes.

10 **Straining the clams.** Line a colander with several layers of moistened muslin and set it over a large bowl. Strain the clams' cooking liquid and add to it the squid's stewing liquor. Set the clams aside. Discard the herbs and the garlic and onion. ▶

11 **Preparing pork and tomatoes.** Cut a piece of shoulder of pork into small cubes. In a little olive oil, fry the pork on all sides until brown. Add chopped garlic, chopped onions and skinned and seeded tomatoes (*above*). Cook the mixture briskly, stirring constantly, until most of the liquid has evaporated.

12 **Heating the rice.** Prick some smoked sausages with a fork. Boil them for 5 minutes in water to attenuate their smokiness, then drain and slice them. Cut a rabbit into eight to 10 pieces. Set aside the liver and brown the other pieces for 10 minutes in olive oil. Add the sausage slices and sauté the meat for another 10 minutes. Heat a little olive oil in a wide, heavy pan. Tip in a measured quantity of rice—Spanish rice is used in this demonstration—and add some powdered saffron (*above*).

15 **Adding prawns.** Strew the artichoke quarters, pepper slices and squid over the surface of the rice. Arrange raw, whole Dublin Bay prawns on top of the other ingredients. Season with salt and pepper. Cover the pan with aluminium foil and place in an oven preheated to 180°C (350°F or Mark 4). Leave the paella in the oven for about 10 minutes to heat through.

16 **Completing the paella.** Bring a pan of water to the boil and throw in the cut-up French beans. Parboil the beans for 2 to 3 minutes, then drain them in a colander. Remove the paella from the oven and scatter the drained beans on top. Add the cooked clams (*above*). Return the pan to the oven and cook the paella, uncovered, for about 10 minutes more, or until the rice has absorbed all of the liquid and is soft.

13 **Adding the meat and tomato to the rice.** With a spatula or wooden spoon, stir the rice gently over a low heat until the grains are coated with oil and have turned opaque—in 2 to 3 minutes. Place the sausage slices and rabbit pieces on top of the rice. Add the pork and tomato mixture (*above*).

14 **Adding the clam liquid.** Dilute the reserved mixture of squid and clam juice with water, until the mixture is almost twice the volume of the rice in the pan. Do not use double the rice's volume of liquid as many of the paella ingredients give off liquid as they cook. Bring the liquid to the boil and pour over the rice and meat.

17 **Garnishing and serving.** Thinly slice the reserved rabbit liver. Sauté the liver lightly in olive oil until it changes colour. Take the paella out of the oven and garnish it with the liver and the previously chopped parsley. Serve directly from the pan (*right*).☐

A Speedy Meal from Leftovers

Rapidly fried with other ingredients, left-over whole grains—whether prepared as a pilaff (*page 20*) or simply boiled (*page 18*)—furnish another meal in minutes. You can include any vegetables, meat or fish that will cook quickly; in this demonstration, sweet peppers and marinated beef slices—flavoured in the Chinese way—accompany long-grain rice (*recipe, page 100*). Eggs lightly cooked in the same pan as the rice enrich and bind the dish.

To retain the ingredients' fresh savour, the cooking should be as brief as possible. The rice need only heat through; to minimize the cooking time, all the other ingredients are cut up finely in advance, then fried very quickly over high heat.

To ensure that nothing is burnt and nothing left underdone, you should add the ingredients in sequence, starting with those that require the longest cooking time. Clear a space in the centre of the pan every time you add another ingredient, so that each item in turn has a brief moment in contact with the hot pan.

1 Slicing vegetables and meat. Halve a sweet green pepper lengthwise; seed it and cut it into strips. Slice spring onions thinly. Peel a section of ginger root and cut it into matchsticks; chop a piece of garlic clove. De-stem coriander leaves. Dice some ham and one or two bacon rashers. Firm a piece of beef fillet in a freezer for 30 minutes, then slice it thinly.

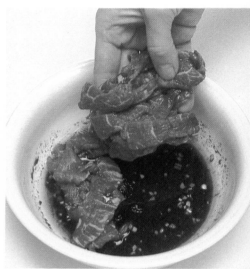

2 Flavouring the beef. In a small bowl, stir together oil, soy sauce, chopped garlic, sugar and pinches of salt and pepper. Mix in a little cornflour to thicken the mixture. Add the beef slices and coat them well with the sauce. Leave the beef to marinate in the sauce for a few minutes, while you prepare the rice.

6 Breaking the eggs into the pan. Again, make a space in the middle of the mixture and break the eggs into it (*above, left*). Season them lightly with salt and pepper. Stir the eggs until they begin to cook but are still very creamy (*above, centre*), then combine them with the rice mixture (*above, right*). Taste the dish for seasoning and, if you like, sprinkle a little soy sauce over it for extra flavour.

3 **Starting to fry the rice.** Heat a few tablespoons of oil in a large, heavy frying pan. Add the pieces of ginger to flavour the oil, then drop in the pepper slices. Fry them over a high heat for about 1 minute, stirring constantly. Loosen the rice grains with your fingers, then throw them into the pan (*above*).

4 **Adding the ham.** Stirring gently with a spatula, cook the rice until the grains are hot and separate. Push the rice to the edge of the pan, making space in the centre. Put the bacon and the spring onions to cook in the space. After a few seconds, add the diced ham.

5 **Adding the coriander leaves.** Stir the mixture, then make space in the centre of the pan and put in the beef with its sauce. Fry the beef slices for a few seconds, turning them to sear all their surfaces. Add the whole coriander leaves and stir the mixture for a few minutes.

7 **Serving the fried rice.** Transfer the mixture to a serving dish (*above*). If you like, garnish the rice with more coriander leaves. Serve immediately, while the egg is soft and the rice is lightly bound. □

Croquettes with a Surprise Stuffing

Leftover cooked rice, bound with egg and moulded into a ball round a morsel of stuffing, is quickly transformed by deep frying into a savoury snack or first course. The stuffing can be a tablespoonful of meat sauce (*recipe, page 101*), a chunk of cooked sausage or a slice of soft cheese such as *fontina* or *mozzarella*. In this demonstration, the cooked rice is stuffed with a slice of *mozzarella* cheese and a piece of ham (*recipe, page 99*). The *mozzarella* melts during the brief cooking so that, when the croquettes are eaten, the cheese forms the strings that earn this dish its Italian name: *suppli al telefono* or "telephone-wire croquettes".

To ensure that the croquettes will hold together, make them from rice which has been cooked to a clinging consistency. Leftover risotto—whose stickiness is augmented with grated cheese—(*page 22*) is ideal. If possible, make the croquettes with rice that has been refrigerated—well covered—for at least a day; rice is easiest to mould into croquettes when it is quite cold. To provide a crunchy coating, and to prevent the oil from penetrating the croquettes, they are rolled in breadcrumbs before being fried.

Successful deep frying depends on preheating the oil to the right temperature—about 190°C (375°F). If the oil gets too hot, the croquettes will burn; if it is too cool, the oil will penetrate the breadcrumbs before the coating crisps, making the croquettes greasy. To test whether the oil is at the right temperature, throw in a small bread cube and time how long it takes to brown; it should change colour after about 1 minute.

Remember that adding the croquettes will lower the temperature of the oil. To minimize this effect, use a deep pan, with enough oil to submerge the croquettes completely, and cook only a few at a time.

1 Binding the rice. Put cold risotto or boiled rice in a large bowl. Reserve a handful of the rice on a plate. Add lightly beaten eggs to the bowl; use your hands to mix the eggs gently with the rice (*above*). If necessary, add enough of the reserved rice to make the mixture in the bowl firm.

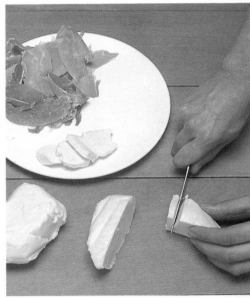

2 Cutting up the cheese. Cut or tear thin slices of ham into small pieces. With a sharp knife, thinly slice some *mozzarella* or similar soft cheese into strips about 2.5 cm (1 inch) long (*above*).

4 Frying the croquettes. Pour oil into a large saucepan to a depth of about 7.5 cm (3 inches). Heat the oil to 190°C (375°F). If you have no deep frying thermometer, throw in a bread cube; when the bread cube browns in about 1 minute the oil is ready for cooking. Fry three or four croquettes at a time, using a slotted spoon to lower them into the oil (*above, left*). Fry the croquettes until they are golden-brown—about 1 to 1½ minutes. Lift out the croquettes with the slotted spoon (*above, right*) and drain on absorbent paper.

3 **Forming the croquettes.** Dust your hands with flour. Place a tablespoon of the rice mixture on one hand. Fold a piece of ham and lay it on the rice, then add a slice of cheese (*above, left*) and another tablespoon of rice (*above, centre*). Shape the rice into a ball between your palms (*above, right*). To coat its surface, roll the croquette on a plate of fine breadcrumbs. Firm the croquettes by putting them in the refrigerator for about 30 minutes.

5 **Serving the croquettes.** When all of the croquettes have drained, pile them on a warm dish (*left*) and serve. Eat them with a knife and fork, or with your hands. As you pull apart the two halves of the croquette, the melted cheese will stretch in strings between them (*above*). □

Couscous: a Full Meal from One Pot

When couscous—semolina formed into tiny pellets—cooks in steam, the pellets become tender and light but remain separate. In North African countries, couscous is often cooked in the steam that rises from poaching meat and vegetables; the whole dish—including the meat and vegetables with their broth—takes its name from the grain and is also known as couscous (*demonstration, right and overleaf; recipes, pages 114-115*). This technique can also be used to cook cracked grains or grits, although such grains will not acquire the light, fluffy texture characteristic of the steamed couscous.

To become tender, the couscous must absorb water before cooking: the pellets are dampened and left to swell. The damp pellets will form lumps, so you should rub them gently at intervals and shake them through a sieve before cooking.

The cooking is done in a two-section vessel called a *couscoussier* (*Step 8, opposite page, below*). Meat and vegetables are kept at a light boil in the bottom part of the *couscoussier*, while the grain cooks in the top compartment; holes in both the base and lid of the top section allow steam to pass through the grain and escape from the pot. The joint between the two sections is sealed, so that all of the steam is driven upwards to cook the grain.

In this demonstration, the meats and vegetables in the lower part of the *couscoussier* include lamb, chicken, carrots and turnips—and dried chick peas, which have been soaked in water overnight and pre-cooked. The meats and vegetables are simmered in water, seasoned with coriander, spices and a hot sauce known as *harissa* (*box, overleaf*) and supplemented later with quick-cooking vegetables such as courgettes and peppers. Because the meats demand longer cooking than the grain, the meat and vegetables are simmered for about 30 minutes before the top section of the *couscoussier* is set in place.

When partly cooked, the grain will cake together; it is removed briefly from the *couscoussier*, separated and moistened. Once it is fully cooked, the grain is served heaped on a large dish, forming a bed for the meat and vegetables. More *harissa* sauce is provided for each diner to season the couscous to his taste.

1 Dampening the couscous. Spread the couscous on a tray or roasting tin and sprinkle it with just enough water to dampen all the grain. Here, the couscous used is made from semolina formed into pellets about the size of millet grains.

2 Stirring the couscous. Rake through the couscous with your fingers so that all the pellets are moistened (*above*). Leave the pellets to absorb the water and swell for about 15 minutes, then sift them through your fingers again.

5 Preparing the ingredients for the stew. Meanwhile, simmer some soaked chick peas for 1 to 1½ hours, until they are tender (*page 78*). Drain them in a sieve set over a bowl. Cut up a chicken or a shoulder of lamb—or, as here, both—into large pieces. Finely chop an onion. Peel carrots and turnips (*above*) and cut them into large chunks. Rinse a bunch of coriander leaves.

3 **Separating the grains.** Roll the grains of couscous gently between your palms to break up any lumps (*above*). Sprinkle the couscous with more water, a little at a time, and gently roll the pellets between your palms after each addition. Continue adding water and rolling until the pellets are saturated, and have swelled to about twice their original size.

4 **Sieving the couscous.** Put the damp couscous pellets in a coarse-meshed sieve, and shake the sieve over the tray so that the couscous passes through. If some of the pellets have lumped together and will not pass through, sprinkle them with a little more water and roll them between your palms again, then re-sieve.

6 **Assembling the stew.** Pour cold water into the bottom part of the *couscoussier* and then drop in the prepared meat, vegetables and coriander (*above*). Add a pinch each of powdered saffron and ground cinnamon and a teaspoon or two of *harissa* sauce (*box, overleaf*).

7 **Adding the second section.** Bring the water slowly to the boil; remove any scum from its surface and cook it at a bare simmer, uncovered, for about 30 minutes. Heap the couscous lightly in the top section of the *couscoussier*. Set the top section on the lower one, and cover the *couscoussier* with its lid.

8 **Sealing the couscoussier.** Mix some flour with about one-third its volume of water. Dip a band of cloth in this paste and squeeze the cloth to rid it of excess moisture. Wrap the cloth round the join between the top and bottom sections of the *couscoussier*. Tuck the end of the cloth under the last layer. ▶

9 **Tipping out the couscous.** Raise the heat slightly, so that the water boils and produces enough steam to cook the grain. After about 30 minutes, the pellets will lump together. To separate them, remove the cloth from the *couscoussier*; lift off the top section, leaving the stew to cook on the stove. Using a fork, push the couscous out on a tray (*above*).

10 **Fluffing up the grain.** Spread the couscous out evenly on the tray. To help separate the pellets, sprinkle cold water over the couscous. Gently rake through the grain with your fingers and break up any lumps. Leave the grain on the tray while you prepare the other ingredients.

11 **Preparing pumpkin.** Slice a pumpkin into quarters and scrape out the seeds with a spoon (*above*). With a small, sharp knife, peel the pumpkin quarters and cut them into large chunks.

12 **Cooking the pumpkin.** Pumpkin easily overcooks and turns mushy: cook it apart from the other stew ingredients so that you can check its progress. Put the pumpkin pieces in a small pan and cover them with liquid ladled from the *couscoussier*. Simmer them over a low heat until soft but not disintegrating—about 20 minutes.

13 **Preparing other vegetables.** Grill peppers, turning them every few minutes, until the skin blisters. Leave the peppers to cool, covered by a damp cloth; peel and seed them. Immerse tomatoes in boiling water, then skin, halve and seed them. Cut courgettes into large pieces. Add the vegetables to the stew.

14 **Completing the cooking.** Return the couscous to the top section of the *couscoussier*; replace the top section on the lower one and seal the joint as before, with a new strip of cloth. Cook for a further 15 minutes so that the peppers and courgettes are tender and the couscous soft and fluffy.

Making harissa sauce. Soak a couple of dried chili peppers in cold water for about 1 hour until they soften. Split the peppers, remove the stalks and seeds. Put the peppers in a mortar with 2 to 3 tablespoons of caraway seeds, a garlic clove and some coarse salt. Pound the mixture to a paste with a pestle. Mix the paste with oil until it reaches a fluid consistency. *Harissa* sauce will keep for up to 3 months in a refrigerator.

15 **Serving the couscous.** Place the grain on a large serving dish and pour over it a few ladlefuls of broth. Add a large chunk of butter and, using two forks, toss the couscous. Arrange the cooked pumpkin round the edge of the serving dish, and place the meat and vegetables on top of the couscous. Serve the couscous with the rest of the broth and a bowl of *harissa* sauce (*above*); those who enjoy the powerful taste of the sauce can mix a little with broth in a spoon, and pour the mixture over their couscous (*right*).□

Permutations of Cornmeal Porridge

Porridges, made by simmering ground, rolled or flaked grains to a thick, smooth mush, are staples regarded with deep affection by many people. The Scots, for example, hold dear their oatmeal porridge, the Italians their polenta made from cornmeal (*right*). Polenta can be served quite plain or can be enriched by being baked or fried with other ingredients.

To make plain polenta, sprinkle the grain into about twice its volume of boiling water, then stir continuously as it cooks to prevent it from sticking to the pan. As the mixture becomes solid, thin it with boiling water.

In this demonstration, the polenta is spread out to cool and set, then cut into shapes and baked with a tomato sauce. Alternative accompaniments include salt cod (*recipe, page 111*) or any of the sauces served with pasta. If you choose to fry the polenta, you can incorporate pre-cooked, finely chopped vegetables or meat before you cut the shapes. In the demonstration here (*box, opposite page*), squares of polenta mixed with cabbage are fried until golden-brown (*recipe, page 112*).

1 Sprinkling in the cornmeal. Bring a large pan of salted water to a rolling boil. Strew in coarse cornmeal from a height to distribute the grain evenly in the water. Add the grain fairly slowly, so that the water remains on the boil; otherwise the grains will form lumps. As soon as you have added the grain, lower the heat and begin stirring with a wooden spoon.

2 Thinning the polenta. Stir the polenta continuously. Each time it becomes too thick to stir easily, add a ladleful of boiling water (*above*). Cook the polenta for at least 30 minutes, until it acquires an elastic texture and comes away from the sides of the pan. A full hour's cooking will give a softer-textured porridge.

3 Turning out the polenta. Serve the polenta at once, if you wish—either with a sauce or quite plain, as a garnish for meat or fish. If you prefer to bake or fry the polenta, turn it out on to a smooth work surface (*above*). With a spoon or spatula, flatten it out to an overall thickness of about 1 cm (½ inch) and smooth the surface. Leave the polenta to cool and set for at least 20 minutes.

4 Shaping the polenta. Use a knife or a pastry cutter to make shapes from the cold slab of polenta: in this case, the polenta is stamped into circles with a pastry cutter. Collect the trimmings and knead them into a ball. Flatten the ball and cut out more shapes.

5 Arranging the polenta shapes. Lay the polenta shapes in an overlapping pattern in a gratin dish, so that they form an even layer. Generously sprinkle the polenta with grated Parmesan cheese. If you like, you can bake the polenta simply with its sprinkling of cheese—or cover it with a tomato sauce (*Step 6*).

Fried Cubes of Polenta with Cabbage

1 **Cooking the cabbage.** Finely chop some cabbage and throw it into a pan of boiling salted water. Cook the cabbage for about 5 minutes, then drain it. Stew it gently, for about 10 minutes, in a pan with a little olive oil. Stir the cabbage, with plenty of grated Parmesan cheese, into hot polenta (*Step 2, left*).

2 **Setting the polenta.** Turn out the mixture into a shallow rectangular dish. Use a metal spatula that has been coated with olive oil to smooth the surface of the mixture (*above*). Leave the mixture to cool and set in the dish for at least 20 minutes. Cut the mixture into large cubes.

3 **Frying the polenta.** Sprinkle some flour on to a plate and lightly coat each cube with the flour. Fry the cubes in olive oil or lard over a medium heat for about 15 minutes, turning them to brown and crisp each surface (*above*). Turn carefully as the cubes break easily. Drain them on absorbent towels and serve at once.

6 **Adding the sauce.** Make a tomato sauce (*page 15*), cooked until it is thick enough to coat the polenta. Ladle the sauce over the polenta (*above*). Sprinkle the sauce with grated Parmesan and bake the dish in an oven preheated to 200°C (400°F or Mark 6) for about 20 minutes, until the polenta and sauce are heated through and the cheese melts (*right*).□

2
Making Pasta
A Rewarding Art

Making your own pasta is one of the most straightforward of culinary techniques: flour is simply moistened with egg and a little oil, kneaded to develop its natural elasticity, and rolled out. The process is closely akin to pastry-making—indeed the identical mixture of flour, egg and oil can double as pasta or pastry, according to whether you boil or bake it (*page 72*). The pasta dough must be rolled out thinner than most pastry, but that is a question of care and patience rather than special skill. Once rolled, the pasta can be formed into any one of a range of shapes—strips, squares, butterflies and figures-of-eight, for example—using a knife, a pastry wheel or your thumbs (*page 48*). Although it may be dried, it is best cooked within a few hours of rolling while it is still moist and flexible.

The reward for your efforts is pasta with a distinctive texture—firm and springy, yet tender—and a delicious fresh flavour. To make a more luxurious pasta, you can moisten the dough with egg yolks alone, instead of whole eggs. And you can add flavour and colour to the pasta with herbs or such natural dyes as spinach, beetroot and saffron (*page 50*).

With a pasta machine (*opposite and page 46*), pasta-making becomes even simpler. The machine both kneads and rolls the pasta. The two processes are achieved by passing the dough between a single set of rollers, which are kept at a set distance apart for the kneading, then brought progressively closer together to squeeze and stretch out the dough. Separate cutting rollers convert the thin sheets of dough to noodles.

Dedicated pasta-eaters claim that because hand-made pasta is treated less roughly than machine-made pasta, its fresh egg flavour is more pronounced. The difference can be minimized by not overdoing the machine kneading; the fewer times the dough is passed through the machine, the more it resembles hand-made pasta. The machine's drawbacks are in any case outweighed by its usefulness. For most cooks, a machine will ensure that home-made pasta makes a regular appearance on the dinner table, instead of being just an occasional treat.

One of the best arguments for making your own pasta is that it allows you to prepare stuffed shapes—ravioli, for instance—with a home-made filling. Possible fillings range from curd cheese with herbs to puréed, spiced peas, fish mixed with spinach and leftovers of all sorts—finely chopped stewed meat is a prime example (*recipes, pages 138-139*).

A strip of floured dough, flattened into a thin sheet by repeated passages between the rollers of the pasta machine, is cranked through a set of cutting rollers that slice it into fine noodles. The pasta machine has a second set of cutting rollers for broader noodles.

First Steps: Mixing, Kneading and Rolling

Making pasta by hand demands only a little time and effort, and no specialized equipment at all. Flour is moistened to produce dough, and the dough is kneaded. Usually, the dough is rolled out (*below*) then cut into various shapes (*page 48*). But to make Hungarian-style pasta shreds, used to garnish soups as well as in the soufflé demonstrated on page 74, the dough is grated (*right*).

While any type of flour can be used in pasta-making, a flour rich in gluten is best for an easily rolled dough that will yield firm, springy pasta. Gluten is a protein that, when moistened, forms an elastic network that strengthens the dough. Fine semolina made from durum wheat, the variety with the highest proportion of gluten, is used for most commercial pasta—but it produces a hard dough that

requires fairly lengthy kneading. Strong flour sold for bread-making is a good choice for hand-made pasta because it is rich in gluten, but requires less kneading and rolling than semolina.

Although the flour can be made into a dough with water, egg confers a richer flavour. If you are making pasta for rolling out, use about one egg for each 100 g (3½ oz) of flour; the exact proportion will depend on the size of the eggs and the type of flour you use. The addition of a little oil or melted butter softens the dough, making it easier to handle (*recipe, page 167*).

Large quantities of dough are most easily mixed on a flat surface, smaller quantities in a bowl. On a flat surface, heap up more flour than you will need, place the liquids in the centre and gradually mix in flour from the perimeter, stopping when the dough forms a coherent mass. In a bowl, it is more difficult to

incorporate the flour progressively, so start with less flour than you think you will need. A little more flour can easily be added, whereas liquid could not readily be blended into a dough that is too stiff.

Once the dough is mixed, it should be kneaded for a few minutes. Kneading is a repetition of two steps—flattening and folding the dough—which develop the gluten network. Kneading should leave the dough smooth and silky—neither dry nor sticky. At this point, the dough is so elastic that it springs back on itself if you try to roll it. If it is left to rest for an hour, however, the gluten relaxes so that the dough can be rolled out thinly.

The dough for shredded pasta (*recipe, page 167*) must be very stiff. Extra flour is incorporated during kneading and the dough is chilled to firm it before grating.

A Standard Dough for Every Purpose

1 Adding egg to flour. Form a mound of flour on a smooth surface. Make a well in the centre of the mound. Break whole eggs into the well, or lightly beat them and pour in the beaten egg (*above*). Add salt and, if you like, pour a little olive oil into the well to soften the dough and make it easier to manipulate.

2 Mixing the dough. With one hand, gradually push the flour from around the edge of the well into the egg mixture. Stir with your fingers to form a batter in the well. To prevent the eggs from flowing out, support the perimeter of the flour with your free hand (*above*). Continue to incorporate flour into the egg mixture until the batter has become a firm paste. Gather it into a ball.

Extra Stiffness for Grated Pasta

1 **Breaking eggs into the flour.** On a smooth surface, form a mound of flour. Make a deep well in the mound. Break eggs into the well (*above*). Add salt; stir the eggs into the flour gradually, working outwards to make a stiff paste.

2 **Incorporating extra flour.** Lightly flour the work surface. Knead the dough, repeatedly folding and pressing it (*above*). During the kneading process, constantly add more flour; the dough should become as stiff as possible without crumbling. Continue kneading until the dough is smooth and firm.

3 **Grating the dough.** Wrap the dough in plastic film. Put it in a freezer for about 30 minutes. Using the large holes of the grater, coarsely grate the dough on to a sheet of greaseproof paper. Use the pasta shreds straightaway or flour them generously in order to prevent them from sticking together.□

3 **Kneading the dough.** With the heel of your hand, press the ball of dough flat on a lightly floured surface. Fold the dough double, then press again. Repeat this procedure for 5 to 10 minutes, until the dough is silky and elastic. Leave the dough, covered with a cloth, for 1 hour.

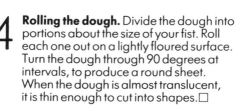

4 **Rolling the dough.** Divide the dough into portions about the size of your fist. Roll each one out on a lightly floured surface. Turn the dough through 90 degrees at intervals, to produce a round sheet. When the dough is almost translucent, it is thin enough to cut into shapes.□

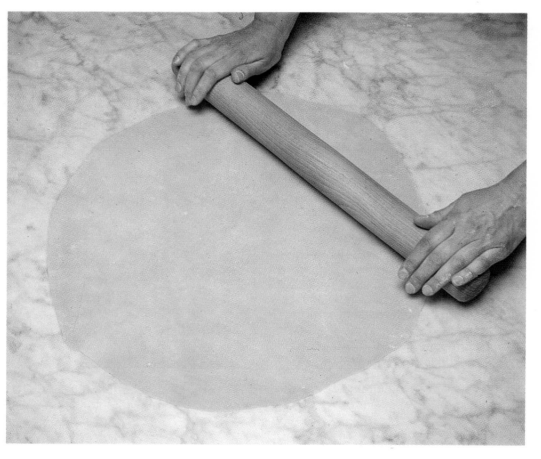

The Versatile Pasta Machine

Most of the work involved in making pasta at home—kneading and rolling out—can be done by a simple, hand-operated machine. The machine not only saves labour but also eliminates the all-manual method's step of resting the dough before rolling out (*page 44*). The entire pasta-making process thus can be completed in a matter of minutes.

There are several types of machine, all of which operate in similar ways. The most common version (*right*) consists of three pairs of rollers set in a sturdy frame. One pair of rollers is smooth, with an adjustable knob at the side of the machine to vary the width of the gap between the pair. These rollers first knead and then roll out the dough. The other rollers are fitted with cutters; they are used to slice the rolled dough into noodles (*page 48*). Each pair of rollers has a socket for the handle that operates the machine.

The dough itself is mixed from the same ingredients as hand-made pasta—flour, eggs, salt and often a little olive oil, manually kneaded just enough to bind them together. Most of the kneading is done by machine. The dough is floured, to prevent it from sticking to the machine, and then passed repeatedly through the smooth rollers. So that the dough is thick enough to be pressed firmly by the rollers—the essence of kneading—rather than slipping easily between them, it must be folded over between passages. If you are making a large quantity of pasta, tear the hand-kneaded dough into portions the size of your fist, so as to produce sheets of manageable proportions.

The kneading is complete when the dough is very smooth and has attained the exact width of the rollers. During the rolling-out stage, the gap between these rollers is decreased after each passage of the sheet through them. The dough is no longer folded between passages and it becomes progressively longer and thinner as the gap narrows. The sheet of dough is very fragile by this point, and careful handling is necessary to prevent it from tearing. When it has attained the thickness you require, the dough can be cut into different shapes—either by hand or with the machine's cutters—or used to enclose small morsels of stuffing (*page 53*).

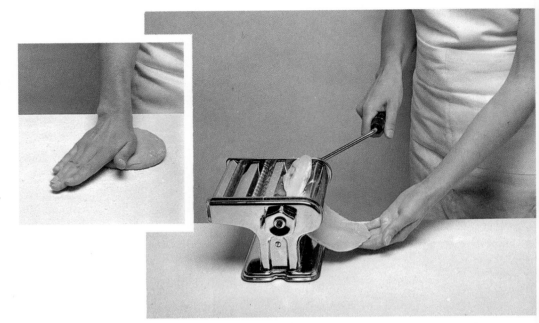

1 **Preparing the dough.** Mix fresh pasta dough (*page 44*) and lightly knead it. Divide it into fist-sized portions. Flatten each portion with your hand (*inset*). Set the adjustable rollers of the machine fully open. Flour the dough and pass it between the rollers. Support the rolled dough with one hand (*above*).

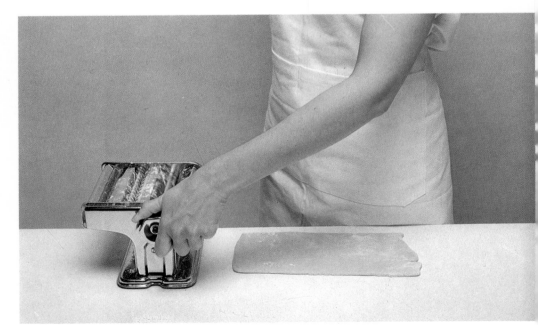

4 **Rolling out the dough.** Decrease the gap between the rollers by turning the knob at the side of the machine round by two or three notches (*above*). Flour the dough and, without folding it, pass it between the rollers. Flour the dough lightly once more.

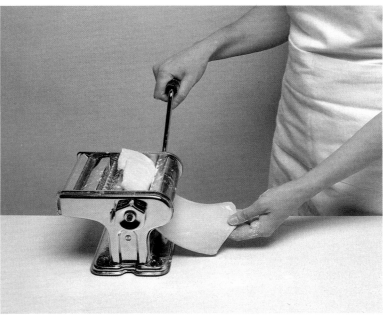

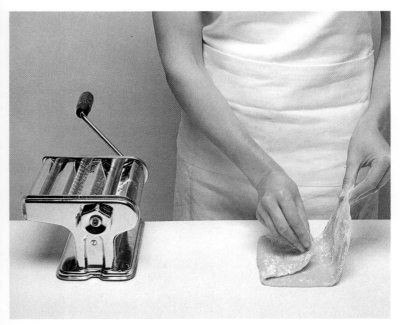

2 **Folding the rolled dough.** Lightly flour a smooth working surface. Lay the rolled dough out on it. Fold one end of the dough towards the middle and fold the other end on top of it to make three layers (*above*) of approximately the original size of the portion. Sprinkle on a little more flour.

3 **Kneading the dough by machine.** Turn the dough 90 degrees, to help produce a neat rectangular shape, and pass it between the smooth rollers again. Repeat the flouring, folding and rolling up to seven or eight times, occasionally turning the dough, until it is very smooth and shaped to the width of the machine.

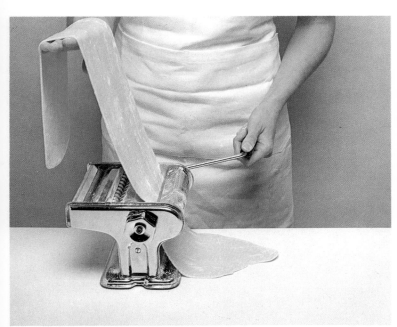

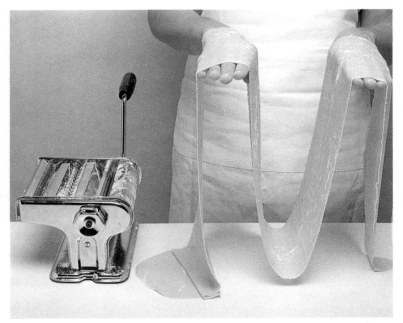

5 **Rolling the dough thinner.** Decrease the gap between the rollers by two or three more notches. Pass the dough through the machine again. Because the pasta sheet will now be quite long, support it with one hand as you feed it into the machine (*above*) and, as it emerges, help it to slide along the work surface rather than letting it fall in folds and sticking together.

6 **Drying out the rolled dough.** Flour the dough and roll it as thin as you require—for most purposes, the machine's next-to-finest setting is the most suitable. Unless you intend to make filled pasta shapes, hang the dough up to dry: an excellent way is to hang it over a broomstick supported by two chairs. When the dough is no longer sticky, cut it into the lengths you require. □

The Knack of Shaping Dough

Home-made pasta can be fashioned into a wide range of flat and rounded shapes, from simple noodles and squares to butterflies. Some of the most rapidly formed pasta shapes are demonstrated here; by using similar techniques you may well devise others of your own.

Noodles can be made either by machine (*right*) or by hand (*below*). Small squares are speedily prepared by cutting through several layers of pasta at once (*opposite page, below, right*). For decorative effect, a pastry wheel will give noodles and squares serrated edges; you can pinch rectangles into butterflies and press discs or balls of pasta into cupped shapes.

For cutting, the pasta dough should be flexible but not at all sticky. To achieve the right state, you may have to leave the rolled-out pasta to dry for a time—from a few minutes to 1 hour, depending on the temperature of the room and its humidity. Do not leave the pasta so long that it becomes leathery: it would crack when cut. After cutting, sprinkle the shapes liberally with fine semolina or flour to prevent them from sticking together.

Rapid Cutting with a Pasta Machine

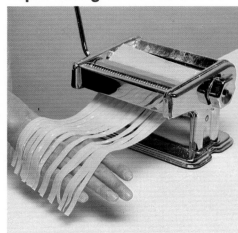 

Making noodles. In addition to the rollers for kneading and stretching dough, pasta machines have two or more cutters of different widths. To prepare medium-sized noodles, insert the handle of the machine beside the wider cutter and crank a length of the machine-rolled dough through the machine. Support the noodles with your hand as they emerge (*above*).

Cutting fine noodles. If you prefer thin noodles, insert the handle of the machine beside the narrow cutter, and pass the pasta sheet through it. Once the cutter has gripped the pasta, there is no need to touch the uncut sheet; leave it draped over the machine and use your free hand to catch the cut noodles as they emerge (*above*) to prevent them from tangling.

Hand-Sliced Noodles

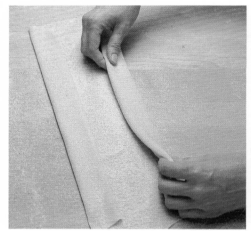 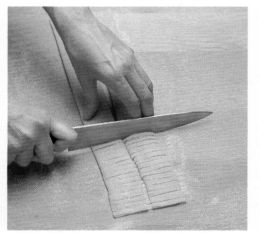 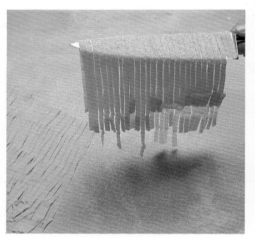

1 **Folding the dough.** On a wooden board, roll out a piece of pasta dough into a roughly circular shape. Sprinkle the sheet with fine semolina to prevent it from sticking. Fold the pasta very loosely over on to itself, working from both sides towards the centre until the two loose rolls meet. Do not press the folded pasta, or it may stick together.

2 **Cutting the noodles.** With a sharp knife, cut the dough into even strips (*above*). One advantage of cutting by hand instead of machine is that there is no restriction on the noodles' width: cut them as wide or narrow as you please.

3 **Unrolling the noodles.** Slide a knife underneath the cut pasta at the point where the two rolls meet. Insert the full length of the blade, then raise the knife, blunt edge uppermost: the rolled-up noodles will unroll, dropping down on either side of the blade (*above*).

Using a Pastry Wheel

Crimping the edges. Place a rectangular strip of either hand-rolled or machine-rolled pasta dough on a floured work surface. Cut round the outside of the strip with a pastry wheel to make a serrated edge. With the wheel, cut the strips into wide noodles (*above*) or lasagne—pieces 12 cm (5 inches) square.

Forming Figures-of-Eight

Pressing with your thumbs. Tear off small, walnut-sized pieces of dough from a larger piece and form them into sausage shapes with your fingers. Flatten the pieces slightly and place them on a floured surface. Using your thumbs, press down firmly at both ends of each shape, leaving an imprint on either side of a central ridge of dough (*above*).

Creating Mushroom Caps

Moulding in your palm. Roll some pasta dough on a floured surface into a cylinder approximately 2 cm ($\frac{3}{4}$ inch) in diameter. Cut the cylinder into 3 mm ($\frac{1}{8}$ inch) thick slices. Place a round in the palm of your hand and, with the thumb of the other hand, make a depression in the round—while twisting it slightly so that it becomes broader and thinner.

Fashioning Butterflies

Pinching neat rectangles. Cut round the edge of a rectangular sheet of pasta dough with a pastry wheel, to give a serrated edge. With the pastry wheel, cut the pasta sheet into small rectangles about 5 by 2.5 cm (2 by 1 inches). Pinch the small rectangles of dough at the centre to form butterflies.

Mass Producing Small Squares

Stacking layers for speedy cutting. Roll out sheets of pasta and cut them into long strips about the width of three fingers (*above, left*). Flour the strips and stack them neatly on top of each other. Cut this stack across into smaller strips about 2.5 cm (1 inch) wide. Cut the strips in half again to make squares (*above, right*).

Incorporating Colour and Flavour

Coloured pasta requires no more effort to make than plain pasta, yet the results, especially if you combine several colours in one dish, as illustrated on page 56, are spectacular. The colourings—herbs for speckled green pasta, beetroot for red, tomato for orange, spinach or chard for solid green and saffron for yellow—also flavour the pasta subtly.

All the colourings, except saffron, require preparation before they are mixed with the other pasta ingredients: flour, eggs, salt and olive oil. The herbs are chopped, the vegetables are cooked then chopped or puréed so that they will be assimilated evenly into the dough. Spinach is parboiled and puréed if the pasta is to be hand-rolled. If you use a machine, however, it is enough to chop the parboiled spinach finely; the machine's rollers will spread the colour uniformly. For a tomato colouring, simply use a little well-reduced tomato sauce (*page 15*). Beetroot must be boiled and puréed, no matter how you make the pasta; you can pound it in a mortar and pestle, but the easiest way to pulp beetroot is in an electric food processor.

To distribute saffron evenly through the dough combine it with the flour before the moist ingredients are added. The vegetable purées and the herbs can be combined with the other pasta ingredients in a single mixing step.

Once the colourings have been incorporated into the dough, the pasta is kneaded and rolled out by hand (*page 44*) or by machine (*page 46*). To compensate for the moistness of most of the colourings, add extra flour to the dough during kneading. Some colourings, such as spinach and herbs, release their moisture progressively and, to counter the stickiness, you will have to dust the pasta with more flour than usual when you roll it out.

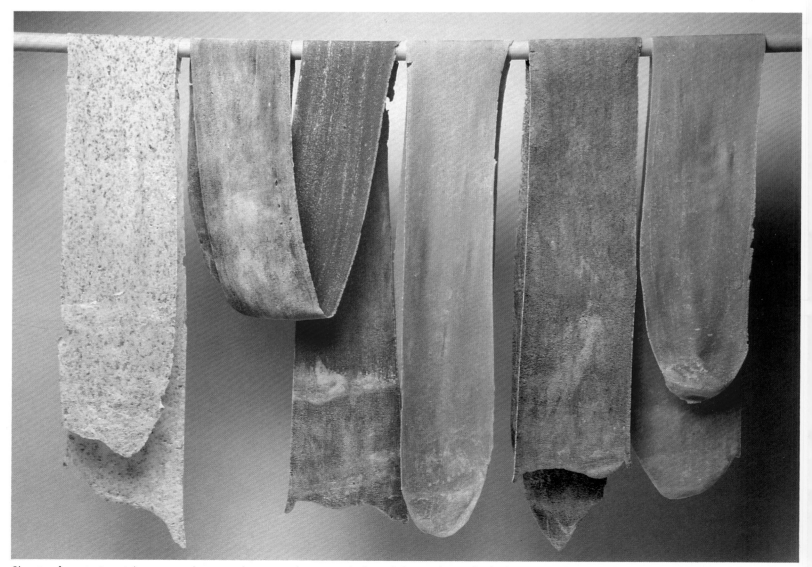

Sheets of pasta in rainbow tones hang to dry over a broomstick. From left to right are herb, beetroot, tomato, spinach and saffron-coloured pasta.

A Muted Green from Spinach

1 **Preparing the spinach.** Cook spinach in boiling salted water for 5 minutes. Drain and rinse it. Squeeze the spinach as dry as possible and chop it finely; then add it to flour, egg, salt and oil.

2 **Kneading the dough.** Mix all of the ingredients for the green pasta thoroughly with a fork. Knead the dough briefly by hand (*above*), then use a pasta machine to knead and roll it out.

An Orange Glow of Tomato

Blending in the tomato purée. To make orange-coloured pasta, stir a well-reduced tomato sauce (*page 15*) into the other ingredients before kneading and rolling out the dough.

A Speckling of Fresh Herbs

1 **Chopping herbs.** Finely chop a selection of fresh herbs—in this case parsley, sorrel, thyme, sage, tarragon and lovage. Basil, marjoram, hyssop and fennel are among other possibilities.

2 **Stirring in the herbs.** Using a fork, stir the chopped herbs into the other pasta ingredients—flour, olive oil, salt and eggs. Knead the pasta and roll it out.

A Warm Glow from Saffron

1 **Mixing in the saffron.** Add a knife-tip of saffron to the dry ingredients—flour and salt—and stir it in well with a fork to ensure the colour is distributed evenly.

A Lively Pink from Beetroot

1 **Puréeing the beetroot.** Boil unpeeled beetroots in salted water until tender—40 minutes to 2 hours, depending on their size. Peel and chop the beetroots and purée them in a food processor (*above*).

2 **Stirring in the beetroots.** Stir the beet purée with the other pasta ingredients in a mixing bowl or on a flat surface. Knead the pasta and roll it out.

2 **Kneading the dough.** When the saffron is evenly spread through the flour, mix in the liquid—eggs and oil. Knead and roll out the dough.

Savoury Fillings for any Shape

Puréed or finely chopped mixtures based on meat, fish, vegetables or cheese all make excellent fillings for pasta shapes. Two contrasting stuffings are demonstrated here, both suitable for filling any shape (*opposite page and overleaf*). A mild curd cheese and spinach stuffing is shown on the right; a sturdier mixture of braised meats with spinach is prepared below (*recipe, page 138*).

Both stuffings readily lend themselves to improvisation: you can vary the proportions as you please, omit spinach or replace it with other leaves such as lettuce or chard, and use any kind of meat, including leftovers. A little egg helps bind the ingredients, but is not essential because the stuffing will be tightly enclosed.

Since fresh pasta needs such brief boiling, any stuffing ingredient that cannot be eaten raw must be pre-cooked. Leaves must be squeezed dry after boiling, otherwise they will make the pasta soggy and easily torn. Similarly, a braising liquid should be reduced—or strained off and used later as a sauce for the pasta.

A Fresh Cheese Mixture

1 **Mixing cheese and egg.** Remove the stalks from spinach leaves. Cook the spinach in boiling water for 2 to 3 minutes. Drain it, rinse it under cold water, then squeeze and chop it finely. Mix *ricotta* cheese with eggs and some grated Parmesan cheese (*above*).

2 **Stirring in the spinach.** Add the chopped spinach to the other stuffing ingredients in the bowl. Stir to combine them all thoroughly (*above*). Season with salt, pepper and ground allspice to taste.

Braised Meats Allied with Spinach

1 **Cooking meats.** Finely chop onions and meat—here raw veal and beef with cooked ham. Sauté the onions in oil until soft. Stir in the meat, turning it until brown. Add thyme, a bay leaf and a glass each of wine and stock. Partially cover and simmer for 1 to 1½ hours, until the meat is tender and the liquid reduced.

2 **Mashing the stuffing.** Parboil trimmed spinach for 2 to 3 minutes in plenty of water. Drain and squeeze it dry. Chop it finely. Remove the thyme and bay leaf from the cooked meat. Transfer the meat and onions to a large bowl (*above*), and mash them thoroughly with a fork.

3 **Mixing in the spinach.** Add egg yolks and the chopped spinach to the mashed meat and onions. Use a fork to blend the ingredients thoroughly. Taste the stuffing and, if necessary, season it with salt and freshly ground pepper.

Enclosing Fillings in Tidy Packets

Small, stuffed pasta shapes are made by one of two methods. The filling is either sandwiched between two sheets of pasta (*below*), or it is placed in the centre of a small pasta square or circle, which is then wrapped around it (*overleaf*).

The ravioli here are of the first type and are the quickest shapes to make, since they lend themselves to mass production. A strip of pasta rolled out with a pasta machine, or a hand-rolled sheet of pasta trimmed to a rectangular shape, is dotted at regular intervals with small heaps of stuffing. The pasta between the mounds is moistened, so that it will stick to a second sheet of pasta laid on top of the stuffing. By running a knife or a pastry wheel carefully between the mounds of stuffing, you can quickly separate the dough into individual ravioli.

For the more complex shapes demonstrated on the following pages, the dough is first cut into squares or circles, then, once the stuffing is in place, folded in vari-

ous ways. A circle of pasta can simply be moistened along the edge, folded over and sealed to give a half-moon; or the half-moon can be curled round to make the compact shapes known as *tortellini* (*overleaf, above*). Folded and sealed like an envelope, a circle yields a neat rectangular package; and squares with adjacent edges pinched together produce attractive star shapes (*box, page 54*).

You can make pasta stars from small squares just lightly pinched together at the corners (*page 55, below*). Most stuffings would fall out of such an open container, but if you use a stiff, coherent mixture—a pounded raw meat stuffing as here, or a combination of curd cheese and grated Parmesan—and smear just a little on each pasta square, the stuffing will cling to the pasta during cooking.

Dough for any stuffed shapes should be rolled to a thickness of 3 mm ($\frac{1}{8}$ inch)—a little thicker than dough for unstuffed pasta: the packages must be fairly strong to hold their contents. So that the pasta can be moulded round the stuffing, it

should be as moist and flexible as possible: use the pasta sheets immediately they are ready. For ravioli, roll out just two sheets at a time; for the other shapes, roll and cut out as many circles or squares as you want; flour them well so that they do not stick together and stack them on top of each other to keep them from drying out while you work.

Each pasta shape needs a margin of at least 5 mm ($\frac{1}{4}$ inch) of sealed pasta round the stuffing to enclose it securely. You should avoid using too much stuffing or, with ravioli, placing the mounds of stuffing too closely together. Make sure no stray stuffing lies between the edges you are trying to seal, or they will not hold together when you press them.

Because of the dough's moistness, stuffed pasta shapes tend to stick to each other and to any surface on which they are laid. To prevent sticking and tearing, place them, well separated, on a floured cloth until you are ready to cook them.

The Knack of Forming Ravioli

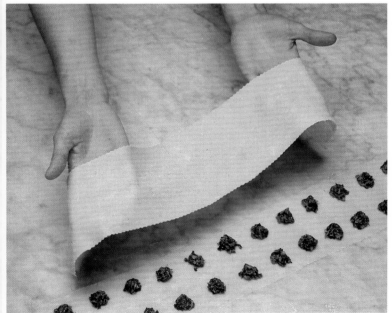

1 Sealing in the stuffing. Roll out two identically sized sheets of pasta; trim their edges with a pastry wheel. Place half-teaspoon portions of stuffing (*opposite page*) on one of the sheets at 5 cm (2 inch) intervals; leave a 2.5 cm (1 inch) margin round the edge of the sheet. Brush the dough with water between the mounds of stuffing. Lay the second sheet of pasta over the first one (*above*).

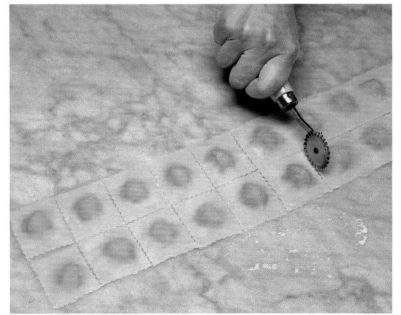

2 Cutting the ravioli. With the side of your hand, press the pasta between the mounds of stuffing, so that the two moistened sheets stick together firmly. Using a fluted pastry wheel, cut along and across the dough, midway between the rows of stuffing to separate the individual ravioli (*above*).□

Moulding Circles into Tortellini

1 **Adding the filling.** With a biscuit cutter, stamp circles about 7.5 cm (3 inches) in diameter from a sheet of pasta dough. In the middle of each circle, put a teaspoon of stuffing—here, a spinach and curd cheese mixture (*page 52*). Using a pastry brush or your finger, moisten the edge of the circle with water (*above*).

2 **Making the first fold.** Fold over the circle of dough to form a half-moon containing the stuffing. To seal in the stuffing, pinch the moistened edges of the dough together between your thumb and forefinger (*above*). If you like, you can cook the pasta in this form—or go on to make *tortellini* (*Steps 3 and 4*).

Two Ingenious Ways to Form a Wrapping

Folding circles for a trim package. With a biscuit cutter, stamp circles about 7.5 cm (3 inches) in diameter from a sheet of pasta dough. Put a teaspoon of stuffing in the centre of each circle. Brush the rim of the circle with a little water. Fold two opposite sides of the circle over the stuffing. Fold the other two sides over the first two (*above*), and press gently to seal the envelope-like container.

Pinching squares for a star-like shape. With a fluted or plain pastry wheel, cut a sheet of pasta dough into squares measuring approximately 7.5 cm (3 inches) across. Place a teaspoon of stuffing in the middle of each square, and brush the edge of the square with water. Pinch together two opposite corners of the square over the stuffing, then fold the other two corners into the centre. To enclose the stuffing securely, pinch the edges together.

3 **Bending the half-moon into shape.** Take each half-moon in both hands and curve it gently into a ring shape around your index finger, until its ends are almost touching. At the same time, fold the sealed margin of the dough up towards the straight edge of the shape, to make a groove around the edge (*above*).

4 **Fixing the shape.** Pinch the ends of the curled half-moon firmly together, so that the shape remains curled round. Lay the completed *tortellini* on a floured towel; be sure that they are not touching, or they may stick together. Leave the *tortellini* to dry out for a few minutes before you cook them.□

Loosely Enclosing a Finely Ground Stuffing

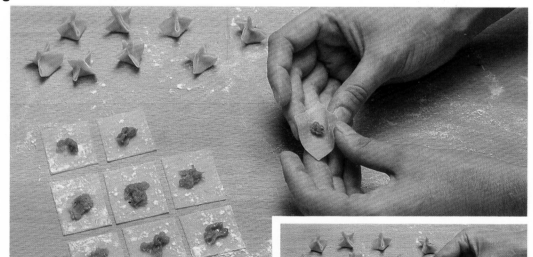

1 **Preparing the stuffing.** Trim fat and connective tissue from a piece of lamb shoulder. Chop the meat into small pieces. In a mortar, pound the lamb with peeled garlic, salt and pepper, and herbs—mint, oregano and parsley are used here—until it is a fairly smooth paste. Alternatively, purée the meat and flavourings in a food processor.

2 **Pinching the corners.** Cut a sheet of pasta dough into 3 cm (1¼ inch) squares. Smear a little stuffing on each square. Bring together two opposite corners of each square (*above*) over the stuffing, then the other two, and pinch all four corners together (*right*). There is no need to seal all the edges: the stuffing will adhere to the pasta during cooking.□

3
Cooking with Pasta
From the Elemental to the Exotic

A selection of differently coloured, tender noodles, together with pasta shapes stuffed with cheese and spinach, are served with chopped ham, cheese and cream from a pie made from olive oil pastry. The moistness of the pie filling contrasts perfectly with the crisp texture of the golden-brown base and lid.

Of all products made from grains, pasta is perhaps the most fascinating: its smooth, succulent texture makes it irresistible, however simply it is cooked. Boiled until barely firm, tossed with butter, cream or olive oil, and sprinkled with grated cheese or herbs, any pasta is delicious; but such restrained treatment is especially appropriate for stuffed pasta shapes, whose delicate fillings make extra flavouring redundant. If you choose to direct the limelight away from the pasta, there is an endless choice of accompaniments—lightly boiled or sautéed vegetables, such delicacies as truffles or wild mushrooms, and any number of fish, meat and vegetable sauces (*recipes, pages 115-123*).

Sauces for pasta—and for dumplings, which are close cousins of pasta in both their making and their cooking (*page 60*)—are often variations on such classics as a white sauce and a tomato sauce (*pages 14-15*). One elaboration on the tomato sauce is a meat sauce, made by simmering chopped beef or other meat with aromatic vegetables and tomatoes. A meat sauce can be enriched with cream, and modified by adding sautéed chicken livers or such vegetables as peas or mushrooms. For a seafood sauce, tomatoes can be paired with mussels or clams and their liquor, or with robustly flavoured fish—tuna and anchovies, for example. Other delicious dressings for pasta include nuts pounded with oil, and poppy seeds or even breadcrumbs fried to crispness in plenty of butter.

Instead of simply having a sauce poured over it, pasta can be combined with other foods in more formal ways. It can make up part of the stuffing for a pie, for example (*opposite and page 72*), or for a dish encased in sautéed slices of aubergines or courgettes (*page 71*). Pasta can even form a casing itself, although it lacks the strength to support a moist stuffing unaided. However, lined with a mousseline forcemeat that firms on cooking to make a delicious cement, coils of long-strand macaroni give a sculptured beehive exterior to a moulded dish (*page 68*).

Less ambitiously, large pasta squares arranged in an overlapping pattern may be layered with sauces and cheese and baked, to produce a dish with alternating textures (*page 62*). Simmered in milk to a creamy consistency, grated pasta shreds form the basis of an unusual soufflé (*page 74*). And rolled up raw with a stuffing, a large sheet of pasta can be poached and sliced into spirally patterned rounds (*page 64*).

Steps in Boiling and Serving Pasta

The most basic way of preparing pasta is to boil it in salted water and mix it with a sauce in its serving dish. The sauce can be no more than a light coating of olive oil or butter—or a rich and savoury meat sauce (*page 14*). The simpler coatings are especially appropriate for fresh home-made pasta, whose delicate flavour would be masked by an assertive sauce. On the right, for example, fresh noodles are simply served with butter and grated Parmesan cheese. In the lower demonstration, dried *trenette* (rippled noodles) are boiled with potatoes and beans; the pasta and vegetables are served with *pesto*, a pungent basil and garlic sauce (*box, opposite page; recipe, page 122*).

Both fresh and dried pasta are boiled in the same way; the only difference is the cooking time. To keep the pasta from clumping together as it cooks, use plenty of lightly salted water—at least 4 litres (6 pints) for every 500 g (1 lb) of pasta—and add a spoonful of oil to the water. Make sure the water is boiling vigorously when you add the pasta: the water's movement will help to keep the pasta separate. Stir the pasta gently at the beginning of cooking to unravel any tangled strands.

Pasta should be boiled until it is tender but not flabby. The Italian expression for perfectly cooked pasta *al dente*—"to the tooth"—means that the pasta should still have a firm, faintly chewy core. Fresh pasta shapes—whether unfilled (*page 48*) or filled (*page 52*)—reach the *al dente* stage after anything from 2 to 5 minutes of cooking. Dried pasta requires at least twice as long. The precise time depends on the thickness and dryness of the pasta, and its constituents: pasta made from semolina, for example, needs more cooking than pasta made from flour. To time the cooking accurately, remove a sample of pasta at regular intervals and pinch it.

Once it is ready, the pasta should be removed from the water immediately so that it stops cooking. You can use a wooden pasta fork (*Step 2, above*) to lift out and drain long pasta shapes, such as noodles and spaghetti, before transferring them to a heated serving dish. Alternatively, long shapes can be drained in a colander—the most appropriate method for draining small pasta shapes.

Fresh Egg Noodles with Butter and Cheese

1 Adding noodles to water. Bring plenty of water to the boil in a large saucepan. Add salt and a spoonful of oil. When the water is boiling rapidly, put in the noodles. Stir them to make sure the strands are not stuck together. Keep the water at a steady boil.

2 Draining the pasta. With a pasta fork, lift out some of the pasta from the pan every 30 seconds or so. Test whether a strand is cooked by pinching it. When the noodles are done, lift them out with the fork. Hold each forkful above the pan for a few seconds to drain, then transfer it to a warmed bowl or individual plates.

Dried Shapes Cooked with Vegetables

1 Cooking trenette. Peel and slice potatoes. Top and tail green beans. In a large pan, bring plenty of lightly salted water to the boil and add a spoonful of oil. Put in the potatoes; 5 minutes later, add the beans. When the water returns to a rapid boil, add the *trenette*, pushing them against the base of the pan until they soften and bend (*above*).

2 Testing for doneness. About 7 minutes after adding the pasta, begin testing for doneness. At 30-second intervals lift out a few strands with a pasta fork and pinch one (*above*). When the pasta is done, add a spoonful of the water to the *pesto* sauce (*box, right*). Empty the remaining contents of the pan into a colander.

3 **Tossing the pasta in butter and cheese.** Grate some Parmesan cheese (*inset*). As soon as all of the pasta is in the serving bowl or on individual plates, add the cheese and a little butter. Toss the pasta well with a spoon and a fork (*above*). Serve at once.□

An Aromatic Fresh Herb Sauce

Pesto—a word that simply means "pounded"— is an uncooked mixture of basil, garlic, pine-nuts and salt, pounded with olive oil to make a smooth paste. Grated Parmesan or *pecorino* cheese gives it body and extra flavour. A little of the pasta's cooking liquid moistens the sauce, making it easier to mix with pasta.

1 **Making a paste.** In a mortar, grind garlic cloves, pine-nuts and coarse salt to a pulp. Tear fresh basil leaves and pound them in. Add grated cheese and a trickle of olive oil.

3 **Adding the sauce.** Immediately, transfer the pasta, potatoes and beans from the colander to a warmed serving bowl or individual plates. Add the *pesto* sauce (*inset*). Toss the pasta and vegetables thoroughly (*above*) with the sauce.□

2 **Completing the sauce.** Add more olive oil in a slow trickle; stir the sauce with the pestle, until the sauce is smooth and creamy. Before using the *pesto* sauce, add a little of the pasta's cooking liquid.

Plump Shapes Cooked Like Pasta

Very similar in composition to pasta, dumplings (*right, below*) and plump batter noodles (*right*) are cooked almost like pasta and are often served with the same range of sauces.

Batter noodles are made from the same ingredients as ordinary pasta—flour, eggs and sometimes a little oil—but a larger proportion of egg (*recipe, page 118*), gives them a consistency too liquid to permit kneading and rolling out. They are shaped at the moment of cooking, setting in the form in which they enter the cooking water. Because rapidly boiling water would break up the noodles, they should be cooked at a bare simmer.

To shape batter into noodles, you can either squeeze it from a piping bag, or trickle it into the water through the holes of a colander. An alternative technique uses a somewhat firmer batter made with slightly more flour. Spread the batter on a board and use a knife to slide small strips into the simmering water (*recipe, page 121*). However they are shaped, the batter noodles need only cook until they become firm—a minute or less. In the demonstration here, they are served with a sauce of butter and breadcrumbs (*Step 4*) whose crispness contrasts with the noodles' soft, springy texture.

Dumplings can be made from the same ingredients as pasta, or you can replace some or all of the flour with semolina, cornmeal, cooked potato or grated raw potato and add some cheese or chopped, cooked spinach for flavour (*recipes, pages 142-145*). The dumplings demonstrated here are made from cooked, puréed potatoes, mixed with eggs and a little flour and butter. The mixture is kneaded briefly and formed into short cylinders before cooking. Each cylinder is rolled against the prongs of a fork to shape it (*Step 3*).

To prevent them from sticking together, dumplings should be cooked in plenty of simmering water, in as wide a pan as possible. If you do not have a pan of at least 3.5 litres (6 pints) capacity, cook the dumplings in batches of 20 to 30; larger dumplings should be cooked in smaller batches. The dumplings sink when first dropped into lightly boiling water; they are cooked when they rise to the surface.

Squeezing Batter into Simmering Water

1 **Whisking the batter.** Put flour into a large bowl. Mix eggs and olive oil in another bowl. With a whisk, beat the eggs and oil into the flour (*above, left*). Continue whisking until bubbles appear and the batter is smooth. Whisk in more flour until the mixture is thick and creamy, but will still trickle from the whisk (*above, right*).

Moulding and Cooking Potato Dumplings

1 **Puréeing potatoes.** Boil potatoes in salted water; drain them well and peel them. With a pestle, force the potatoes through a metal sieve set over a bowl (*above*). Add butter, as here, or lard and stir it in; the heat of the potatoes will melt it. Stir in flour, beaten eggs, salt and pepper. Add more flour, if necessary, to give a stiff but workable dough.

2 **Rolling the dough.** Lightly knead the dough in a bowl for about 2 minutes. Divide it into fist-sized portions. On a floured board, roll each portion into a cylinder about the thickness of a finger (*above*). Divide each cylinder into approximately 2.5 cm (1 inch) lengths.

2 **Filling a piping bag.** Insert a plain nozzle into a piping bag. To prevent the batter from escaping as you fill the bag, fold the nozzle back against the bag. Turn the upper half of the bag inside out and spoon the batter into the lower half. Fold back and twist the upper part of the bag to enclose the mixture.

3 **Piping the noodles.** Holding the piping bag closed at the top, squeeze it gently until batter emerges through the end of the nozzle. Squeeze the batter, in approximately 7.5 to 12 cm (3 to 5 inch) lengths, into a large pan of simmering, lightly salted water. Cover the pan and cook the noodles for about a minute, until the water returns to the boil.

4 **Serving the noodles.** Drain the noodles in a colander and transfer them to a heated serving dish. To make a sauce, sauté fresh breadcrumbs in a generous quantity of butter until they are golden. Pour the butter and the breadcrumbs over the noodles.□

3 **Shaping the dumplings.** Place each dumpling on the underside of the prongs of a fork. Press the centre of the dumpling with your finger (*above, left*), giving the dumpling a crescent shape. Roll the dumpling back along the fork to emboss it with a pattern (*above, right*).

4 **Cooking the dumplings.** Bring a large pan of salted water to a simmer. Drop the dumplings into the water. Cook the dumplings, uncovered, for about 3 minutes or until they rise to the water's surface. Drain them in a colander or with a slotted spoon (*above*) transfer the cooked dumplings to a dish.

5 **Covering with sauce.** Prepare a sauce—here, a meat sauce (*page 14*)—and pour it over the heaped dumplings (*above*). Serve the dumplings at once or sprinkle the sauce with grated cheese and place the dish in an oven set at 200°C (400°F or Mark 6) until the cheese has melted and lightly browned.□

Baking with Sauces and Flavourings

Although any pasta shape can be combined with a sauce and then baked, the large flat squares or rectangles known as lasagne are particularly suited to this purpose. Arranged side by side to form wide sheets, the pasta squares are usually layered with different sauces to produce a dish whose texture alternates appetizingly between firm and creamy.

The parboiled green lasagne used below are layered with a meat sauce, a white sauce (*page 14*) and grated cheese. To keep the sauces from spilling out of the dish, and to make a decorative rim, the first layer of pasta is arranged so that it does not simply cover the base of the dish, but also lines the sides and overhangs the edges. When the subsequent layers of pasta are in place, the overhanging pasta is flipped back into the centre of the dish.

To bake noodles or other smaller shapes, the parboiled pasta can be simply mixed with a sauce before being transferred to a baking dish. If you want to make a layered dish, you can alternate the mixture of pasta and sauce with additional flavouring, such as tomatoes, mushrooms or ham. On the opposite page (*box*), small pasta squares are combined with egg yolks, soured cream and melted butter and the mixture is lightened with beaten egg whites and layered with chopped ham (*recipe, page 127*).

1 **Parboiling the lasagne.** Bring a large pan of salted water to the boil. Add lasagne—in this demonstration, coloured green with spinach (*page 51*)—a few at a time and boil them until they are barely cooked: this should take about 1½ to 2 minutes for fresh pasta and about 5 minutes for dried pasta.

2 **Rinsing and drying the lasagne.** Remove the lasagne from the pan with a wide spatula and briefly immerse them in a bowl of cold water in order to stop the cooking. Place the lasagne side by side on a towel to drain (*above*). Make sure that the squares are not touching each other, or they may stick together.

3 **Layering the lasagne.** Butter a shallow ovenproof dish and cover the bottom with a layer of meat sauce (*page 14*). Arrange lasagne over the meat sauce so that the squares overlap by about 1 cm (½ inch), and the outer edges overhang the rim of the dish (*above*). Cover the sauce with more overlapping squares.

4 **Adding the white sauce.** Coarsely grate *mozzarella* and finely grate Parmesan cheese and blend them together with your hands. Spoon a layer of meat sauce over the lasagne lining the dish; follow with a layer of white sauce (*page 14*). Sprinkle the mixture of grated cheeses over the white sauce.

Layering with Chopped Ham

1 Adding egg whites. Parboil small pasta squares (*page 48*) in salted water. Drain them and cool them briefly in a bowl of cold water. Separate eggs and whisk the yolks with melted butter and soured cream. Add the mixture to the pasta. Whisk the egg whites until they are stiff and form peaks and add them to the pasta, egg yolks and cream (*above*).

2 Adding the ham. Use a spoon to gently fold the egg whites into the moistened pasta. Place a layer of the mixture at the bottom of a buttered ovenproof dish. Sprinkle with diced cooked ham (*above*). Continue to build up the dish with alternate layers of the pasta mixture and ham, finishing with the pasta.

3 Cooking the dish. Put the assembly in an oven preheated to 180°C (350°F or Mark 4) and cook it for about 1 hour. The top of the dish should be a light golden colour. Allow the dish to settle for a few minutes before serving (*above*).

5 Building up the layers. Place another layer of lasagne on top of the cheese, but arrange the squares inside the dish instead of overhanging the edge (*above*). Add more layers of meat sauce, white sauce and cheese. Flip the overhanging lasagne back over the cheese so that it borders the dish.

6 Cooking the lasagne. Brush the border with melted butter and cover the dish with foil. Cook it in an oven preheated to 180°C (350°F or Mark 4), for about 25 minutes, removing the foil after about 12 minutes to let the top brown. Leave the dish at room temperature to firm for a few minutes before serving it (*above*).□

Filled Rolls to Feed Two or Twenty

Stuffing and Poaching a Giant Sheet

A roll of pasta and stuffing can be made on any scale—from a huge cylinder that is sliced into spiral-patterned rounds for serving (*right*) to packages small enough for individual portions (*opposite page, far right*). The preparation and method of cooking must be adjusted according to the size of the roll.

For a large roll (*recipe, page 140*) home-made pasta is essential: commercial pasta is not available in large enough sheets. The simplest way to prepare a large sheet is by hand; the pasta must be rolled fairly thick, so that the sheet is not too fragile.

The raw pasta is laid on a large piece of muslin and spread evenly with a stuffing of a contrasting colour, which will give a decorative effect when the finished roll is sliced. Here, a spinach and *ricotta* stuffing (*page 52*) is used; a meat stuffing is another possibility. The pasta and stuffing should be rolled firmly, but with the minimum of handling: the best method is to lift one end of the muslin on which the pasta lies off the work surface, so that the sheet will roll up almost unaided.

Poaching is the only cooking method suitable for the large roll; if it were baked, it would have to be parboiled until tender before being rolled, and such an unwieldy sheet of pasta dough would inevitably be damaged during parboiling. The large roll should be wrapped in muslin to hold its form during cooking. A fish kettle (*Step 5*) is the most logical poaching vessel: not only will its shape accommodate a very long roll, but its integral rack simplifies lifting the roll in and out. If you do not have a fish kettle, make a shorter roll that can be lifted with the help of two spatulas.

Small rolls, called cannelloni, can be prepared from either home-made pasta—here, coloured with saffron (*page 51*)—or commercial pasta squares; the large tubes sold as cannelloni are also intended for stuffing, but are less easy to handle than squares that you roll up yourself. Small squares can easily be rolled round a stuffing by hand, without the help of a piece of muslin. They are generally baked: the preliminary parboiling presents no problems, and baking provides the opportunity for cooking the roll with a sauce—a white sauce, for example, or the tomato sauce used here.

1 **Unrolling a large pasta sheet.** Mix, knead and roll out a sheet of pasta to a thickness of about 5 mm (¼ inch) (*page 44*). Lightly flour a large piece of muslin. Roll the pasta sheet loosely round a rolling pin, then carefully unroll it from the rolling pin on to the muslin (*above*).

2 **Spreading the stuffing.** Prepare a stuffing—here, a mixture of spinach and *ricotta* (*page 52*) with some chopped ham. Spoon the filling on to the pasta sheet (*above*) and spread to an even thickness of about 1 cm (½ inch). Leave a 2.5 cm (1 inch) uncovered border all round the edge of the pasta sheet.

5 **Poaching the roll.** Place the wrapped roll on the rack of a fish kettle and lower it into the kettle (*above*). Pour on boiling water to immerse the roll. Place the fish kettle over two stove burners and simmer the roll for about 40 minutes. Lift the rack out of the kettle and allow the roll to drain. Leave it to cool slightly so that it is easier to handle. Cut off the strings and unwrap the roll (*inset*).

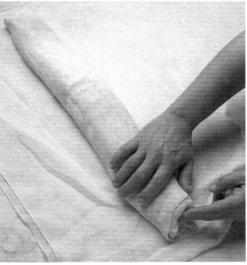

3 **Rolling the pasta.** Lift one end of the muslin a little way off the work surface, so that the end of the pasta sheet rolls over. Gradually gather up more of the muslin, to nudge the pasta along. During the rolling, regularly press the roll with your hands to compact it. Leave the rolled-up pasta near the end of the piece of muslin.

4 **Folding in the ends.** Tuck in the ends of the pasta roll, so that the filling is well enclosed. Roll the muslin around the pasta, so that the roll is tightly cocooned in layers of cloth. Tie the cloth with string to enclose the two ends of the roll.

Rolling and Baking Cannelloni

1 **Mixing a stuffing.** Gradually add beaten whole eggs and egg yolks to a bowl of *ricotta* cheese, stirring to blend them in evenly (*above*). Add some grated Parmesan cheese and chopped parsley. Season with salt, pepper and nutmeg.

2 **Rolling the pasta.** Parboil squares of pasta and drain them. For extra flavour, line each square with prosciutto. Spread the filling on to one end. Roll up the squares, brush them with melted butter and place in a buttered baking dish.

6 **Slicing and serving the roll.** Slide the roll from the muslin to a heated dish and serve the roll as quickly as possible. Use a sharp knife to slice the roll, first dipping the knife into hot water so that the pasta does not stick to it. Serve the slices with a sauce (*above*)—in this case, a chunky tomato sauce (*page 15*) with basil leaves.□

3 **Serving the rolls.** Pour tomato sauce between the rolls and sprinkle them with grated Parmesan. Bake at 190°C (375°F or Mark 5) for 20 minutes. Cover the dish with foil for the first 10 minutes to prevent drying. Serve hot (*above*).□

Noodles Fried to Golden Crispness

Once they have been made tender by parboiling or soaking, noodles, spaghetti and all small pasta shapes can be fried until richly coloured and crisped. Fried pasta can serve as a garnish or as an integral part of a whole meal dish, as in this demonstration, where Chinese egg noodles are fried with shrimps, crab and pork and seasoned with sesame-seed oil and vinegar (*recipe, page 124*).

Wheat-based pasta should first be parboiled until it softens but still has a firm core. The parboiling time depends on the pasta. Fresh noodles are ready in a few seconds—indeed, fresh noodles are sometimes sautéed without any parboiling at all, to accompany a dish of boiled and butter-tossed pasta. The thin dried noodles used here require about 3 minutes of parboiling, and thicker dried shapes may take 7 to 8 minutes to become flexible. Dried rice noodles need only be soaked in cold water for about 15 minutes; they are then soft enough to be fried.

Before you fry the pasta, set it aside in a colander to drain completely dry while you prepare all the other ingredients. Here, boned shoulder of pork has been chopped into small cubes, shrimps shelled, and the flesh of a boiled crab extracted from its body and claws.

The meat and shellfish are first fried separately from the noodles; the rapid stirring and turning necessary to cook these ingredients evenly would break up the fragile pasta. When the time comes to cook the noodles, they must be stirred gently, with a wooden spoon or spatula; keep them moving, so that they brown evenly and do not burn on the bottom of the pan. When the pasta is well coloured, the prepared ingredients are mixed with the noodles, reheated, seasoned and then served at once, piping hot.

1 Boiling noodles. On a high heat, bring a large saucepan of salted water to a rolling boil. Immerse the noodles in the boiling water. Keep the water at a vigorous boil: the constant motion will prevent the noodles from sticking to the bottom of the pan and to each other.

2 Testing for doneness. Boil the noodles for about 3 minutes or until they are barely tender to the bite; from time to time, lift the noodles from the boiling water to check on their progress. Drain the parboiled noodles in a sieve, rinse under cold running water to stop them cooking and set them aside.

6 Seasoning the dish. Pour sesame-seed oil over the contents of the pan (*above, left*). Add a dash of vinegar; add salt if necessary. Quickly, but carefully, toss the ingredients together until they are all coated with oil (*above, right*); the delicate flavour of the sesame-seed oil would be destroyed if it were heated for too long.

3 **Cooking meats.** Heat oil in a frying pan. Sauté shelled shrimps for 5 minutes or until they are golden-brown, then set them aside on a plate. Sauté boiled crab meat for about 2 minutes and set it aside with the shrimps. Add the cubes of pork to the pan. Stir and turn them (*above*) for about 10 minutes or until they are well browned. Set the pork aside.

4 **Sautéing the noodles.** Heat some oil in a large frying pan. Add the noodles to the hot oil. Cook them for about 3 minutes or until they are golden-brown, turning them frequently with a spatula (*above*).

5 **Adding the meats.** Using a spatula, add the crab, shrimps and pork to the fried noodles. Gently fold them into the mass of noodles and heat all of the ingredients together for about 3 minutes, stirring occasionally, until warmed through.

7 **Serving the dish.** The noodles should be served as hot as possible. Transfer them, using a spatula and spoon, on to a well-heated serving dish (*right*), or into heated individual-sized bowls.☐

A Casing of Coiled Macaroni

Long strands of macaroni, packed side by side in a single layer, can make a striking container for a savoury filling. The macaroni lines a butter-coated mould, which supports both pasta and filling as they cook; the dish is unmoulded for serving. In this demonstration, the macaroni is coiled in a hemispherical mould, which gives the dish a beehive aspect when it is turned out (*overleaf; recipe, page 132*).

As well as providing the casing, pasta also forms part of the stuffing. Cut-up macaroni left over from lining the mould can be mixed with all sorts of pre-cooked and chopped meat, fish and vegetables: sautéed chicken livers, for example, or fish and shellfish in a sauce. For this demonstration, the macaroni is mixed with veal sweetbreads in a thick sauce. The sweetbreads—calf thymus glands—require advance preparation: first, they are soaked to draw off blood, then parboiled, trimmed, weighted to compact them and, finally, braised with wine and aromatic vegetables. The braising liquid, thickened with a flour and butter roux, becomes the sauce.

To support the casing, and to prevent the macaroni from unravelling, the pasta is coated with a mousseline forcemeat. The forcemeat—a very fine purée of flesh, bound with egg white and enriched with cream—firms as it cooks; liberally applied to the inside of the macaroni, it forms a wall that prevents the unmoulded beehive from collapsing.

The chicken forcemeat used in this demonstration will go well with any meat stuffing; substitute a forcemeat made from whiting, hake or pike if you choose a fish or shellfish stuffing. The proportions of a mousseline can vary, within limits. More cream makes the mousseline rich and delicate, but it is the egg white that provides the support for the timbale. Safe proportions to use are one large egg white and a maximum of $\frac{1}{4}$ litre (8 fl oz) of double cream for 250 g (8 oz) of flesh.

1 Preparing sweetbreads. In a bowl of cold water, soak veal sweetbreads for an hour. Transfer them to a saucepan and cover them with fresh cold water. Bring the water to the boil, simmer the sweetbreads for 2 minutes, then drain them. Plunge them into cold water to stop the cooking. Remove gristle and fat and peel off the surface membrane.

2 Flattening the sweetbreads. Place the sweetbreads side by side on a towel. Place another towel over them (*above*). Compress the sweetbreads underneath a board which is pressed down with kitchen weights or heavy cans. Leave them to firm for about 2 hours.

6 Straining the liquid. Remove the sweetbreads from the pan and let them cool. Tip the rest of the contents of the pan into a fine sieve set over a bowl. Using a pestle, press the vegetables firmly, but without grinding, to extract the liquid and flavour (*above*). Discard the vegetables and herbs left in the sieve. Slice the sweetbreads and reserve them.

7 Making the sauce. In a small pan, make a roux by gently heating butter and stirring in a little flour. Add the strained liquid, whisking constantly. Put the pan half off the heat and simmer the sauce gently for about 40 minutes, to reduce it by about half. Remove the fatty skin that repeatedly forms on the side of the surface furthest from the heat.

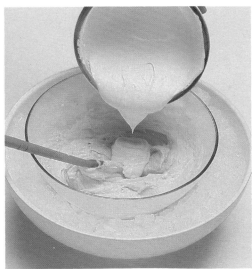

3 **Puréeing chicken flesh.** Bone and skin a chicken breast. Chop the flesh into small pieces. In a food processor, grind the pieces to a purée, then combine them with an egg white. To make the purée very smooth, press it through a fine drum sieve (*above*). Transfer the purée to a bowl set on a bed of cracked ice; press a piece of plastic film against its surface.

4 **Incorporating the cream.** Chill the purée in the refrigerator for about an hour. Slowly mix in unwhipped cream until the purée is soft enough to stir easily. Whip the rest of the cream until it can still just be poured, then blend it in (*above*). Reserve the mousseline in the bowl set over ice.

5 **Braising the veal sweetbreads.** Chop carrots and onions finely. Sauté them in butter, with a sprinkling of mixed herbs, until softened—about 10 minutes. Add the sweetbreads, in a single layer (*above*). Pour in a good splash of white wine, and boil to reduce by half. Add a bay leaf and cover the sweetbreads with stock. Simmer, covered, for 40 minutes.

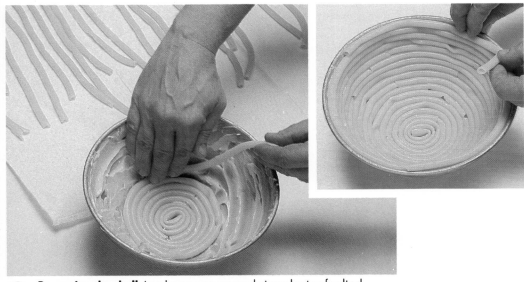

8 **Preparing the shell.** In a large saucepan, bring plenty of salted water to the boil. Add long macaroni and cook it until it is *al dente*. Drain the macaroni in a colander. Place the strands on a towel; make sure the strands are not touching or they may stick together. Thickly butter a hemispherical mould or a metal bowl. Starting at the centre of the mould (*above*), coil the macaroni so as to leave no gaps between the strands. Continue until the inside of the mould is completely lined (*inset*).

9 **Spreading the mousseline.** Leave the mould in the refrigerator until the butter has set firmly enough to hold the macaroni in place. Spoon three-quarters of the mousseline into the mould, and spread it evenly over the surface of the coiled macaroni (*above*). ▶

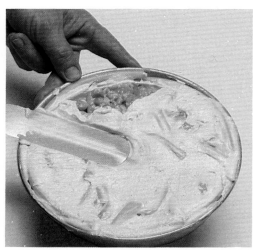

10 **Mixing the stuffing.** Cut the leftover macaroni into 5 cm (2 inch) lengths. Put them in a large bowl with the sliced sweetbreads. Add enough of the sauce to the bowl to bind the mixture (*above*), and stir it in.

11 **Stuffing the shell.** Fill the macaroni case with the stuffing. To eliminate any air pockets, gently press the stuffing down. Level the top and, using a metal spatula, spread over it the remainder of the mousseline (*above*).

12 **Cooking the dish.** Press a round of buttered greaseproof paper over the mousseline. Place a trivet in a large pan, lift the mould into the pan (*above*) and half fill the pan with hot water. Poach the dish in a moderate oven—180°C (350°F or Mark 4)—for 45 minutes, then remove the pan from the oven and lift out the mould.

13 **Turning out and serving.** Take the paper off and leave the dish to firm for 10 minutes. Place a preheated plate on top of the mould. Turn the plate and mould over together. Lift off the mould. Cut the case into wedges (*left*). Serve with tomato sauce (*page 15*) enriched with cream.□

Sliced Vegetables to Enclose a Stuffing

To encase a pasta filling, sliced and fried aubergines make an interesting alternative to the coiled macaroni demonstrated on the opposite page. Aubergines yield slices large and flexible enough to fold around a stuffing, and strong enough to hold the dish together. Among vegetables, only courgettes, which yield narrower slices, can be used in the same way.

Since the casing itself makes a substantial contribution to the dish's flavour, the stuffing can be as assertive as you like; a subtly flavoured mixture, such as the sweetbread filling used on page 68, would be out of place. The stuffing in the demonstration below consists of parboiled *penne* macaroni, vegetables, hard-boiled eggs and cooked meats, united by a tomato sauce (*recipe, page 128*).

The aubergines are cooked before being arranged to form the casing. A single frying will soften them enough to line the mould; in this demonstration, the fried slices are coated in flour, dipped in beaten egg and cheese, and briefly fried again to set the coating. The cheese flavours the aubergines and the flour and egg batter gives them additional firmness to help support the stuffing.

The aubergines can line several individual-sized moulds or, as here, a single large one. To make a decorative pattern, arrange the slices radially (*Step 2, below*). Once the filling is in place and completely enclosed by aubergine slices, the dish need only be baked long enough for all its flavours to mingle.

1 Frying the aubergines. Slice aubergines lengthwise. Fry them in olive oil over a medium heat. When they are tender—after about 10 minutes—drain them on absorbent paper. Coat the slices in flour and dip them in egg mixed with grated Parmesan cheese. Fry them again.

2 Preparing the case. Cut a circle from an aubergine slice and place the circle in the centre of a deep mould. Lay three-quarters of the remaining aubergine slices in an overlapping radial pattern in the mould so that they completely cover the mould's base and sides (*above*).

3 Preparing the stuffing. In a bowl, mix parboiled *penne* macaroni with chopped cooked tongue, white chicken meat, sautéed chicken liver and hard-boiled egg. Add fried sausage-meat, boiled peas, and grated cheese. Stir in the tomato sauce (*page 15*).

4 Filling the case. Fill the aubergine-lined mould with the stuffing (*above*). Level the stuffing and arrange the remaining aubergine slices in an overlapping radial pattern on top of it. Tuck the ends of the topmost aubergines inside the slices that line the side of the mould.

5 Topping with sauce. With a spoon, spread tomato sauce over the top of the aubergines. Sprinkle the sauce with Parmesan cheese. Cover the dish with foil and bake it in a fairly hot oven—190°C (375°F or Mark 5)—for 25 to 30 minutes to heat the stuffing through.

6 Serving the dish. Remove the mould from the oven and leave it to settle for 10 minutes. Remove the foil and turn out on to a serving platter. Pour tomato sauce round the dish (*above*). Serve it hot. □

Pre-Baked Case for Pasta Pie

The juxtaposition of a crisply baked pastry case and a smooth pasta filling makes a pie with a memorable contrast of textures. The pie in this demonstration is filled with a selection of differently coloured pasta, pre-cooked then moistened with cream and flavoured with grated cheese and ham. More elaborate mixtures of pasta and meat in a sauce (*pages 68-71*) would make an equally suitable filling, or you could combine the pasta with sautéed vegetables: mushrooms or courgettes or artichoke heart quarters, for example. If you like, you can include stuffed pasta in the pie. Here, *tortellini*, which have been filled with spinach, are mixed with the noodles (*page 54*) to add an extra dimension of flavour to the pie.

All kinds of pastry are suitable for the crust—from a butter or lard shortcrust to the olive oil used in this demonstration. In fact, the pastry's ingredients, flour, eggs and oil (*recipe, page 166*) are the same as those of the pasta; a higher proportion of

olive oil is included, however, giving the pastry its distinctive taste and a pleasantly crumbly texture.

Because the pie is removed from its tin after cooking, the pastry should be rolled out thickly enough to make a sturdy case that will stand unsuppported. Bake the pie in a spring-form tin, whose sides can be unclipped and separated from the base at the end of cooking (*Step 8, right*).

It is possible to make a pasta pie by enclosing the pasta in raw pastry. However, the pastry will be crisper if you cook it partially, as here, before adding the filling. For the preliminary baking, the base is weighted down with dried beans to prevent air bubbles from forming blisters and buckling the pastry. The lid of the pie is pre-baked separately from the base; it is put in place on the pastry base once the filling has been added, so that the creamy pasta does not dry out.

1 **Mixing the pastry.** Sieve some flour into a large mixing bowl; add an egg, salt and olive oil. Pour on a little tepid water (*above*) and mix the ingredients with a fork until all the mixture is loosely bound together.

5 **Trimming the base.** Assemble the spring-form baking tin and close the spring clip. Brush the inside of the tin with oil. Roll out the remaining dough into a large circular shape. Roll the dough loosely around the rolling pin and transfer it to the tin. Gently press the dough into the tin. Trim the edge of the dough with a knife, leaving a 2.5 cm (1 inch) overhang (*above*).

6 **Weighting the dough.** Fold back the overhanging dough, pressing the double thickness of dough on to the lip of the tin and fluting it with the side of your thumb. Line the pastry case with a piece of greaseproof paper and fill it with a thick layer of dried beans (*above*). Bake the case and lid in a moderate oven—180°C (350°F or Mark 4)—for about 15 minutes or until lightly coloured. Remove the greaseproof paper and the beans from the pastry case, and return it to the oven for a few minutes to dry out.

2 **Kneading the dough.** Knead the dough with your knuckles (*above*), lightly sprinkling over more flour if the dough becomes sticky. Form the dough into a ball. Leave it in the bowl in a cool place, covered with a cloth, for about 1 hour to make the dough easier to roll out.

3 **Making the lid.** Take slightly less than half of the dough from the bowl. On a smooth, floured surface, roll the dough out into a roughly circular shape. Then lay the base of the spring-form baking tin in the middle. Trim the dough with a knife to make a circle about 2.5 cm (1 inch) wider than the tin (*above*).

4 **Completing the lid.** Remove the baking tin base. To form a double-thickness rim that will make the lid less fragile, curl back the edge of the dough up to the circular impression left by the edge of the tin. For a decorative effect flute the rim with your thumbnail (*above*) or a fork. Lift the dough carefully by hand and place it on a greased baking sheet.

7 **Filling the case.** Boil *tortellini* (*page 54*) and green, orange and yellow noodles (*page 51*) separately until *al dente*. Drain the pasta and mix it with double cream and chopped ham. Place the pasta mixtures in the pastry case with plenty of grated Parmesan cheese (*above*) and more cream. Brush the rims of the case and lid with olive oil, so that they will acquire a good colour. Put the lid on the case (*inset*). Bake the pie in an oven preheated to 180°C (350°F or Mark 4) for about 20 minutes.

8 **Serving the pie.** Take out the pie when it is a rich golden-brown colour. Remove the lid. Release the spring clip and lift off the wall of the tin (*above*). Leave the case on the base of the tin and transfer it on to a serving plate. Replace the lid for serving, but remove it before cutting the dish into portions.☐

The Unique Texture of Pasta Soufflé

Home-made pasta shreds (*page 44*) can be used as the basis for an attractive and unconventional soufflé. The most common foundation for a soufflé is a white sauce (*page 14*), which is enriched with egg yolks, flavoured and finally lightened with beaten egg whites. But because grated pasta cooks in milk to a creamy, almost sauce-like consistency, it can serve in place of a white sauce. The pasta shreds retain their shape during cooking, giving the soufflé a pleasantly varied texture.

In the grated pasta soufflé demonstrated here, the cooked pasta, enriched with egg yolks, is not mixed evenly with a flavouring. Instead, the pasta mixture is combined with whisked egg whites and then transferred to a soufflé dish, and a flavouring is placed in its centre. The flavouring here (*recipe, page 133*) is minced and sautéed calf's lung; you could substitute any chopped meat bound by a sauce, or lightly cooked, sliced or puréed vegetables, such as mushrooms or peas.

A topping of soured cream provides a foil to the savoury calf's lung filling. As the soufflé bakes, the cream in part penetrates the soufflé mixture, while the surface turns a light biscuit colour.

Forms of pasta other than grated noodles can play a part in a more orthodox soufflé—but only as an optional addition to the basic soufflé mixture. In the demonstration opposite (*box*), fresh, thin green noodles, together with ham and grated cheese, flavour a soufflé with a white sauce base (*recipe, page 134*). The final step in the preparation of the soufflé is to fold in the beaten egg whites. Because the egg whites are not very stable, no time must be lost between beating them and putting the soufflé in a hot oven. The oven must be preheated and the mould buttered in advance. With these precautions, the soufflé will rise dramatically.

1 Sautéing minced lung. Boil a calf's lung for about 30 minutes and let it cool. Cut it into large chunks and put it through the medium blade of a mincer. In a frying pan, melt some lard and sauté the minced meat with finely chopped onion. Off the heat, bind the mixture together with a lightly beaten egg.

2 Stirring the pasta shreds. Prepare a stiff dough and grate it (*page 44*). Add the pasta shreds to the boiling milk in a pan and simmer gently for about 30 minutes, stirring constantly, until the pasta absorbs most of the milk.

3 Adding the egg yolks. Toss chopped parsley into the pasta mixture. Separate egg yolks from whites. Off the heat, blend the yolks into the pasta mixture, stirring well with a wooden spoon.

4 Folding in the egg whites. Whisk the egg whites in a copper bowl until they stand in stiff peaks. To lighten the soufflé base, stir into it a large spoonful of the beaten egg white. Add the soufflé base to the remaining whites and, with a wooden spatula, fold it in gently but quickly, to avoid loss of volume.

Special Colour and Flavour from Green Noodles

1 Adding flavourings. Parboil fresh green noodles for 20 seconds and drain them. With a wooden spoon, stir egg yolks into a thick white sauce (*page 14*). Add chopped ham and grated Parmesan cheese, together with the noodles. Season the sauce with salt, freshly ground pepper and grated nutmeg.

2 Folding in egg whites. Whisk egg whites in a copper bowl until they form stiff peaks. Stir some of the whites into the sauce to lighten it. Add the sauce to the remaining whites, folding in quickly but gently to avoid breaking the noodles.

3 Serving the soufflé. Butter a soufflé dish. Spoon the soufflé into the dish. Cook the soufflé in an oven preheated to 190°C (375°F or Mark 5) for about 40 minutes. Remove it when its surface is well browned (*above*), and serve it quickly.

5 Adding soured cream. Transfer the soufflé mixture to a well-greased baking dish. Spoon the prepared calf's lung into the centre of the soufflé: the meat will sink in under its own weight. Cover the soufflé with a generous layer of soured cream. Put the soufflé in an oven preheated to 190°C (375°F or Mark 5).

6 Serving the soufflé. The soufflé is ready to serve in about 45 minutes, when well risen and lightly coloured. Use a large spoon to serve it; each portion should include both the meaty filling and the lighter-textured soufflé (*right*).□

4
Cooking with Pulses
Lengthy Simmering for Succulent Results

Tactics for soaking and boiling
Purées smooth or coarse
How to assemble a cassoulet
Beans baked overnight with flavourings

A spoonful of molasses is added to a round-bellied pot of red kidney beans together with other flavourings—mustard powder, brown sugar and salt. The water in which they were boiled stands ready to cover the beans so they do not dry out during long, slow baking.

Subtly different in taste and texture, attractively varied in appearance, the scores of commonly available pulses offer a multitude of options to the discerning cook. The pulses can be served as simply as you like: a chunk of butter or a dash of olive oil, for example, is sufficient embellishment for a dish of plump haricot beans or fragile lentils. They may be matched with grains: pulses with rice (*recipe, page 163*) are a well-loved combination, where the contrast of red, black or beige beans against the white grain presents an appetizing display. Or, for the heartiest of meals, they may be allied with meats. Traditionally, pulses have always been eaten with such preserved meats as salt pork—largely because there was little else to be found in a winter larder in the days before refrigeration. Pulses are equally delicious with fresh meats, however, and their mealy texture makes them an excellent foil for fatty meats, both preserved and fresh.

No matter how they are presented, most pulses require lengthy cooking, often preceded by soaking, in order to reabsorb the water lost when they were dried. Gentle simmering and a minimum of stirring are necessary to keep them intact. Even such careful treatment will not prevent split pulses from disintegrating. It is best to make a virtue of necessity and serve them as purées. In fact, all pulses can be sieved into smooth purées or mashed and formed into a pancake-like roll (*page 81*). Flour milled from pulses, moistened into a stiff paste with water or milk, offers other possibilities: it can be cut into shapes and deep-fried (*recipe, page 155*) or, like the polenta on page 40, sautéed or baked with a sauce.

When pulses are served with meat, it is often best to cook them apart, so that the pulses' flavour remains distinct and stands in clear contrast to the meat. But pulses cooked together with meats make a warming one-course meal, whether they are baked covered for hours in a slow oven (*opposite and page 86*) or pre-cooked and baked without a lid to produce a crusty gratin, such as the celebrated cassoulet (*page 82*). A cassoulet is the consummation of pulse dishes, worth every moment of its unhurried preparation. It can contain a choice from any number of different meats—goose, duck or game, lamb and sausages; usually it includes pork rind and feet which have a high gelatine content and contribute greatly to the dish's richness. Layered between the meats, haricot beans cook until they barely retain their shape, but acquire a memorable succulence.

77

Boiling: the Simplest Approach

The simplest way to cook pulses is by simmering them gently in water, perhaps with a flavouring of herbs and aromatic vegetables. At the end of cooking, you can dress the pulses with butter or oil or serve them with a garnish. In this demonstration, black-eyed peas are garnished with sautéed tomatoes, parsley and garlic.

The first step in preparing pulses is to spread them out on a tray or a large plate and pick them over for foreign matter. When you have checked all of the pulses, rinse them under running water.

Once clean, most pulses must be soaked in water to reabsorb moisture and swell. Most large beans and peas need up to 8 hours' soaking; some smaller types require only about an hour. Split pulses, with no hard outer skin to slow down absorption of water, need a similarly short time; lentils require no soaking at all.

The chart on the right gives soaking times, in cold water, for the pulses illustrated on pages 12-13. If you soak the pulses in hot water (*Step 1, below*) they will need less time to swell. Both methods produce equally good results. A pinch of bicarbonate of soda can be added to the

water to speed up the swelling process.

Because soaking draws indigestible substances from the pulses, discard the water after soaking and replace it with fresh for cooking. Beans of the kidney bean family, particularly red and black ones, contain a potentially dangerous toxin rendered harmless by boiling. After soaking, these beans should be cooked for 10 minutes at a light boil—100°C (212°F)—before they are simmered. The chart gives approximate simmering times; precise timing depends on age and variety and some recipes call for pulses to simmer for an hour or more after they become tender for a more velvety texture.

The cooking time will be noticeably longer if there are minerals—including salt—dissolved in the water. Cooks who live in hard-water areas sometimes offset the water's effect by adding a pinch of bicarbonate of soda. But soda should be reserved for the soaking period; if cooked with the pulses, it detracts from their flavour. In any case, add salt only after the pulses are tender. Acid foods, such as tomatoes, also slow down the cooking and should be added towards the end.

Soaking and Cooking Times

Pulse	Soaking time in cold water	Cooking time
Aduki beans	1 hr	1 - 1½ hrs
Black beans	7 - 8 hrs	1 - 2 hrs
Black-eyed peas	7 - 8 hrs	1 - 1½ hrs
Borlotti beans	7 - 8 hrs	1 - 2 hrs
Broad beans	7 - 8 hrs	1 - 2 hrs
Butter beans	7 - 8 hrs	1 - 2 hrs
Cannellini beans	7 - 8 hrs	1 - 2 hrs
Chick peas	7 - 8 hrs	1½ - 3 hrs
Dutch brown beans	7 - 8 hrs	1 - 2 hrs
Field beans	7 - 8 hrs	1 - 2 hrs
Flageolet beans	7 - 8 hrs	1 - 2 hrs
Haricot beans	7 - 8 hrs	1 - 2 hrs
Lentils:		
Puy	—	1 hr
Large beige	—	1 hr
Red	—	20 - 30 mins
Mung beans	1 hr	45 - 60 mins
Peas:		
Green or yellow:		
Whole	7 - 8 hrs	1 - 1½ hrs
Split	1 hr	45 - 60 mins
Pigeon peas	7 - 8 hrs	45 - 60 mins
Pinto beans	7 - 8 hrs	1 - 2 hrs
Red kidney beans	7 - 8 hrs	1 - 2 hrs
Soya beans	7 - 8 hrs	45 - 60 mins

1 Soaking pulses. Pick over and wash pulses—here, black-eyed peas. Put the peas in a heavy pan with about double their volume of cold water. Bring the water to the boil slowly: gentle treatment helps to tenderize them evenly. Turn off the heat, and leave the peas to soak for about 1 hour. Drain the peas in a colander.

2 Adding aromatics. Return the peas to the pan and cover them with at least twice their volume of fresh water. Stud an onion with 1 or 2 cloves and place it in the water, with a few unpeeled garlic cloves and a carrot. Tie parsley, thyme and a bay leaf in a bundle with a stick of celery; add this bouquet garni to the pan (*above*).

3 **Cooking the pulses.** Bring the peas to the boil slowly, then reduce the heat so that they simmer. Cover them with a lid, and cook the peas for about 1½ hours, until they feel tender when pressed. At intervals check that the peas have enough liquid. When the peas are cooked, discard the herbs and vegetables; add salt to taste.

4 **Preparing a garnish.** Skin, seed and coarsely chop tomatoes. Sauté them briefly in a little butter until they have heated through; season them with salt and pepper. Drain the cooked peas in a colander and transfer them to a heated serving dish. Surround the peas with the sautéed tomatoes (*above*).

5 **Serving the pulses.** Finely chop peeled garlic cloves or grind them to a pulp in a mortar. Finely chop a large bunch of parsley and mix it thoroughly with the garlic. Scatter the parsley and garlic over the peas and tomatoes and serve (*left*). □

Beans Pounded in the Frying Pan

The soft flesh of cooked pulses, enhanced with butter or other fat, makes a rich and satisfying purée, whether the pulse is merely mashed over high heat or sieved to velvety smoothness.

For the simplest, least refined purées there is no need to rid pulses of their skins. In the demonstration on the right (*recipe, page 156*), boiled red kidney beans are gradually added to onions frying in lard in a wide pan. Some of the beans' liquid is added also, to keep them from burning, and the mixture is mashed with a broad wooden pestle. The purée can be served fairly moist or, as here, cooked until it is dry enough to be flipped over and served like a rolled pancake; the wide pan allows the beans' liquid to evaporate quickly.

A really smooth purée is best prepared in two steps. First, the cooked pulses are ground to a coarse pulp in a food mill—a little of their cooking liquid can be added when the dryness of the pulses makes the mill difficult to turn.

Next, the pulp is pressed through a sieve, which separates out the skins and leaves a fine-textured purée. (With pulses sold ready-skinned, such as split peas, this second step can be omitted.)

The lentil purée shown here (*box, opposite page*) is served with butter, which helps bind the purée as well as providing the best complement to the lentils' taste. Purées made from blander pulses such as split peas can be flavoured with a little finely chopped onion or garlic, or mixed with egg and steamed to make a firm pudding (*recipe, page 157*).

1 **Frying beans with onion.** Simmer beans—here, red kidney beans—until they are soft (*page 78*). In a large frying pan, melt a little lard. Chop an onion finely. Fry the onion over a low heat until it is soft. Add a ladleful of beans and cooking liquid to the onion (*above*).

2 **Mashing the beans.** Increase the heat until the liquid comes to the boil. Keeping the liquid boiling, mash the beans with a pestle (*above*). Continue mashing until the beans form a coarse purée.

3 **Adding more beans.** Add another ladleful of beans, with their cooking liquid (*above*). Mash them thoroughly into the purée. Continue adding and mashing the beans a ladleful at a time, until they are all coarsely pulped. You can serve the purée at this stage, or continue to cook the beans until they form a dry, pancake-like dish (*Step 4*).

A Buttery Purée of Lentils

1 Milling lentils coarsely. Cook lentils with herbs and aromatic vegetables (*page 78*). Drain them thoroughly and reserve the liquid. Put a few spoonfuls of the lentils at a time into a food mill set over a bowl, and grind them, using a medium disc. Wash the last batch of cooked lentils through the food mill with a little of the reserved liquid.

2 Sieving the milled lentils. Set a fine-meshed drum sieve over a plate. Using a plastic scraper, press the lentils through the sieve a few spoonfuls at a time. Discard the skins from the top.

3 Reheating the purée. Heat the purée over a fairly high heat, stirring and beating continuously. Add some more of the reserved cooking liquid if the purée seems very stiff and dry. Remove the pan from the heat. Cut a generous quantity of butter into small knobs and stir the butter into the purée until it has disappeared.

4 Boiling off the liquid. Keep the pan over a fairly high heat, shaking it now and then, until the purée begins to dry out and sizzle at the edges. Tilt the pan from side to side so that the purée comes cleanly away from the sides.

5 Turning out the beans. Roll the beans towards the side of the pan furthest from the handle. With the edge of the pan touching the rim of a serving dish, invert the pan over the dish (*above*) so that the bean pancake rolls on to the dish.

6 Serving the beans. You can serve the mashed beans plain, or with a topping of grated or crumbled cheese. Accompany the beans with a moist or crisp dish—a plain green salad, for example—that will balance their dryness.□

Moist Beans and Meats with a Crisp Topping

When baked with a variety of meats, beans or other pulses make satisfying and well-balanced whole meal dishes. Fatty meats produce especially rich dishes: the beans absorb the fat and their flavour mingles deliciously with that of the meat. Such a combination may involve nothing more complicated than beans with a slice of bacon or lamb, or be as all inclusive as the French cassoulet demonstrated here and overleaf. In this version, haricot beans, goose, lamb and various forms of pork are separately pre-cooked—each in the way that best reinforces its own flavour—then layered in a casserole and baked for several hours (*recipe, page 160*).

Preserved goose—salted, cooked, then potted in its own fat—is a traditional ingredient. Preserved goose is not always available, however. An effective substitute is used in this demonstration, where a fresh goose is simply salted overnight to give it the same pungent, briny taste as salt goose, then cooked in its fat.

The beans are simmered with pork or bacon rind, salt pork belly or green bacon, trotters and sausages; gelatine from the rind and the trotters adds a velvety smoothness to the cooking liquid. The lamb is browned in fat, then braised with vegetables in some of the liquid from the pork and beans. Nothing is wasted: at the end of the braising, the liquid is strained off the lamb and is used later as a sauce for the cassoulet.

Once everything has been pre-cooked, the cassoulet is assembled. Layers of beans alternate with the various meats in a large casserole, and the whole is then moistened with the liquids from the lamb stew and the pork and beans. Breadcrumbs sprinkled with goose fat form a topmost layer that crisps during baking. From time to time as the cassoulet cooks, its top surface is broken up with a spoon and basted: the result is a deep crust that contrasts with the moist meats and the creamy beans beneath.

1 Salting a goose. Pull out the fat from the cavity of a goose. Cut the goose into eight or ten pieces, sprinkle them with salt and herbs, and leave overnight. Next day, heat the goose fat gently in a pan with a glass of water until the fat melts; strain the fat through a muslin-lined sieve into a large pan. Wipe the goose pieces (*above*) and put them in the fat.

2 Cooking the goose. If there is not enough goose fat to cover the pieces, supplement it with lard. Simmer the goose slowly in the fat, uncovered, for about 2 hours, until it is tender. Remove the goose pieces from the pan with a fork (*above*). Strain and reserve the fat.

5 Removing the bacon. Bring the water to the boil, cook for 10 minutes then reduce to a simmer. After 40 minutes, remove the sausages and reserve them. After a further 20 minutes, or when it is tender, take out the bacon (*above*) and set it aside. Continue to simmer the remaining ingredients for another hour, or until the beans are tender but intact.

6 Cutting up the trotter. Drain the beans and bacon, and reserve the liquid. Cut the trotter in half lengthwise. Remove the bones and discard them. Cut the meat into small chunks. Untie the rind and chop it into small squares. Chop up the carrots, but discard the onion: it will have surrendered all its flavour to the cooking liquid. Discard the bay leaf.

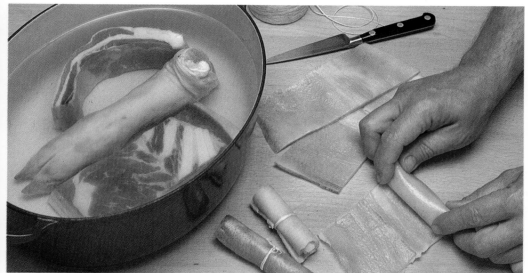

3 **Rolling the rind.** Slice the rind thinly off a large piece of green bacon. Cut the rind into several rectangles. Roll up the rectangles tightly and tie them into neat bundles (*above*). Put the rind in a casserole with a pig's trotter and the bacon. To cleanse the meat of the albuminous substances that form a grey scum during cooking, cover it with cold water, bring the water to the boil, and simmer for a few minutes. Remove the meat and rinse it under running water.

4 **Adding beans.** Transfer the green bacon, rind and trotter to a clean pan. Add soaked (*page 78*), drained haricot beans (*above*), together with herbs and aromatic vegetables—here, thyme, bay, garlic, carrots and an onion studded with cloves. Prick 2 or 3 garlic sausages with a fork and add them to the pan. Cover the ingredients with cold or tepid water.

7 **Browning lamb.** Coarsely chop fresh carrots and onions. Add them to goose fat melted in a heavy sauté pan. Cook them until they are lightly browned, then tip them into a sieve set over a bowl. Reserve the vegetables; when the fat has drained from them, pour it back into the sauté pan. Cut a shoulder of lamb into large pieces. Put the lamb pieces into the pan, salt them and brown them on all sides. Sprinkle flour over the meat (*above*). After 2 to 3 minutes, return the carrots and onions to the pan. Add peeled, seeded and chopped tomatoes, garlic and a bay, thyme and parsley bouquet.

8 **Deglazing the lamb.** Pour some red or white wine into the sauté pan (*above*). Stir gently with a wooden spoon to loosen any scraps of meat and vegetables adhering to the sides and bottom. Add enough of the beans' cooking liquid to cover the contents of the pan. Put a lid on the pan and simmer gently for about 1½ hours. Skim off any fat from the stew two or three times during the cooking period. At the end of cooking, discard the bouquet of herbs. ▶

9 **Making a sauce.** Reserve the lamb and carrots. With a pestle, press the other contents of the pan through a sieve into a saucepan (*above*). Simmer the resulting sauce in the pan half off the heat for about 15 minutes, removing the fat that will collect on the cooler side.

10 **Assembling the first layer.** Rub the inside surface of a large, deep earthenware casserole with cloves of garlic. Distribute the squares of bacon rind on the bottom of the dish. Place the goose pieces on top of them. With a ladle, spread about a third of the drained beans over the goose (*above*).

13 **Spooning in the sauce.** Without displacing the breadcrumb topping, gently spoon the strained sauce from the lamb stew over the assembled casserole. Continue adding the sauce until it just reaches to the level of the breadcrumbs. If there is not enough sauce, supplement it with cooking liquid from the bean stew.

14 **Adding the goose fat.** Dust the surface of the casserole with more fine breadcrumbs. Sprinkle 2 to 3 tablespoons of the goose fat over the top (*above*). Place the casserole, uncovered, in an oven preheated to 170°C (325°F or Mark 3).

15 **Breaking the crust.** Baste the dish every 20 minutes or so with either the leftover lamb sauce or, if that is used up, with the bean cooking liquid or the cassoulet's own liquid. When the top begins to turn golden, after about 1½ hours, break up the surface with the side of a spoon (*above*).

11 **Arranging the second layer.** Arrange the pieces of cooked lamb over the first layer of beans. Add the chopped carrots that cooked with the bacon and beans, and the pieces of pig's trotter. Cover the meat with about half of the beans remaining in the colander, spreading them evenly.

12 **Adding the third layer.** Slice the garlic sausages into pieces about 1 cm (½ inch) thick. Scatter the sausage slices and the bacon on top of the second layer of beans (*above*). Ladle the remaining beans over the bacon and sausage to form the final layer. Sprinkle the surface with fine breadcrumbs.

16 **Forming a perfect crust.** Baste the broken surface of the cassoulet with the bacon and bean cooking liquid. Return the dish to the oven for 1½ hours. Repeat the surface breaking and basting two or three times until a thick crust has formed (*above*). Serve the cassoulet—make sure each diner receives some crust, each type of meat and plenty of beans (*right*). □

Leisurely Baking for a Fusion of Flavours

Prolonged baking in a gentle oven—for most of the day or overnight—provides ample opportunity for beans and meats to exchange flavours. The lengthy cooking also allows any additional flavourings to disperse thoughout the dish, permeating the pulses. In this demonstration, for example, molasses, brown sugar, mustard and onions impart a sweet-sharp flavour to red kidney beans baked with salt pork or green streaky bacon (*recipe, page 164*).

Before baking, the kidney beans must be soaked to tenderize them (*page 78*). They are then boiled in a change of water to start off the cooking.

The beans must not be allowed to dry out during their long cooking. Traditional bean pots have a stout profile narrowing at the neck to reduce evaporation. You can cook the beans in any vessel of similar shape, provided you start the cooking with the beans covered by at least 2.5 cm (1 inch) or so of the water in which they were brought to the boil.

1 Assembling the ingredients. Soak beans—haricot or pinto beans or, as here, red kidney beans—in cold water for several hours. Drain them and cover them with fresh water. Boil for 10 minutes. Drain the beans again, and reserve the water. Assemble the other ingredients—here, an onion, molasses, dry mustard, brown sugar, coarse salt and a piece of green bacon cut into sections.

2 Preparing the bean pot. Pour the beans into a bean pot or casserole. Add the brown sugar, salt, dry mustard and molasses. Pour in enough of the reserved water to cover the beans by about 2.5 cm (1 inch). Add the onion and bacon.

3 Cooking the dish. Cover the bean pot with a lid and place it in an oven set at 130° to 140°C (250° to 275°F or Mark ½ to 1) for 7 to 8 hours, or overnight, until the beans are very soft but still intact. Remove the onion before serving.□

Anthology of Recipes

In choosing the grain, pasta and pulse recipes for the Anthology that follows, the Editors and consultants for this volume have drawn upon the cooking literature and culinary traditions of more than 36 different countries. The selections range from the simple to the sophisticated—from plain pease pudding to a luxurious casserole of wild rice and oysters. The Anthology spans more than three centuries and includes recipes by 112 writers, many of them distinguished exponents of the culinary art. Some of the recipes in this Anthology have never before been published in the English language. Whatever the sources of the recipes, the emphasis is on authentic dishes meticulously prepared with fresh, natural ingredients. Exotic cuisines are well represented, with, for example, couscous from North Africa, *falafel* from the Middle East and *frijoles refritos* from Mexico. There are pasta recipes in abundance from Italy and also from those other places where pasta is a staple—the Middle East, Eastern Europe and South East Asia among them. The pasta selection is complemented by recipes for dumplings.

Since many early recipe writers did not specify amounts of ingredients, these have been judiciously included; and, where appropriate, introductory notes printed in italics have been added by the Editors. Modern terms have been substituted for archaic language, but to preserve the character of the original recipes, and to create a true anthology, the authors' texts have been changed as little as possible. Some instructions have necessarily been expanded, but in any circumstances where cooking directions still seem somewhat abrupt, the reader need only refer to the appropriate demonstration at the front of the book to find the technique explained. Cooking terms and ingredients that may be unfamiliar are explained in the combined Index and Glossary at the end of the book.

The Anthology is grouped, like the first half of the book, into grain, pasta and pulse dishes but, for ease of use, it has been further subdivided. Recipes for standard preparations—basic doughs, stocks and sauces—appear at the end. The serving suggestions included in some recipes are, of course, optional.

In the ingredients list that begins each recipe, the main or title ingredients of each dish are listed first; the other ingredients are given in order of use. Metric and imperial weights for each ingredient are listed in separate columns. The two sets of figures are not exact equivalents, but are consistent for each recipe. Working from either metric or imperial weights and measures will produce equally good results, but the two systems should not be mixed. All spoon measures are level.

Whole Grains

Red Rice

In this recipe, Italian Piedmont (round-grain) rice may be substituted if glutinous rice is not available.

To serve 8 to 10

1 kg	glutinous rice, washed and drained	2 to 2½ lb
30 g	aduki beans, soaked for 1 hour and drained	1 oz
About 1.75 litres	water	About 3 pints
1 tbsp	salt	1 tbsp
3 tbsp	black sesame seeds, mixed with 1 tsp salt	3 tbsp

Boil the beans in the water, without covering the pot, for 1½ to 2 hours or until soft, adding more boiling water if necessary. Drain the beans in a strainer, reserving the beans' cooking water to colour the rice.

Combine the rice with the beans, 1.25 litres (2 pints) of the bean water and the salt, and cook, covered, over a low heat for about 30 minutes. Serve on plates or in bowls. Sprinkle the sesame seed and salt mixture over the rice.

AYA KAGAWA
JAPANESE COOKBOOK

Pilaff with Pine-Nuts

To serve 6

375 g	long-grain rice	13 oz
150 g	butter	5 oz
1 litre	boiling water	1¾ pints
	salt	
60 g	currants	2 oz
60 g	pine-nuts or slivered, blanched almonds	2 oz
2 tbsp	chopped parsley	2 tbsp
1 tbsp	finely slivered orange rind	1 tbsp

Melt 30 g (1 oz) of the butter in a large saucepan, add the rice and stir until it is coated with butter. Pour in the boiling water, add salt, cover and simmer for 25 minutes. Add the currants, fluff with a fork, and remove the pan from the heat.

In a small pan, melt the remaining butter, add the pine-nuts, and heat until the nuts are lightly toasted and the butter starts to brown; pour the nuts and butter over the rice and mix gently. Transfer the rice to a serving dish and sprinkle with parsley and orange rind.

JOSÉ WILSON (EDITOR)
HOUSE AND GARDEN'S PARTY MENU COOKBOOK

Rice and Lentils

Khichhari

To serve 6

175 g	rice, washed and drained	6 oz
250 g	beige lentils or green split peas or mung beans, soaked for 1 hour and drained	8 oz
2 tbsp	chopped coriander leaves	2 tbsp
2.5 cm	piece fresh ginger root, peeled and chopped	1 inch
4	garlic cloves	4
½ tsp	ground turmeric	½ tsp
½ tsp	paprika or cayenne pepper	½ tsp
½ tsp	*garam masala*	½ tsp
2 tbsp	*ghee*	2 tbsp
1	onion, finely chopped	1
½ tsp	cumin seeds	½ tsp
2	green chili peppers, seeded and finely chopped (optional)	2
2	tomatoes, skinned, seeded and quartered	2
1	potato, diced	1
1 tsp	salt	1 tsp

In a mortar, pound 1 tablespoon of the coriander leaves with the ginger, garlic, turmeric, paprika or cayenne pepper, and *garam masala*. Heat the *ghee* and lightly fry the onion. Stir in the *masala* paste with the cumin seeds and chili peppers. Fry for a few minutes and add the rice, the lentils, split peas or mung beans, and the tomatoes. Fry for a further 5 minutes and cover with water. Add the diced potato. Salt and bring to the boil. Reduce the heat and simmer for about 20 minutes, or until the rice is cooked. Add extra water to the pan if necessary to avoid drying up. Serve sprinkled with the rest of the chopped coriander leaves.

JACK SANTA MARIA
INDIAN VEGETARIAN COOKERY

Cauliflower Pilaff

Phūlgobi Pulau

To serve 6

275 g	rice, soaked for 1 hour and drained	9 oz
250 g	cauliflower florets	8 oz
	salt and pepper	
30 g	*ghee* or clarified butter	1 oz
1	onion, finely chopped	1
6	garlic cloves, finely chopped	6
2	green cardamom pods	2
5 cm	stick cinnamon, broken up	2 inch
6	cloves	6
2.5 cm	piece ginger root, finely chopped	1 inch
2	green chili peppers, stemmed, seeded and chopped (optional)	2
½ tsp	paprika or cayenne pepper	½ tsp
1 tsp	cumin seeds	1 tsp
½ tsp	*garam masala*	½ tsp
¼ litre	yogurt	8 fl oz
90 cl	hot water	1½ pints

Sprinkle the cauliflower with salt and pepper and fry the florets in *ghee* until they begin to turn golden. Remove them, add the onion and garlic to the pan, and fry until the onion is soft. Add the cardamoms, cinnamon, cloves and rice. Stir-fry until the rice turns opaque, about 5 minutes. Add the cauliflower florets, ginger, chili peppers, paprika, 2 teaspoons of salt, the cumin seeds and *garam masala*. Fry for a further 5 minutes. Stir in the yogurt. Add the hot water, bring to the boil, cover the pan and simmer until the rice is cooked and has absorbed the water.

JACK SANTA MARIA
INDIAN VEGETARIAN COOKERY

Lamb Pilaff with Double Stock

Yakhni Pilau

The jellied stock should be prepared from a little mutton and such gelatinous bones as shin, knuckle, trotters or cow heel. Strain the stock and skim off all fat when it cools. This stock can be made plain or with the addition of a few strips of lemon rind or a handful of lemon leaves, parsley or coriander leaves, 2 cm (1 inch) ginger root, chopped, 5 cm (2 inches) cinnamon stick, 1 or 2 green chili peppers or a sweet green pepper, 1 teaspoon of peppercorns and a few chopped chives. The pilaff can be garnished with blanched almonds, slivered and fried; sweet pepper rings, salted then roasted or grilled; sautéed onion rings; and raisins, soaked, drained and lightly fried.

To serve 4

250 g	long-grain rice, soaked for 1 hour and drained	8 oz
600 g	boned lamb, cubed	1¼ lb
2	limes, juice strained	2
8	anise or fennel seeds, ground	8
15 cl	double cream, lightly whipped	¼ pint
15 cl	yogurt	¼ pint
125 g	clarified butter	4 oz
4	cloves, bruised	4
60 cl	jellied stock	1 pint
7	cardamom pods, bruised	7
5 cm	stick cinnamon	2 inch
2 tbsp	poppy seeds, roasted and ground	2 tbsp
2	bay leaves	2
	salt	
6 tbsp	chopped watercress or raw spinach	6 tbsp

Prick the lamb cubes all over with a fork and rub them with lime juice and anise or fennel. Lightly beat the cream and yogurt together and pour this mixture over the pieces of lamb. Leave the lamb to marinate.

Heat 30 g (1 oz) of the butter in a small pan and add the cloves. Splash in 6 cl (2 fl oz) of stock and stir. Cover, and leave on a low heat for 5 minutes. Heat 60 g (2 oz) of the butter in another pan, add the cardamoms, cinnamon, poppy seeds and the bay leaves. Add the rice and cook over a medium heat, stirring until the rice becomes translucent—about 6 to 8 minutes. Then add the cream and yogurt sauce strained from the meat and enough stock to cover the rice by 3 cm (1¼ inches). Bring to the boil, add salt and chopped watercress or spinach. Cover, and bake in an oven preheated to 180°C (350°F or Mark 4) for 12 minutes. Meanwhile, fry the lamb in the remaining butter and when it is crisp and well browned, mix it into the rice. Cover the pilaff, reset the oven to 170°C (325°F or Mark 3) and bake for 15 minutes. Leave in a warm place for 5 minutes before serving.

DHARAMJIT SINGH
INDIAN COOKERY

Yellow Rice Nepalese-Style

To serve 4

250 g	long-grain rice, soaked in water for 30 minutes	8 oz
4 tbsp	oil	4 tbsp
8	spring onions, sliced	8
5 cm	stick cinnamon	2 inch
3	cardamoms, seeds extracted	3
4	cloves	4
	ground turmeric	
$\frac{1}{4}$ litre	hot water	8 fl oz
300 g	fresh coconut flesh, peeled, grated, soaked for 30 minutes in $\frac{1}{4}$ litre (8 fl oz) water and squeezed through a towel to extract the coconut milk	10 oz
	salt	
3 or 4	sprigs fresh coriander	3 or 4

Heat the oil in a frying pan and fry the sliced onions until they are brown. Remove the onion slices and drain them on paper towels. Drain the rice; add it to the pan with the spices and turmeric and fry for 3 minutes. Add the hot water, coconut milk and a little salt. Cook, covered, over a low heat for about 20 minutes or until the rice is cooked. Add the coriander. Place, uncovered, in a 150°C (300°F or Mark 2) oven for 5 to 10 minutes to evaporate the excess moisture. Serve hot, garnished with the fried onions.

E. MAHESWARI DEVI
HANDY RICE RECIPES

Paella with Chicken, Pork and Seafood

Paella Valenciana

The ingredients of this paella may be varied according to availability or taste; a rabbit may be substituted for the chicken, clams may be substituted for the mussels, or the snails and eel may be omitted altogether.

To skin the eel, first stun it by knocking its head against the table; then slit the skin all around the head, loosen the skin with pliers, and peel it back from the head as if removing a

glove. The technique of cleaning squid is demonstrated on page 28. Mussels may be cooked and shelled in the same way as clams (page 29). To prepare them, see opposite page.

To serve 6 to 8

400 g	rice	14 oz
One 1.5 kg	tender chicken, cut into 6 or 8 serving pieces	One 3 lb
200 g	lean pork, cut into pieces	7 oz
100 g	ham, thinly sliced	$3\frac{1}{2}$ oz
8	small smoked sausages, pricked and parboiled	8
2	squid, cleaned, pouches cut into rings	2
12	snails, cooked, removed from their shells	12
1	small live eel, skinned, cleaned and cut into 6 or 8 sections	1
24	mussels, cooked and shelled, cooking liquid reserved	24
8	prawns or Dublin bay prawns	8
20 cl	olive oil	7 fl oz
2	medium-sized onions, finely chopped	2
4	sweet red peppers, skinned, seeded and chopped	4
2	artichokes, trimmed and quartered, chokes removed	2
100 g	French beans, topped and tailed, sliced into short lengths	$3\frac{1}{2}$ oz
2	tomatoes, skinned, seeded and chopped	2
2	garlic cloves, chopped	2
6 to 8 tbsp	chopped parsley	6 to 8 tbsp
	white pepper	
	freshly grated nutmeg	
	salt	
$\frac{1}{2}$ tsp	powdered saffron	$\frac{1}{2}$ tsp
1 tsp	paprika	1 tsp
200 g	shelled peas, parboiled	7 oz
1	bay leaf	1

Place a paella dish, with the oil, over a medium heat and add the chicken pieces, pork, ham and sausages. Once these have turned a golden colour, add the onions, peppers, artichokes and beans and cook for a few more minutes then add the squid, snails and pieces of eel. Toss in the prawns and tomatoes.

Continue to cook over a low heat, adding the garlic and parsley, and seasoning with white pepper, nutmeg and salt. Add the rice, stir well and season with a little saffron and paprika. Pour in the mussels' cooking liquid and enough water to make twice as much liquid, in volume, as rice—about

1 litre (1¾ pints)—then add the peas and the bay leaf. Turn up the heat and cook over a high heat until the liquid comes to the boil; then place the pan in an oven preheated to 180°C (350°F or Mark 4) for 15 to 20 minutes. A few minutes before removing the paella from the oven add the mussels. The paella should be served in the dish in which it was cooked.

CANDIDO LOPEZ
EL LIBRO DE ORO DE LA GASTRONOMÍA

Paella Valenciana

The cleaning and preparation of squid is shown on page 28. To prepare the mussels, scrape off the beard and other growths on the shell with a sharp knife and leave them in clean, cold salted water for about 3 hours, during which time they should discard the sand and mud they have absorbed. Change the water as it becomes muddied. Discard any opened shells. Cooked shrimps may be used in this recipe if uncooked ones are unavailable; add them to the other ingredients in the pan for the final 5 minutes of cooking time.

To serve 8 to 10

600 g	rice	1¼ lb
12.5 cl	oil	4 fl oz
1 kg	chicken, jointed	2 to 2½ lb
	salt	
200 g	lean pork, chopped	7 oz
200 g	squid, cleaned and chopped	7 oz
100 g	onion, chopped	3½ oz
1	sweet red pepper, grilled, skinned, seeded and chopped	1
300 g	tomatoes, skinned, seeded and chopped	10 oz
200 g	live mussels	7 oz
200 g	*chorizo* or other spicy frying sausage, cut into pieces	7 oz
60 cl	boiling water	1 pint
200 g	shrimps, uncooked	7 oz
100 g	small French beans	3½ oz
200 g	shelled peas, blanched for 5 minutes in salted water	7 oz
4	garlic cloves	4
	powdered saffron	

In a large pot, brown the chicken in 2 tablespoons of the oil and season it with salt. When it is half-cooked, about 10 minutes, add the pork and squid. Cover and simmer for 10 minutes. Add the onion and sweet pepper; when the vegetables begin to brown, add the tomatoes. Simmer the mixture, uncovered, until the tomatoes have reduced to a pulp, about 10 minutes.

Then add the mussels and sausage. Cover and cook for about 2 to 3 minutes or until the mussels have opened. Remove the pan from the heat.

Heat 4 tablespoons of the remaining oil in a paella pan or large frying pan. When the oil begins to smoke, add the rice and fry it until it begins to colour. Then add the contents of the pot to the paella pan. Stir and pour in 60 cl (1 pint) of boiling water. Add the uncooked shrimps, French beans and peas. Pound the garlic with a pinch of powdered saffron and the remaining 2 tablespoons of oil. Add this to the paella pan, cover, and cook the mixture for a further 15 minutes. Set aside to rest for 5 minutes, then serve the paella in the pan.

VICTORIA SERRA
TIA VICTORIA'S SPANISH KITCHEN

Tunisian Fish with Rice

Riz au Poisson à la Tunisienne

The technique of making harissa, the fiery pimento sauce used in North African cooking, is shown on page 39.

Any large white fish can be used, such as angler fish, swordfish, sea bass and sea bream; or use tuna or bonito.

To serve 4

300 g	rice, washed and drained	10 oz
750 g	fish, scaled, cleaned and cut into 4 thick slices	1½ lb
	salt and pepper	
10 cl	oil	3½ fl oz
1	small onion, chopped	1
1 tbsp	puréed tomato	1 tbsp
1 tsp	*harissa*, mixed with 10 cl (3½ fl oz) water	1 tsp
About 8 tbsp	water	About 8 tbsp
30 g	butter	1 oz

Season the fish with salt and pepper. Heat the oil in a saucepan large enough to hold the fish slices placed side by side. Add the onion, and cook until the fish is lightly browned on both sides. Add the puréed tomato and the *harissa*, simmer for 10 minutes, then pour on enough water to cover the fish. Bring to the boil, reduce the heat and simmer gently until cooked—about 12 to 15 minutes.

Remove the fish slices from the broth and keep them warm. Add enough water to the broth to make it up to ¾ litre (1¼ pints) and bring it to the boil. Add the rice, reduce the heat, cover, and simmer until all the liquid has been absorbed, about 20 minutes. Then add the butter.

Adjust the seasoning, heap the rice on a serving dish, garnish with the fish, and serve hot.

M. KOUKI
POISSONS MÉDITERRANÉENS

Country Dirty Rice

To serve 4 to 6

400 g	long-grain rice	14 oz
10 cl	oil	3½ fl oz
3 tbsp	flour	3 tbsp
125 g	onions, finely chopped	4 oz
750 g	chicken livers, finely chopped	1½ lb
60 g	celery, chopped	2 oz
30 g	parsley, finely chopped	1 oz
100 g	spring onions, chopped	3½ oz
75 g	sweet green pepper, chopped	2½ oz
1 tsp	finely chopped garlic	1 tsp
	salt and pepper	
⅛ tsp	cayenne pepper	⅛ tsp
1 litre	stock (*page 165*)	1¾ pints

In an iron pot, make a brown roux with the oil and flour by cooking them over a low heat. Add the onion, and stir until brown. Add the chicken livers, celery, parsley, spring onions, sweet green pepper and garlic, and stir. Season with a little salt, pepper, and the cayenne pepper. Cook for 5 minutes over a medium heat; then add 10 cl (3½ fl oz) of the stock and cook for a further 15 minutes. Skim any excess oil from the top of the mixture and remove the pan from the heat.

In a separate pan cook the rice in the rest of the stock for 18 to 20 minutes or until the liquid is absorbed and the rice is fluffy. Fold the rice into the vegetable mixture and correct the seasoning. Before serving, warm in an oven preheated to 180°C (350°F or Mark 4) for 20 minutes.

THE JUNIOR LEAGUE OF NEW ORLEANS
THE PLANTATION COOKBOOK

Chilean Eel Curry

Chilenischer Aal-Curry

To kill a live eel, bang its head against the table. Cut off the head to a length of about 7.5 cm (3 inches). This section also contains the viscera. To skin it, slit the skin all the way round just beneath the head. Loosen it with pliers and peel back the skin as if removing a glove.

To serve 6

500 g	rice	1 lb
500 g	fresh eel	1 lb
½ litre	dry white wine	16 fl oz
2	bay leaves	2
3	cloves	3
6	juniper berries	6
30 g	butter	1 oz
	salt	
3 tsp	curry powder	3 tsp
1 tbsp	chopped fresh dill	1 tbsp

Bring the white wine to the boil with the bay leaves, cloves and juniper berries. Simmer for 5 minutes. Put in the eel and poach it for about 10 minutes; remove it and set it aside, reserving the liquid.

Wash the rice and fry it briskly in the butter. Strain the poaching liquid and add it to the rice. Simmer for 10 minutes or until the liquid is almost entirely absorbed. Season with salt and add the curry powder. Skin the eel, remove the bones and cut the eel into pieces 3 cm (1 inch) long. Add the pieces to the rice with the chopped dill. Cover the pan and cook for 10 minutes over a very low heat.

LILO AUREDEN
WAS MÄNNERN SO GUT SCHMECKT

Milanese Risotto

Risotto alla Milanese

To serve 5 or 6

500 g	round-grain rice	1 lb
1	small onion, finely chopped	1
40 g	beef marrow	1½ oz
75 g	butter	2½ oz
15 cl	dry white wine	¼ pint
¼ tsp	powdered saffron, mixed with 2 tbsp stock	¼ tsp
1.25 litres	stock (*page 165*)	2 pints
About 90 g	Parmesan cheese, grated	About 3 oz

Cook the onion and the marrow in half of the butter in a shallow pan until the onion is soft and the marrow well browned. Stir in the rice and, after a few minutes, add the wine, 15 cl (¼ pint) of the stock and the saffron. With the heat on low, stir the mixture, slowly, until the liquid is almost absorbed, then add a ladleful more of the stock. Continue stirring and adding stock a little at a time each time it is absorbed. When the rice is just tender, take the pan off the heat and stir in the remaining butter and the Parmesan cheese. Serve with more Parmesan cheese on the side.

PELLEGRINO ARTUSI
LA SCIENZA IN CUCINA E L'ARTE DI MANGIAR BENE

Chicken and Pork Stew with Rice

Diabo

For this dish, which comes from Mação, the rice should be cooked as for a pilaff (page 20). Mustard greens are a very spicy vegetable obtainable from Oriental food shops. Usually preserved in brine, they need to be soaked in water before use.

To serve 6 to 8

300 g	rice	10 oz
1 kg	chicken, cut into 10 pieces	2 to 2½ lb
400 g	boneless lean pork, cut into large cubes	14 oz
130 g	lard	4 oz
1	large onion, chopped	1
	salt and pepper	
2	bay leaves	2
3	cloves, tied in a piece of muslin	3
1 tbsp	vinegar	1 tbsp
	freshly ground allspice	
10 cl	puréed tomato	3½ fl oz
750 g	mustard greens or other greens	1½ lb

In a sauté pan, cook the onion in the lard until golden, then add the meats, salt and pepper, bay leaves, cloves, vinegar, a pinch of allspice and the puréed tomato. Cover and simmer gently for about 45 minutes, or until the meats are tender, adding a little water if the stew becomes too dry.

Put the rice to cook 30 minutes before the stew is ready, and the mustard greens 10 minutes before. Arrange the rice on a warmed serving plate and set the mustard greens on top of the rice. Discard the cloves from the stew. Pour the stew over the rice and greens and serve.

MARIA ODETTE CORTES VALENTE
COZINHA REGIONAL PORTUGUESA

Catalan Rice

Arros à la Catalane

To serve 6

500 g	rice	1 lb
400 to 500 g	pork chops or pork fillet or boned pork loin	14 oz to 1 lb
2 tbsp	olive oil	2 tbsp
1	onion, chopped	1
2 to 3 tbsp	puréed tomatoes	2 to 3 tbsp
150 g	*chorizo* or other spicy frying sausage, diced	5 oz
30 g	shelled green peas	1 oz
3	garlic cloves, chopped	3
¼ tsp	powdered saffron	¼ tsp
1 to 1.5 litres	stock or water	1¾ to 2½ pints
	salt and pepper	

In a large saucepan, brown the pork in the olive oil over a medium heat for about 2 minutes. Add the onion and cook for a further 3 minutes until the onion is transparent. Add the puréed tomatoes, the diced sausage and a little water. Cook for 10 minutes, then add the peas and the garlic. Bring to the boil and add the rice, saffron and the stock or water. Cook for 15 to 20 minutes or until the rice is soft and the liquid has been absorbed. Season with salt and pepper to taste.

MARIE-THÉRÈSE CARRÉRAS AND GEORGES LAFFORGUE
LES BONNES RECETTES DU PAYS CATALAN

Risotto with Parmesan

Risotto alla Parmigiana

To serve 4

500 g	round-grain rice	1 lb
1	small onion, chopped	1
80 g	butter	3 oz
1.5 litres	stock (*page 165*)	2½ pints
60 g	Parmesan cheese, grated	2 oz

Heat the onion in a pan with 40 g (1½ oz) of butter. Fry the onion until it turns golden. Add the rice to the onion, and after a few minutes add 15 cl (¼ pint) of the stock. Stir the mixture continually, gradually adding more stock as it is absorbed. When the rice is cooked, that is, when it is *al dente* and not too dry, remove the pan from the heat, add the rest of the butter, cut into pieces, and the Parmesan cheese. Stir and serve.

STELLA DONATI
LE FAMOSE ECONOMICHE RICETTE DI PETRONILLA

Risotto with Chanterelle Mushrooms

Risotto de Chanterelles

To serve 4

400 g	round-grain rice	14 oz
500 g	chanterelle mushrooms	1 lb
3	onions, finely chopped	3
1	garlic clove, finely chopped	1
3 tbsp	olive oil	3 tbsp
	paprika	
100 g	butter	3½ oz
2	carrots, grated	2
	salt and pepper	
	powdered saffron	
1 litre	boiling meat stock (*page 165*)	1¾ pints
2 tbsp	chopped mixed parsley, tarragon, chervil and chives	2 tbsp
60 g	Parmesan or Gruyère cheese, grated	2 oz

Lightly sauté one of the chopped onions and the garlic in the oil, adding a pinch of paprika. Add the mushrooms, cover the pan and cook for a further 12 minutes over a low heat. Keep the contents of the pan hot.

Heat 40 g (1½ oz) of the butter in a heavy casserole and, stirring constantly, add the rest of the onion. Add the rice and continue stirring until it turns a light golden colour. Add the carrots, stir for a moment and add the mushrooms. Season with salt and pepper. Add a pinch of saffron and moisten with the boiling stock (about double the volume of the rice). Cover the casserole and put in an oven preheated to 180°C (350°F or Mark 4) for about 20 minutes without stirring again.

Remove from the oven and gently stir in the rest of the butter, the parsley, tarragon, chervil, chives and the grated cheese. Return to the oven, uncovered, for a further 5 minutes, mix and serve very hot.

F. AND T. RARIS
LES CHAMPIGNONS, CONNAISSANCE ET GASTRONOMIE

Risotto with Green Peas

Risi e Bisi

Risi e bisi, a Venetian dish, is not cooked in quite the same way as the ordinary risotto, for it should emerge rather more liquid; it should not be stirred too much or the peas will break. It is to be eaten, however, with a fork, not a spoon, so it must not be too soupy. To make a less rich dish, cook the rice with lightly salted water instead of stock, which will produce soothing food for tired stomachs.

To serve 4 to 6

400 g	round-grain rice	14 oz
1 kg	green peas, shelled	2 lb
1	small onion, chopped	1
40 g	butter	1½ oz
60 g	ham, equal quantities of fat and lean, chopped	2 oz
About 1.75 litres	hot chicken or meat stock (*page 165*)	About 3 pints
60 g	Parmesan cheese, grated	2 oz

Put the onion to soften in about 15 g (½ oz) of the butter. Add the chopped ham. Let the ham melt slightly, then add the shelled peas. When the peas are impregnated with the butter, pour in a large cupful of hot stock and, when it is bubbling, add the rice. Now pour over more hot stock, about 60 cl (1 pint), and cook gently without stirring. Before all of the stock is absorbed, add more. When the rice is cooked, stir in 30 g (1 oz) each of butter and Parmesan cheese, and serve the rest of the cheese separately.

ELIZABETH DAVID
ITALIAN FOOD

Risotto with White Truffle Slices

Risotto aux Truffes

To appreciate fully the flavour and aroma of the truffle, it should be served with very simple accompanying dishes. In fact, it goes perfectly with plain boiled rice tossed with butter and cheese. But if you prefer risotto, here is the recipe.

To serve 4

400 g	round-grain rice	14 oz
1	white truffle, thinly sliced	1
1	onion, finely chopped	1
90 g	butter	3 oz
	salt and pepper	
10 cl	white wine	3½ fl oz
1.5 litres	hot meat stock (*page 165*)	2½ pints
75 g	Parmesan or Gruyère cheese, grated	2½ oz

Over a low heat sauté the onion in a pan with three-quarters of the butter. Add the rice, stir it around for a few minutes, season with salt and pepper, increase the heat and pour in the wine. Mix, and cook until the wine has evaporated. Using a ladle, add the hot stock, little by little, stirring all the time. After 15 to 18 minutes, the risotto will be cooked. Turn off the heat and add the grated cheese and the rest of the butter. Mix again, then serve covered with the truffle slices.

F. AND T. RARIS
LES CHAMPIGNONS, CONNAISSANCE ET GASTRONOMIE

Cabbage Risotto
Riz au Chou

To serve 4

300 g	long-grain rice	10 oz
750 g	cabbage, halved, cored, coarse outer leaves discarded, stalks and ribs removed, shredded	1½ lb
	olive oil	
125 g	smoked bacon, diced small	4 oz
2	onions, roughly chopped	2
	salt and pepper	
60 g	Gruyère cheese, grated	2 oz

Heat the oil in a large saucepan. When it is hot, put in the bacon and onion to colour. Add the cabbage and cook for 15 minutes, stirring frequently with a wooden spoon.

Add the rice. Mix thoroughly. Cook for 10 minutes without the lid, then pour in enough boiling water to cover the rice and cabbage completely. Season and cover the pan. Simmer over a low heat for about 25 minutes. At the end of this period, remove the lid, add the grated cheese and gently mix it in with a fork. Put in a warm serving dish and serve very hot.

MYRETTE TIANO
PÂTES ET RIZ

Cuttlefish Ink with Risotto
Risotto al Nero di Seppie

Cuttlefish can be cleaned in the same way as squid (page 28). The ink sac can be clearly seen among the rest of the viscera, which is discarded. If the cuttlefish is fresh, the ink will be liquid and will flow from the ink sac when it is broken. If frozen, the ink will have solidified and will have to be forced out of the sac and dissolved in a tablespoonful of boiling liquid (water, stock or wine). To make the fish stock, boil 1 kg (2 to 2½ lb) fish head, bones and trimmings, rinsed and roughly chopped, one onion, one carrot, one leek, one stick of celery and a bouquet garni in 2.5 litres (4 pints) water. Season with salt

and keep on a low boil until scum rises. Skim until no more scum rises, then reduce the heat and simmer for 30 minutes. Strain the stock.

To serve 6

600 g	round-grain rice	1¼ lb
850 g	cuttlefish, cleaned and sliced into strips, ink sac from one reserved	1¾ lb
¼ litre	dry white wine	8 fl oz
1	garlic clove, finely chopped	1
2	bay leaves	2
12.5 cl	olive oil	4 fl oz
1	onion, chopped	1
About 1.5 litres	boiling fish stock	About 2½ pints
	salt and pepper	
2 tbsp	chopped parsley	2 tbsp
100 g	butter, cut into small pieces	3½ oz
75 g	Parmesan cheese, grated	2½ oz

Dilute the ink with half the white wine. Gently fry the garlic and bay leaves in half the oil until the garlic is lightly coloured. Remove and chop the bay leaves. Increase the heat to medium, add the cuttlefish strips to the pan and, after a few minutes, stir in the diluted ink and the bay leaves. Reduce the heat and cook uncovered for 15 minutes.

Meanwhile, in another pan, prepare the risotto. Stew the onion slowly in the remaining oil until soft. Add the rice and cook over a medium heat, stirring constantly. Add the remaining wine, leave to evaporate, then add some of the stock. Simmer, stirring occasionally, until the rice is nearly cooked, about 15 minutes, adding more stock as necessary.

Add the ink and cuttlefish mixture, season with salt and pepper, stir and cook uncovered for a further 18 to 20 minutes. Add the parsley, butter and Parmesan cheese and mix well.

LUIGI VOLPICELLI AND SECONDINO FREDA
L'ANTIARTUSI: 1000 RICETTE

Squid and Scampi Risotto

Risotto con Moscardini e Scampi

Moscardini *are small squid found in the Genoa region of Italy. Use the smallest squid available, preferably not more than 5 cm (2 inches) long. The technique of cleaning and preparing squid is shown on page 28.*

The sauce for this risotto is also excellent served with spaghetti or other kinds of pasta.

To serve 6

600 g	round-grain rice	1¼ lb
3	*moscardini* or small squid	3
10	scampi or large prawns, cooked or raw	10
1.5 litres	water	2½ pints
	salt	
2	carrots, scraped and diced	2
1	onion, diced	1
4	celery stalks, diced	4
60 g	butter	2 oz
5 to 6 tbsp	oil	5 to 6 tbsp
350 g	tomatoes, scalded, skinned and chopped	12 oz
4 tbsp	finely chopped parsley	4 tbsp
2	garlic cloves, finely chopped	2
2 tbsp	finely chopped basil	2 tbsp
500 g	green peas, shelled	1 lb
35 cl	good dry white wine	12 fl oz
60 g	butter	2 oz
30 g	Parmesan cheese, grated (optional)	1 oz

To prepare the broth in which the rice is to be cooked, put the water, salt, carrots, onion and celery into a large pan and simmer for 30 minutes.

Prepare the *moscardini,* slicing off the heads and removing the ink sacs. Leave the heads whole, but slice the rest of the flesh into strips and rings.

Put the butter and oil in a deep saucepan in which the rice is to be cooked. Place over heat, and when the butter has melted, add the tomatoes. Mix the parsley, garlic and basil and add to the tomatoes. Cook, stirring constantly, until the garlic browns. Then add the *moscardini,* including the heads and the peas, and reduce the heat. If the sauce becomes too thick, add a few tablespoonfuls of the vegetable broth which is cooking separately.

If the scampi are raw, now is the time to plunge them into the broth, for a scant 5 minutes. Remove, drain and cool. Remove the heads of the cooked scampi (they will be used to decorate the serving dish), shell the tails and add to the sauce.

Continue to cook the sauce over a low heat, making sure it does not stick to the bottom of the pan. When *moscardini* and peas are tender, add the rice and stir to coat evenly with the sauce. Gradually add white wine. As soon as this is absorbed, gradually add the hot, strained vegetable broth and simmer until the rice is cooked; it should be tender but still firm.

Just before serving, dot the rice mixture with the butter and sprinkle with Parmesan cheese. However, remember that connoisseurs do not like cheese to be added to fish dishes. Serve piping hot, decorating the serving dish with the heads of the scampi arranged in a ring round the risotto.

MARIÙ SALVATORI DE ZULIANI
LA CUCINA DI VERSILIA E GARFAGNANA

Chard and Squid Risotto

Risotto con Bieta e Seppie

The technique of cleaning and preparing squid is demonstrated on page 28.

To serve 6

600 g	round-grain rice, washed	1¼ lb
250 g	Swiss chard, washed, dried and coarsely chopped	8 oz
3	squid, thinly sliced	3
6 tbsp	oil	6 tbsp
6 tbsp	finely chopped parsley	6 tbsp
2	garlic cloves, chopped	2
17.5 cl	dry white wine	6 fl oz
	salt and pepper	
	grated nutmeg	
350 g	tomatoes, scalded, skinned and chopped	12 oz
1.5 litres	stock, preferably fish stock, brought to boiling point	2½ pints

Heat the oil in a deep pan, and add the parsley and garlic. When browned, add the squid and simmer for at least 20 minutes. Then add the white wine. Season with salt, pepper and grated nutmeg. When the wine has been absorbed into the mixture, add the Swiss chard and simmer for 10 minutes, to allow it to absorb the flavours in the pan, then add the tomatoes. Pour in the rice, mix well and gradually add the stock, continuing to stir until the rice is cooked. The rice should be moist and tender, but still firm.

MARIÙ SALVATORI DE ZULIANI
LA CUCINA DI VERSILIA E GARFAGNANA

Spanish Rice with Squid

Arroz a la Bruta

In this recipe, the rice turns black when cooked with the squid's ink. For the technique of cleaning and preparing squid see page 28. The ink sac can be clearly seen among the rest of the viscera, which is discarded.

To serve 4

250 g	rice	8 oz
1	large squid, about 500 to 750 g (1 to 1½ lb), or cuttlefish, cleaned, ink sac reserved, body pouch cut into rings	1
	oil	
1	large onion, chopped	1
1	tomato, skinned, seeded and chopped	1
3 or 4	garlic cloves, finely chopped	3 or 4
3 tbsp	finely chopped parsley	3 tbsp
	salt and pepper	
	cayenne pepper	
	ground cinnamon	
About ½ litre	boiling water	About 16 fl oz

Heat the oil in a fireproof earthenware pan, and lightly fry the onion, tomato, garlic and parsley. Add the squid, season with a little salt and black pepper, the cayenne pepper and a little cinnamon, cover, and simmer for about 30 minutes.

Add the rice and leave it to cook for a few moments. Cover with boiling water and bring to the boil over high heat.

Meanwhile, break the ink sac into a cup and dilute it with a few spoonfuls of the hot cooking liquid. Add this to the rice when it begins to boil. Mix very well, cover, and continue to cook the rice, adding more boiling water as necessary, for 15 to 20 minutes or until a tender, very dry black rice is achieved.

JUAN CASTELLÓ GUASCH
BON PROFIT! EL LIBRO DE LA COCINA IBICENCA

Spinach and Rice

Spanakorizo

A similar dish, *prassorizo*, is made with leeks and rice: substitute 750 g (1½ lb) sliced leeks for the spinach and add the leeks at the same time as the liquid.

To serve 6 to 8

125 g	long-grain rice	4 oz
1 kg	spinach, stems removed, washed and drained	2 lb
2 tbsp	olive oil or 30 g (1 oz) butter	2 tbsp
1	small onion, chopped	1
12.5 cl	tomato sauce or canned tomatoes, drained	4 fl oz
10 cl	water	3½ fl oz
4 tbsp	chopped parsley	4 tbsp
2	sprigs fresh mint, chopped	2
	salt and freshly ground pepper	
	nutmeg	
3	rashers bacon, fried until crisp and crumbled (optional)	3
4	eggs, hard-boiled and sliced (optional)	4
1	lemon, cut into wedges	1

Heat the oil or butter in an enamelled pan, then add the onions and cook over a low heat until soft and transparent. Add the rice and sauté for a few minutes, stirring constantly, then add the tomato sauce or tomatoes and the water. Cover the pan and simmer until the rice is almost tender (about 10 minutes). Uncover the pan and stir in the spinach, parsley and mint; season with salt and pepper. Partially cover the pan and continue cooking, stirring with a wooden spoon until the spinach has wilted. Grate a little nutmeg over the top and continue cooking until all of the liquid has been absorbed and the *spanakorizo* is tender, not mushy. Remove from the heat and drape the *spanakorizo* with a dry towel, set beneath the lid of the pan, until ready to use. Transfer to a warmed serving dish, sprinkle with bacon bits, if desired, and garnish with the sliced eggs and lemon wedges. Serve warm.

VILMA LIACOURAS CHANTILES
THE FOOD OF GREECE

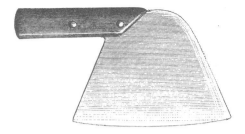

Dill and Broad Bean Polo

Sheved Baghala

If small, tender, fresh broad beans are used for this dish it is not necessary to soak them.

To serve 8

400 g	long-grain rice, washed and soaked in water for at least 2 hours or overnight	14 oz
1 kg	fresh broad beans, or 125 g (4 oz) dried beans soaked in water overnight and cooked for about 2 hours, or until tender	2 lb
	salt	
4 tbsp	hot water	4 tbsp
¼ tsp	saffron threads (optional)	¼ tsp
125 g	butter	4 oz
1	bunch fresh dill, stems removed, leaves finely chopped	1

If using fresh beans, remove them from their pods, and soak the beans in cold water for 1 to 2 hours. Peel off the inner skins, which will slip off the beans easily.

Fill a large saucepan with cold water, place over a high heat and bring to the boil. Add the rice, 2 tablespoons of salt and the beans. Boil, uncovered, over a high heat, stirring occasionally, for 7 to 8 minutes. Remove from the heat and drain the rice and beans in a colander. Rinse with water.

In the pot in which the rice cooked, put the hot water, saffron (if desired), butter and ½ teaspoon of salt, and bring to the boil. Pour half the buttery liquid into a cup and reserve.

Mix the dill with the rice and return the rice to the pot. Mound the rice and, with the handle of a spoon, make a deep hole in the centre. Cover and cook over a medium heat for 5 minutes; uncover, and sprinkle the rice with the reserved buttery liquid, then cover and steam over a very low heat for about 40 minutes.

Remove the pan and place it on a cool surface for about 5 minutes to loosen the bottom crust. Uncover, and fluff the rice on to a serving dish. Remove the bottom crust and arrange it around or on top of the rice.

DAISY INY
THE BEST OF BAGHDAD COOKING

Persian Rice with Lentils and Chicken

To serve 4 to 6

250 g	long-grain rice	8 oz
150 g	whole lentils	5 oz
3	whole chicken breasts, boned, skinned and cut into 1 cm (½ inch) cubes	3
60 g	dried apricots, coarsely chopped	2 oz
2.25 litres	water	3¾ pints
3 tbsp	salt	3 tbsp
60 g	almonds, blanched and sliced or salted pecans, coarsely chopped	2 oz
300 to 350 g	unsalted butter	10 to 12 oz
1	medium-sized onion, chopped	1
1 tsp	pepper	1 tsp
3 tsp	chopped fresh dill	3 tsp

Cover the apricots with warm water and allow them to soak for 30 minutes before the cooking time, unless they are very soft, in which case soak them only when you begin to cook.

Bring ¾ litre (1¼ pints) of the water to the boil, seasoning it well with 1 tablespoon of the salt. Add the lentils and cook until they are slightly more than half done, about 30 minutes. Remove the lentils from the heat, pour them into a colander in the sink and keep them warm under warm running water.

Sauté the nuts in 60 g (2 oz) of the butter until golden. Remove from the pan, leaving any remaining butter in the pan. Sauté the onion in this butter, adding a little more butter if necessary, until it is soft and just beginning to brown lightly. Remove the onion from the heat and set it aside with the sautéed nuts.

Bring 1.5 litres (2½ pints) of water to the boil and season well with 2 tablespoons of salt. Sprinkle in the rice. Stir with a wooden spoon, so that the rice does not stick to the bottom of the pot, until the water boils again. Then boil without stirring for 7 to 8 minutes, or until the rice is just about half cooked. Pour the rice into a colander and rinse with very hot water.

Drain both rice and lentils well, combine them, sprinkle with pepper, and toss lightly with two forks so that they are evenly mixed together.

Melt 250g (8 oz) of the butter. Pour a quarter of this into a heavy 4 litre (6 to 7 pint) pot. Sprinkle in the rice and lentil mixture very lightly, forming a sort of pyramid on top of the butter. Pour the remaining melted butter over the mixture. Cover the pot with a clean, folded cloth and a tight-fitting lid. Place over a low heat for about 1 hour. Remove the lid and allow the rice and lentil mixture to dry out for about 5 minutes. Taste for salt and sprinkle more on if necessary.

While the rice and lentil mixture is cooking, drain the apricots, squeezing out water with your hand. Have the raw chicken cubes at room temperature. Add the chicken to the rice mixture and toss in gently with a fork. The heat of the rice will cook the chicken sufficiently.

As soon as the chicken is mixed into the rice, add the nuts, onion, apricots and dill. Toss in gently without disturbing the crisp bottom layer of rice and lentils. Serve at once, scooping up a little of the crisp bottom layer to top each serving.

JOSÉ WILSON (EDITOR)
HOUSE AND GARDEN'S PARTY MENU COOKBOOK

Rice Balls

Suppli

Suppli are rice croquettes containing in the centre a slice of *mozzarella* cheese and a piece of ham or mortadella sausage. They can be made most successfully with leftover *risotto* (*page 22*), and are so good that when making a *risotto* it is worth cooking enough to have some left to make the *suppli*.

To serve 4 to 6

About 500 g	leftover cooked round-grain rice, or *risotto*	About 1 lb
2	eggs, lightly beaten	2
100 g	ham, thinly sliced and cut into small squares	3½ oz
100 g	*mozzarella* cheese, thinly sliced and cut into small squares	3½ oz
	fine breadcrumbs	
	oil or fat	

Stir the eggs into the cooked rice to bind it. Take about 1 tablespoon of the rice and put it flat on the palm of your hand; on the rice, lay a little slice of ham and one of cheese. Place another tablespoon of rice on the top of the ham and cheese and form the mixture into a ball the size of a small orange, so that the ham and the cheese are completely enclosed. Roll each *suppli* very carefully in fine breadcrumbs, then fry them in hot oil or fat, turning them over and round so that the whole of the outside is nicely browned. Drain them on brown or kitchen paper. The cheese inside should be just melted, stretching into threads (to which the dish owes its nickname of *suppli al telefono*) as one cuts into the rice, so a hard cheese such as Gruyère is not suitable.

ELIZABETH DAVID
ITALIAN FOOD

Malaysian Fried Rice

Nasi Goreng

This dish, one of the most common in Malaysia, always includes prawns, which give it a strong marine flavour. In other respects it is subject to small variations. The Chinese make it with pork, decorate it elaborately with slivers of omelette, chopped spring onion, red chili peppers and parsley, and serve it with a thick chili sauce. The Malay people use beef as the meat, adding onions and sometimes green peas. They present the dish in a neat mould surrounded by shredded lettuce, decorate it with chili peppers cut into flower shapes and a single fried egg on top and serve it with soy sauce containing thin slices of chili pepper. The following recipe provides what many Malaysians would regard as generous quantities of prawn and meat. Less may be used. There does exist in coastal villages a *nasi goreng* which has fish in place of meat. I recommend trying it by substituting 150 g (5 oz) of chopped fish for the meat.

To serve 4

200 g	rice, cooked	7 oz
150 g	shelled prawns	5 oz
150 g	pork or beef, trimmed of fat and finely chopped	5 oz
1	garlic clove, finely chopped	1
5	small onions, finely chopped (optional)	5
1 tbsp	sultanas	1 tbsp
1 tbsp	light soy sauce	1 tbsp
	Suggested garnishes	
4	small red onions, sliced or chopped and fried	4
4	lettuce leaves, shredded	4
2	fresh red chili peppers, seeded and cut into slivers or flower shapes	2
3	spring onions, finely chopped	3
1	one-egg flat omelette, cooked like a pancake, rolled up and cut into strips, or 1 fried egg	1
1 tbsp	chopped parsley	1 tbsp
	croûtons	

Fry the prawns and meat with the garlic and onions until brown. Stir in the cooked rice, sultanas and soy sauce and continue to fry gently until the mixture is thoroughly heated and evenly browned.

Garnish the dish according to taste with red onions, lettuce, chili peppers, spring onions, egg, parsley and croûtons. Serve with chili, Tabasco or soy sauce.

ALAN DAVIDSON
SEAFOOD OF SOUTH-EAST ASIA

Fried Risotto
Risotto al Salto

This is one of the ways of using leftover *risotto alla Milanese (page 23)*. However, this fried risotto is often considered to be superior to that which has been freshly made and so *risotto alla Milanese* should be made in larger quantities than are needed for one meal in order to make this second dish.

To serve 8		
1 kg	leftover *risotto alla Milanese*	2 lb
60 to 90 g	butter	2 to 3 oz

Butter a piece of greaseproof paper and on it shape the risotto into eight patties. In a heavy frying pan heat 15 g (½ oz) of the butter. Put in one rice patty, taking care not to let it break. Move the pan about during the cooking as for an omelette, to prevent the patty sticking to the pan. Fry until a crust has formed on the bottom of the patty. Turn it out on to a plate, and return it to the pan to fry on the other side. Fry the remaining patties, one at a time, in the same way, adding butter as required. Serve immediately.

OTTORINA PERNA BOZZI
VECCHIA MILANO IN CUCINA

Fried Rice

To serve 4		
600 g	boiled rice, at least one day old	1¼ lb
60 g	beef fillet, chilled	2 oz
¼	garlic clove, finely chopped	¼
	salt and pepper	
½ tsp	cornflour	½ tsp
½ tsp	sugar	½ tsp
2 tbsp	soy sauce	2 tbsp
5 tbsp	vegetable oil	5 tbsp
2	slices ginger root, peeled and cut into *julienne* strips	2
1	sweet green pepper, seeded and cut into *julienne* strips	1
2	rashers lean smoked bacon, diced	2
6	spring onions, thinly sliced	6
4	slices ham, diced	4
2 to 4 tbsp	chopped parsley or coriander leaves	2 to 4 tbsp
6	eggs	6

Slice the fillet of beef paper thin and combine the slices with the garlic, a little salt and pepper, the cornflour, sugar, 1 tablespoon of the soy sauce and 2 tablespoons of the oil. Set aside to marinate.

Heat the remaining oil in a large skillet. Add the ginger, sweet pepper and a little salt and pepper, and fry for 1 minute. Loosen the rice with your hands to separate the grains, and add them to the pan. When the grains are hot and separated, form a well in the centre of the rice. Toss the bacon, spring onions and ham into the well and fry them for a moment; then thoroughly mix them into the rice. Form another well in the centre of the rice, drop in the beef mixture, fry for 30 seconds, then add 2 tablespoons of parsley or coriander leaves. Fry for another 30 seconds, then mix thoroughly into the rice. Form yet another well in the centre of the rice, drop in the eggs, and fry them until they reach the consistency of creamy scrambled eggs; then mix the eggs into the rice. Sprinkle with the remaining soy sauce.

Transfer to a warm serving dish, and serve garnished with the remaining parsley or coriander leaves if desired.

DOREEN YEN HUNG FENG
THE JOY OF CHINESE COOKING

Rice and Meat Balls
Boulettes de Kefta au Riz

Kefta *is finely minced lamb or beef mixed with spices. The North Africans pound it in a mortar, but putting it twice through the mincer instead should be sufficient. When the meat has been minced, mix it with 1 teaspoon each of ground cinnamon, paprika and coriander. Prepared* kefta *is available from Arab butchers.*

To serve 8 to 10		
200 g	rice, washed and drained	7 oz
500 g	*kefta*	1 lb
150 g	butter	5 oz
2	onions, finely chopped	2
¼ tsp	powdered saffron	¼ tsp
½ tsp	pepper	½ tsp
½ litre	water	16 fl oz
3 tbsp	chopped parsley	3 tbsp
8 tbsp	lemon juice	8 tbsp

Mix the rice with the *kefta* and shape the mixture into 20 small balls. Melt the butter in a deep casserole over medium heat, and put in the rice and *kefta* balls as you make them.

When all the balls are brown, add the onions, saffron and the pepper. Pour in the water, cover and cook over a medium heat, stirring from time to time for about 40 minutes until cooked through. At the end of the cooking time, add the parsley and lemon juice. Simmer for another few minutes, then remove from the heat before the sauce thickens.

If you prepare this dish in advance and the sauce becomes too thick as it cools, add a little water when you reheat it. Serve the *kefta* very hot.

AHMED LAASRI
240 RECETTES DE CUISINE MAROCAINE

Fried Rice Croquettes

Arancine e Suppli di Riso

If prosciutto is not available, gammon can be substituted.

The veal, chicken livers and ham for these croquettes may be cooked separately and each rice ball filled with a different mixture, so that each will be a surprise for the taste-buds.

	To serve 6	
400 g	round-grain rice	14 oz
1	onion, thinly sliced	1
100 g	butter	3½ oz
60 cl	meat stock (*page 165*), heated	1 pint
60 g	Parmesan cheese, grated	2 oz
2	eggs, beaten	2
30 g	dried mushrooms, soaked for 2 hours in at least 3 changes of warm water, drained and sliced	1 oz
100 g	lean veal, diced	3½ oz
100 g	chicken livers, diced	3½ oz
100 g	prosciutto, diced	3½ oz
	salt and pepper	
60 g	fine dry breadcrumbs	2 oz
1.25 litres	oil for frying	2 pints

Brown half of the onion in 30 g (1 oz) of the butter. Add the rice, and stir until the grains are evenly coated with butter. Gradually add 30 cl (½ pint) of the hot stock. Cover the pan and cook over a medium heat for about 15 minutes. A few minutes before the end of the cooking time, add the Parmesan cheese and 40 g (1½ oz) of the remaining butter. Stir thoroughly, then remove the rice from the heat. Leave to cool, then add the beaten eggs to the mixture.

Brown the remaining onion in the rest of the butter. Add the mushrooms and simmer for a few minutes; then add the diced meats. Add half the remaining stock, season lightly with salt and pepper, and cover the pan. Cook for at least 20 minutes, or until all of the liquid has been reduced to a thick sauce, stirring occasionally, and adding up to 15 cl (¼ pint) more stock if the liquid dries up before the end of the cooking time. Leave the mixture to cool.

Shape the cooked rice into six balls or cylinders. Remove a little rice to make a hollow in each ball or cylinder, and fill the hollow with some of the meat mixture. Close up the holes with the rice taken from the hollowed-out shapes. Roll these croquettes in the breadcrumbs and quickly deep fry in hot oil until golden-brown, about 1½ minutes. Drain the croquettes on brown paper and serve.

IL MONDO IN CUCINA:
MINESTRE, ZUPPE, RISO

Rice with Spinach and Ham

Reis mit Spinat und Schinken

	To serve 4	
250 g	rice, boiled	8 oz
750 g	spinach, cooked and drained	1½ lb
250 g	raw ham, diced	8 oz
30 g	butter, softened	1 oz
125 g	Gruyère cheese, grated	4 oz
45 cl	tomato sauce (*page 166*)	¾ pint

Mix the spinach while it is still warm with the softened butter. Butter a pudding basin and fill it with alternate layers of rice, ham and spinach. Top with a layer of rice. Sprinkle with half of the grated cheese. Cover the top with buttered greaseproof paper or aluminium foil and cook in a water bath in an oven preheated to 180°C (350°F or Mark 4) for about 30 minutes. Turn the pudding out on to a warmed dish, pour on the tomato sauce and sprinkle with the remaining cheese.

LILO AUREDEN
WAS MÄNNERN SO GUT SCHMECKT

Salted Salmon Pudding with Rice

Laxpudding med Risgryn

If salted salmon is not available, use either lightly salted smoked salmon or fresh salmon strewn with coarse salt, peppercorns and a little sugar and refrigerate for up to 4 hours, turning the fish in the liquid which will accumulate.

The Swedes cure salmon with a mixture of salt and sugar and nitrate of potassium, to produce what they call salt *lax* or *rimmad lax*. This salted salmon will keep for months. It is used in this recipe for a salmon pudding. Making a pudding is a good way of stretching a small quantity of salmon.

To serve 3 or 4

175 g	rice	6 oz
350 g	salted salmon, rinsed and sliced	12 oz
1 litre	skimmed milk	1¾ pints
15 cl	milk	¼ pint
100 g	butter, chilled	3½ oz
2	eggs, yolks separated from whites, yolks beaten, whites stiffly beaten	2
2 tsp	salt	2 tsp
½ tsp	white pepper	½ tsp
2 tsp	sugar	2 tsp
3 tbsp	dry breadcrumbs	3 tbsp

Soak the salmon in the skimmed milk for 3 hours. Remove the salmon, dry it well on a tea towel, and cut it into cubes. Discard the skimmed milk.

Bring the 15 cl (¼ pint) of fresh milk to the boil. Add the rice, and cook it, stirring occasionally and adding a little more fresh milk if necessary, until it is almost soft, about 15 minutes. Then take the rice off the heat, beat in 60 g (2 oz) of the butter at once and leave the mixture to cool. When it is quite cold, stir in the beaten egg yolks, the salmon and the salt, pepper and sugar.

Finally, fold in the stiffly beaten egg whites. Adjust the seasoning, and pour the mixture into a buttered 1 litre (1¾ pint) pie dish sprinkled with 2 tablespoons of breadcrumbs. Top the mixture with the remaining breadcrumbs. Bake in an oven preheated to 180°C (350°F or Mark 4) for 1 hour or until lightly browned. Serve with the remaining butter, melted.

ALAN DAVIDSON
NORTH ATLANTIC SEAFOOD

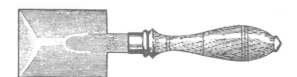

Kedgeree

To serve 4

175 g	long-grain (Patna) rice, cooked so that each grain is dry and separate	6 oz
175 g	smoked haddock, poached, bones and skin removed, finely flaked	6 oz
2	eggs, hard-boiled and finely chopped	2
	salt and freshly ground pepper	
About 60 g	butter	About 2 oz
1 tbsp	finely chopped parsley, or parsley and chives	1 tbsp

Lightly mix the rice, the fish and the eggs, and season this kedgeree with a little salt and plenty of freshly ground pepper. Melt 30 to 40 g (1 to 1½ oz) of the butter in a saucepan without allowing it to colour. Stir in the kedgeree and toss it till it is hot through; or put in a covered dish with plenty of butter in a preheated 170°C (325°F or Mark 3) oven.

Pile the kedgeree in a flat dish, place the remaining butter, cut into pieces, on the pile, and sprinkle with the parsley or parsley and chives. Serve very hot with toast and butter.

ELISABETH AYRTON
THE COOKERY OF ENGLAND

Bari Rice and Vegetables with Mussels

Tiedda alla Barese

To serve 8

500 g	short-grain rice	1 lb
1 kg	tomatoes, peeled	2 to 2½ lb
1 kg	potatoes, sliced into rounds	2 to 2½ lb
500 g	onions, sliced	1 lb
500 g	courgettes, sliced into rounds	1 lb
1 kg	mussels, cooked and shelled	2 to 2½ lb
30 g	butter	1 oz
	salt and pepper	
100 g	breadcrumbs	3½ oz
100 g	*pecorino* cheese, grated	3½ oz
6 tbsp	chopped parsley	6 tbsp
1	garlic clove, chopped	1
4 tbsp	olive oil	4 tbsp
1.25 litres	meat stock (*page 165*)	2 pints

Arrange a layer of the tomatoes in the bottom of a buttered pie dish or deep earthenware casserole, and season. Seasoning each layer, add a layer of potatoes, a layer of onions and courgettes, then a layer of mussels, followed by one of un-cooked rice, and a second layer of tomatoes. Put in a layer of breadcrumbs, cheese and parsley, add the garlic and sprinkle with 2 tablespoons of oil. Add another layer of the remaining vegetables and top with plenty of breadcrumbs, cheese and parsley. Pour in the stock and the remaining oil and bake uncovered in an oven preheated to 230°C (450°F or Mark 8) for 1 hour or until both rice and vegetables are tender. The dish is excellent hot or cold.

LUIGI VOLPICELLI AND SECONDINO FREDA
L'ANTIARTUSI: 1000 RICETTE

Squid Baked with Rice

Kalamarakia Pilafi

The technique of cleaning squid is explained on page 28.

	To serve 4	
250 g	long-grain rice	8 oz
500 g	medium-sized squid, cleaned, rubbed with salt, rinsed and sliced into rings 1 to 2.5 cm (½ to 1 inch) thick	1 lb
4 tbsp	olive oil	4 tbsp
3	garlic cloves, sliced	3
4 tbsp	dry white wine	4 tbsp
2	tomatoes, skinned, seeded and sliced	2
40 g	butter	1½ oz
About 5 tbsp	chopped parsley	About 5 tbsp
1 tbsp	chopped fresh rosemary or 1 tsp dried rosemary	1 tbsp
	salt and freshly ground pepper	
About 30 cl	hot water	About ½ pint

Heat the oil in a frying pan, add the squid and garlic, and sauté for 5 minutes. Stir in the wine and tomatoes, cover, and simmer until the squid is almost tender (approximately 30 minutes). Transfer to a baking dish.

Meanwhile, heat the butter and, stirring constantly, sauté the rice, without browning, until it is opaque. Add the rice to the squid and tomatoes and sprinkle with 4 tablespoons of the parsley, the rosemary, and salt and pepper to taste. Add enough hot water to cook the rice. Cover and bake in an oven preheated to 180°C (350°F or Mark 4) for 30 to 40 minutes, or until the rice is tender. Sprinkle with the remaining chopped parsley and serve hot.

VILMA LIACOURAS CHANTILES
THE FOOD OF GREECE

Rice with Pork and Vegetables

Arroz Murciano

	To serve 6 to 8	
500 g	rice	1 lb
500 g	lean pork, cut into pieces	1 lb
20 cl	oil	7 fl oz
2	garlic cloves	2
6	sweet red peppers, seeded and sliced	6
500 g	tomatoes, skinned, seeded and chopped	1 lb
3 tbsp	chopped parsley	3 tbsp
½ tsp	powdered saffron	½ tsp
About 1.25 litres	boiling water	About 2 pints
	salt and freshly ground pepper	

In a fireproof casserole, sauté the pork in the oil until browned and set the pork aside. Over a low heat, fry the garlic in the same casserole, until lightly coloured, then remove it and put to one side. Put the peppers and tomatoes in the casserole and cook them for 10 minutes or so.

Pound the garlic, with the parsley and saffron, to a paste and add this to the casserole with the peppers and tomatoes. Add a few tablespoons of water and the pork. Cook for a few minutes, or until the broth has evaporated. Add the rice, stir it well and then pour in the boiling water. Season the mixture with a little salt and pepper and bring to the boil. Then place the casserole in an oven preheated to 170°C (325°F or Mark 3), cover and let it cook for 1 hour.

MANUAL DE COCINA

Rice Timbale from Lombardy

Timballo di Riso

To serve 6 to 8

500 g	rice	1 lb
125 g	butter, cut into pieces, at room temperature	4 oz
5 tbsp	freshly grated Parmesan cheese	5 tbsp
4	egg yolks	4
	fine dry breadcrumbs	
	tomato sauce (*page 166*)	
	Meat filling	
250 g	boneless veal, trimmed free of fat and gristle, minced twice	8 oz
250 g	boneless lean pork, trimmed free of fat, minced twice	8 oz
250 g	chicken livers, trimmed and chopped	8 oz
30 g	butter	1 oz
4 tbsp	finely chopped onion	4 tbsp
1	garlic clove, finely chopped	1
75 g	sweet red pepper, grilled, peeled, seeded and chopped	2½ oz
125 g	shelled peas, parboiled	4 oz
4 tbsp	puréed tomato, flavoured with basil	4 tbsp
2 tbsp	dry white wine	2 tbsp
1 tsp	salt	1 tsp
½ tsp	sugar	½ tsp
½ tsp	dried oregano	½ tsp
¼ tsp	freshly ground pepper	¼ tsp
	Tabasco sauce	

Cook the rice in plenty of boiling, salted water for about 15 minutes until it is almost, but not quite, tender. Drain well and place in a bowl. Mix in the butter, Parmesan cheese and egg yolks. Generously butter a 3 litre (5 pint) mould or casserole and coat the bottom and sides thoroughly with breadcrumbs; there must not be any uncovered spots or the timbale will not unmould. Spoon two-thirds of the rice mixture into the casserole. Press the rice against the bottom and sides, leaving a well in the middle.

To make the filling, heat the butter in a deep frying pan. Add the onion and garlic and cook, stirring constantly, until the onion is soft and golden. Add the veal and pork; stir well to blend them together. Stir in the chicken livers. Cook over low heat, stirring frequently for about 15 minutes, or until the meats are cooked through. Add the remaining ingredients, including a dash of Tabasco sauce, and mix well. Stirring frequently, cook over a low heat for about 15 minutes. The filling must be very thick but, if necessary, add a little more wine, a tablespoon at a time, to prevent sticking.

Spoon the filling into the well in the rice, pressing it into place and smoothing the surface. Spoon the remaining rice over the filling and smooth over the top surface of the mould, taking care that the meat is well covered. Bake without a cover in an oven preheated to 180°C (350°F or Mark 4) for about 1 hour, or until the rice is thoroughly set. Unmould carefully on to a heated platter, first running a knife blade round the edge of the mould. Cut the timbale into wedges and serve immediately with tomato sauce on the side.

NIKA HAZELTON
THE REGIONAL ITALIAN KITCHEN

Herbed Wild Rice

If wild rice is not available, brown rice can be substituted.

This wild rice recipe will enhance the mild flavours of a veal roast or the freshest of fish.

To serve 4 to 6

175 g	wild rice	6 oz
125 g	butter	4 oz
2 tbsp	finely chopped spring onion	2 tbsp
2	garlic cloves, finely chopped	2
2	bay leaves	2
1 tsp each	chopped fresh thyme, basil and marjoram	1 tsp each
¾ litre	chicken stock (*page 165*)	1¼ pints
	salt	
	pepper	

Melt the butter in a heavy 2 litre (3½ pint) saucepan. Add the spring onions, garlic and wild rice and sauté, stirring constantly, until the onion is limp, about 3 minutes. Add the bay leaves, thyme, basil, marjoram and chicken stock. Bring to the boil, reduce the heat to maintain a simmer, cover and cook for about 1 hour, or until the rice is tender. Remove and discard the bay leaves. Fluff the rice with a fork, and cook, uncovered, until any excess moisture has evaporated.

BETH ANDERSON
WILD RICE FOR ALL SEASONS COOKBOOK

Wild Rice and Oyster Casserole

To shell an oyster, insert the tip of an oyster knife into the small gap in the hinge of the shell and twist the blade to snap the upper and lower shells apart. Slide the blade along the inside of the upper shell to sever the muscle, then run the blade under the oyster to free it from the lower shell. The technique of cooking wild rice is demonstrated on page 18.

To serve 4

350 g	cooked wild rice	12 oz
8	live oysters, shelled, liquor reserved	8
90 g	butter	3 oz
125 g	shallots or mild onion, chopped	4 oz
90 g	celery, chopped	3 oz
	milk	
1 tsp	salt	1 tsp
¼ tsp	pepper	¼ tsp
¼ tsp	ground cardamom	¼ tsp
175 g	Emmenthal cheese, grated	6 oz

Heat 30 g (1 oz) of the butter in a frying pan and cook the shallots and celery until soft and barely golden. Combine them with the wild rice. Add enough milk to the reserved oyster liquor to make 17.5 cl (6 fl oz) of liquid. Butter a 1.25 litre (2 pint) casserole and in it arrange alternate layers of rice and oysters, ending with a layer of rice. Add the salt, pepper and cardamom to the milk mixture and pour it over the contents of the casserole. Top with the grated cheese. Melt the remaining butter and sprinkle it over the cheese. Bake, covered, in an oven preheated to 200°C (400°F or Mark 6) for 25 minutes or until the melted cheese is beginning to brown.

JOSÉ WILSON (EDITOR)
HOUSE AND GARDEN'S NEW COOKBOOK

Wild Rice Petit Pois

The technique of cooking wild rice is shown on page 18.

To serve 6

175 g	wild rice, cooked	6 oz
850 g	small young peas, shelled, cooked until just tender, and drained	1¾ lb
40 g	butter	1½ oz
60 g	almonds, blanched and slivered	2 oz
1 tbsp	grated orange rind	1 tbsp

Melt the butter in a 2 litre (3½ pint) casserole and lightly toss the almonds in the butter. Put the casserole and almonds into an oven preheated to 170°C (325°F or Mark 3) for 10 to 15 minutes, stirring frequently, until the almonds are lightly toasted. Add the peas, wild rice and orange rind to the casserole and toss lightly to mix. Return the dish to the oven and bake, uncovered, until all the ingredients are heated through, about 15 minutes.

BETH ANDERSON
WILD RICE FOR ALL SEASONS COOKBOOK

Casserole of Carrots and Wild Rice

The technique of cooking wild rice is shown on page 18.

This creamy casserole of wild rice and carrots goes well with game or poultry. You can prepare it early in the day and bake it when needed: allow an extra 10 minutes baking time if you have kept it in the refrigerator.

To serve 6

175 g	wild rice, cooked	6 oz
200 g	carrot, finely grated	7 oz
4	rashers lean bacon, chopped	4
15 g	butter	½ oz
1	large onion, chopped	1
¼ litre	single cream	8 fl oz
1	egg, lightly beaten	1
1 tsp	salt	1 tsp

Fry the bacon over a low heat, adding the butter, if necessary. Remove and set aside. Sauté the onion in the bacon fat until it is lightly browned. Add the wild rice, bacon and carrot to the sautéed onion, stirring to mix well. Combine the cream with the egg and salt. Fold this into the rice and bacon mixture.

Turn into a buttered 2 litre (3½ pint) casserole and bake, covered, in an oven preheated to 180°C (350°F or Mark 4) for about 30 minutes. Remove the casserole's cover, stir the rice mixture thoroughly and bake, uncovered, for another 10 minutes or until the rice is firm.

BETH ANDERSON
WILD RICE FOR ALL SEASONS COOKBOOK

Wheat with Meat

Soweeta

This dish should be served with a green vegetable or salad; eaten with yogurt, it makes a complete, filling meal.

To serve 4

400 g	whole wheat, washed and drained	14 oz
750 g	lean boneless lamb, cut into 5 cm (2 inch) cubes	1½ lb
3 to 6	whole dried red chili peppers about 10 cm (4 inches) long, seeded	3 to 6
125 g	ginger root, scraped and finely chopped	4 oz
60 g	ground coriander	2 oz
3 tsp	salt	3 tsp
125 g	clarified butter	4 oz
400 g	onions, cut in half from top to root and across the grain into thin, even slices	14 oz
¼ litre	yogurt, beaten with a fork until soft	8 fl oz
¾ litre	milk	1¼ pints

Preheat the oven to 180°C (350°F or Mark 4). Set the chili peppers to soak in a cup of hot water. Place the ginger root, coriander and 2 teaspoons of the salt in a blender with 6 tablespoons of water and reduce them to a fine paste. Remove the paste from the blender and put it on a plate by the stove.

In a medium-sized ovenproof casserole, heat 60 g (2 oz) of the clarified butter and fry 125 g (4 oz) of the onions until they are just crisp. Add the meat pieces. Stir, and immediately add the reserved, blended mixture. Fry, turning with a spatula, for 5 minutes over a medium heat. Add ½ litre (16 fl oz) of water and simmer, uncovered, until the liquid is nearly absorbed. Add the yogurt and the remaining onions. Stir and continue to simmer until the yogurt is nearly absorbed. While the meat is cooking, bring ¾ litre (1¼ pints) of salted water to the boil in a saucepan. Stir in the wheat and boil it, uncovered, until all the water is absorbed, about 30 minutes.

When the meat has absorbed all the yogurt, stir the wheat

into the meat casserole. Heat the milk in a saucepan, then pour it down the sides of the casserole and bring it to the boil. Cover the casserole tightly with foil, crimping the edges to form a seal. Cover and bake for 30 minutes or until the liquid is absorbed. It will keep in the oven when it is ready.

Drain the chili peppers, chop them finely and mix them with 1 teaspoon of salt. Sauté them gently in butter for 5 minutes. Pass them separately as a sauce for the meat for those who like a very hot dish.

SHIVAJI RAO AND SHALINI DEVI HOLKAR
COOKING OF THE MAHARAJAS

Moroccan Wheat Casserole

Orissa

To caramelize the sugar, gently heat 1 tablespoon of sugar with half a tablespoon of water, stirring constantly until the sugar has dissolved. Then turn up the heat slightly and bring the syrup to the boil. Do not stir. Remove from the heat as the syrup begins to brown.

The quantity of wheat may be increased or decreased, as long as two parts of water are used to one part of wheat.

To serve 6 to 8

600 g	whole wheat	1¼ lb
1.5 litres	water	2½ pints
¼ litre	oil	8 fl oz
1 tbsp	chopped red chili peppers	1 tbsp
1 tbsp	chopped sweet red pepper	1 tbsp
2	heads garlic, peeled	2
1 tbsp	caramelized sugar	1 tbsp
2 tbsp	salt	2 tbsp
500 g	beef brisket	1 lb
6 to 8	eggs in shell	6 to 8
	small peeled new potatoes (optional)	

Place all the ingredients together in a large deep pot with a tight-fitting lid. No air must enter the pot, so seal the lid with a flour and water paste. It is advisable to add a few drops of oil to the paste, to facilitate its removal after cooking. Roll the paste into a long narrow strip, and press it to the rim of the pot before putting on the lid. Preheat the oven to 140°C (275°F or Mark 1) and cook the stew for 7 hours or overnight, to be reheated and served at lunchtime the following day.

IRENE F. DAY
KITCHEN IN THE KASBAH

Barley with Raisins and Currants

Herren- und Damen-Brei

On the island of Helgoland this dish is served as an accompaniment to *Bachsold,* a dish of dried, salted haddock.

	To serve 2 or 3	
100 g	pearl barley	3½ oz
125 g	raisins, washed	4 oz
125 g	currants, washed	4 oz
	salt	
2	lemons, rind grated, juice strained	2
	sugar	

Cook the pearl barley in about 40 cl (14 fl oz) of salted water with the raisins and currants for about 1 hour. Add the rind of the lemons. Season with lemon juice and sugar to taste.

JUTTA KÜRTZ
DAS KOCHBUCH AUS SCHLESWIG-HOLSTEIN

Smoked Cod and Pot Barley Cutlets

Kotlety Mielone z Dorsza Wędzonego i Pęczaku

	To serve 4	
200 g	pot barley, washed	7 oz
400 g	smoked cod, scaled and boned	14 oz
90 to 100 g	fat	3 to 3½ oz
50 g	onion, finely chopped	2 oz
1	egg	1
	salt and pepper	
40 g	breadcrumbs	1½ oz
	chopped fresh herbs	
	tomato sauce (*page 166*)	

Cover the pot barley with about three times its volume of boiling water and add 20 g (¾ oz) of the fat. Mix in the fat, cover the pan and cook slowly over a low heat for about 45 minutes. When the barley has absorbed the water, put it into a baking dish and bake in an oven preheated to 180°C (350°F or Mark 4) for about 1 hour. Remove from the oven and cool.

Fry the onion in a further 30 g (1 oz) of the fat until it turns a light golden colour. Put the fish, barley and onion through a mincer. Then pass the mixture through a fine sieve. Add the egg, salt and pepper. Mix thoroughly, then divide the mixture into 12 cutlet-shaped patties and roll each cutlet in breadcrumbs. Over a high heat, fry the cutlets in the remaining fat on both sides until they are golden-brown. Lay them out on a long plate and sprinkle with the chopped herbs. Serve with tomato sauce and a salad.

HELENA HAWLICZKOWA
KUCHNIA POLSKA

Barley Casserole (from Mildred Oakes)

	To serve 4	
300 g	pearl barley	10 oz
150 g	butter	5 oz
250 g	mushrooms, quartered	8 oz
2	medium-sized onions, finely chopped	2
About ¾ litre	hot beef or chicken stock (*page 165*)	About 1¼ pints
	salt	
	chopped parsley	

Melt about 40 g (1½ oz) of the butter in a heavy skillet and sauté the mushrooms over a medium-high heat for 4 minutes. Transfer the mushrooms to a small dish. Add the remaining butter to the skillet and heat until the foam has subsided. Add the onions and cook them until they are just wilted. Add the barley and stir over a medium-high heat until the barley has a golden colour. Combine the barley and onions with the mushrooms in a 1.5 litre (2½ pint) casserole or baking dish. Add about 35 cl (12 fl oz) of hot beef or chicken stock, cover and bake in an oven preheated to 180°C (350°F or Mark 4) for 30 minutes. Add another 35 cl (12 fl oz) of hot stock, cover again and bake for a further 30 minutes. Add salt to the casserole if necessary (the stock should be well seasoned) and more stock if the barley has absorbed too much liquid before it is tender. Serve, sprinkled with chopped parsley.

JAMES BEARD
JAMES BEARD'S AMERICAN COOKERY

Mr. Herbert Bower's Frumenty

To make cree'd wheat, wash 250 g (8 oz) of whole wheat grains, and put them in a pan or stoneware jar with a lid. Cover the wheat with cold water three times its own measure. Put the wheat into the oven overnight or for at least 12 hours, at the lowest temperature setting. If the grains are not burst and set in a thick jelly when the cooking time is over, boil up the contents of the pan for 5 minutes or perhaps a little longer, depending on how far the grains are already cooked.

To serve 6

60 cl	cree'd wheat	1 pint
1.30 litres	milk	2⅛ pints
1 tsp	ground allspice	1 tsp
2 tbsp	flour	2 tbsp

Put the cree'd wheat and all but 8 cl (3 fl oz) of the milk into a pan and boil them for 10 to 15 minutes. When the mixture begins to thicken, add the allspice. Finally, make the flour into a thin cream with the remaining cold milk and stir it into the frumenty. Boil until it is thick and creamy, and serve.

FLORENCE WHITE (EDITOR)
GOOD THINGS IN ENGLAND

Tchoomak Hash with Mushrooms

To serve 4

350 g	millet	12 oz
1 kg	mushrooms, washed and coarsely chopped	2 to 2½ lb
100 g	lean green or smoked bacon, diced	3½ oz
45 g	butter or lard	1½ oz
1½	onions, chopped	1½
55 cl	water	18 fl oz
	salt	
1½ tsp	finely chopped mint	1½ tsp

Fry the mushrooms with the bacon in the butter or lard over a medium heat until half cooked, about 2 minutes. Add the onion and cook for 1 more minute.

Wash the millet, first in warm water, then in hot water. Drain. Bring the measured water to the boil and add the millet. Cook until half done, about 45 minutes. Mix in the fried mushrooms, bacon and onions. Season with salt and stir. Place in a 20 cm (8 inch) ovenproof flan dish. Bake, uncovered, in an oven preheated to 180°C (350°F or Mark 4) for 45 minutes to 1 hour until ready. See that the hash is dry and crisp. Before serving, garnish with finely chopped mint.

N. I. GEORGIEVSKY, M. E. MELMAN, E. A. SHADURA
AND A. S. SHEMJAKINSKY
UKRAINIAN CUISINE

Cracked Grains, Meals and Couscous

Cracked Wheat with Mushrooms

To serve 6

250 g	cracked wheat	8 oz
75 g	mushrooms, sliced	2½ oz
90 g	onion, chopped	3 oz
60 g	butter	2 oz
90 cl	chicken stock (*page 165*)	1½ pints
1 tsp	salt	1 tsp
	freshly ground black pepper	

Sauté the mushrooms and onion in butter for 5 minutes or until lightly browned, stirring occasionally. Add the cracked wheat and cook for 5 minutes, stirring constantly. Add the stock, salt and pepper. Bring to the boil, reduce the heat, cover and simmer, stirring occasionally, for 30 minutes, or until all the stock is absorbed and the wheat is soft.

PICTURE COOK BOOK

Cracked Wheat Pilaff

Bulgur Pilavi

Bulgur *is the Turkish name for* burghul.

To serve 6

175 g	large grain *burghul*, washed and drained	6 oz
75 g	butter	2½ oz
1	large onion, coarsely grated	1
1 tbsp	puréed tomato or 1 small tomato, skinned, seeded and diced	1 tbsp
35 cl	beef or chicken stock (*page 165*)	12 fl oz
	salt and freshly ground pepper	

Place 30 g (1 oz) of the butter in a heavy saucepan, add the onion and sauté it, stirring constantly, until golden-brown, about 6 minutes. Add the tomato sauce or the diced tomato and cook for 5 minutes. Add the stock, the rest of the butter, and season with a little salt and pepper; bring to the boil. Add the *burghul*, stir once, cover and boil for 5 minutes over a high heat. Then reduce the heat, cover and cook, until the *burghul* absorbs all of the broth, which should take about 25 minutes. Remove the pan from the heat, remove the cover, place a napkin over the saucepan and replace the cover. Leave the pan to stand in a warm place for 40 minutes. The *burghul* should be flaky and not mushy.

NEŞET EREN
THE ART OF TURKISH COOKING

Burghul Pilaff

This well-flavoured pilaff is delicious with a curry.

	To serve 4	
325 g	*burghul*	11 oz
140 g	butter	4½ oz
1	medium-sized onion, chopped	1
90 cl	boiling stock (*page 165*)	1½ pints
	salt and pepper	

Simmer the *burghul* in 125 g (4 oz) of the butter for about 5 minutes or until thoroughly coated and bubbly. Fry the chopped onion separately in the remaining butter until soft and yellow. Mix the *burghul* and onion together and stir in the boiling stock and the seasonings.

Stir well and place in a buttered casserole. Bake, uncovered, in an oven preheated to 180°C (350°F or Mark 4) for 30 minutes, then stir the pilaff gently with a fork. Bake 15 minutes more, by which time the liquid should all be absorbed and the *burghul* moist but fluffy.

MARIE KARAM KHAYAT AND MARGARET CLARK KEATINGE
FOOD FROM THE ARAB WORLD

Buckwheat Groats with Almonds

	To serve 6	
400 g	buckwheat groats	14 oz
100 to 125 g	blanched almonds, slivered	3½ to 4 oz
12.5 cl	olive oil	4 fl oz
1	garlic clove, finely chopped	1
4 tbsp	chopped onion	4 tbsp
4 tbsp	chopped sweet green pepper	4 tbsp
1 litre	chicken stock	1¾ pints

Sauté the almonds in the olive oil until they are golden-brown. Remove the almonds and set them aside. Add the garlic, onion and green pepper to the oil remaining in the pan

and sauté until the onion is golden-brown, stirring frequently. Add the buckwheat groats and the stock and mix well. Pour into a casserole and bake in an oven preheated to 170°C (325°F or Mark 3) for 30 minutes. Stir in the almonds and bake for a further 15 minutes so that the groats are soft and plump and all the liquid is absorbed.

PICTURE COOK BOOK

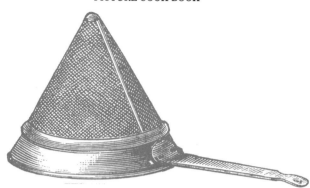

Buckwheat Groats Baked with Meat

*Kasza Gryczana Zapiekana z
Mięsem Lub Podrobami*

Buckwheat groats are often sold under the name of "kasha".
This dish should be served with fresh cabbage or sauerkraut.

	To serve 4	
300 g	buckwheat groats	10 oz
50 g	lard	2 oz
1 litre	water	1¾ pints
50 g	onion, chopped	2 oz
200 g	roast meat (pork, beef or lamb), finely chopped or minced	7 oz
4 tbsp	beef stock (*page 165*)	4 tbsp
	salt and pepper	
12.5 to 25 cl	double cream	4 to 8 fl oz
1 tbsp	chopped fresh herbs	1 tbsp

Heat half of the lard in a saucepan, stir in the buckwheat groats, then pour in the water. Bring to the boil and simmer, covered, for 20 minutes or until all the water has been absorbed. Stir, then cover the pan and set it aside until the groats are soft and dry, about 10 minutes.

Brown the onion to a light golden colour in the remaining lard. Add the meat to the onion with the stock. Bring to the boil, mix with the groats and season with salt and pepper. Put the mixture into a buttered shallow baking dish. Pour the cream over the top and bake in an oven preheated to 200°C (400°F or Mark 6) for 20 minutes. Garnish the dish with chopped herbs before serving.

HELENA HAWLICZKOWA
KUCHNIA POLSKA

Buckwheat Groats with Noodles

Kasha Varnishkas

The technique of shaping bow knot—or butterfly—noodles is demonstrated on page 49.

	To serve 4 to 6	
200 g	buckwheat groats	7 oz
100 g	bow knot noodles, cooked and drained	3½ oz
1	egg	1
	salt and pepper	
2 tbsp	rendered chicken fat or 30 g (1 oz) vegetable margarine	2 tbsp
½ litre	boiling water	16 fl oz

Place the buckwheat in a large frying pan. Add the unbeaten egg and mix well. Place over low heat and stir constantly until each grain is coated with egg.

Transfer the buckwheat to a 1.5 litre (2½ pint) casserole; add half a teaspoonful of salt, and the fat and pour in the boiling water. Cover and bake in an oven preheated to 180°C (350°F or Mark 4) for about 1 hour, or until the groats are fluffy and dry; or, if desired, simmer on top of the stove for 30 to 45 minutes adding more water and fat as necessary. Add the noodles to the cooked groats and mix lightly together. Season to taste. Cook gently for a few minutes until heated through. Serve as an accompaniment to a meat course.

FANNIE ENGLE AND GERTRUDE BLAIR
THE JEWISH FESTIVAL COOKBOOK

Down South Raisin Rye

This may be served as an accompaniment to chicken or ham. If served as a main dish, a cupful or more of diced cooked ham may be added for the last 5 minutes of cooking.

	To serve 4	
200 g	cracked rye	7 oz
250 g	smoked ham hocks (about 2 good-sized pieces)	8 oz
60 g	raisins	2 oz
1 litre	water	1¾ pints
	salt	

Put the ham hocks, raisins and water in a heavy 2 litre (3½ pint) pot and bring to the boil. Sprinkle in the cracked rye. When the water has returned to the boil, reduce the heat and simmer, covered, for 45 minutes, or until the rye is tender. Taste for seasoning and add salt if necessary.

ELIZABETH ALSTON
THE BEST OF NATURAL EATING AROUND THE WORLD

Turkey-Hominy Croquettes

Cooked ham or chicken may be substituted for the turkey.

	To serve 4	
175 g	hominy grits, boiled	6 oz
125 g	cold roast turkey meat, finely minced	4 oz
1 tbsp	finely chopped onion	1 tbsp
40 g	butter, melted	1½ oz
12.5 cl	milk	4 fl oz
2 tbsp	chopped parsley	2 tbsp
	salt and freshly ground black pepper	
2	eggs, beaten separately	2
	breadcrumbs	
	oil or fat for deep frying	

In a saucepan, sauté the onion in 15g (½ oz) of the butter until it is soft. Add the milk, and stir in the hominy grits, cold meat, butter and parsley; season with salt and a generous grinding of black pepper. Stir the mixture well and when it is heated through, remove it from the heat and add one of the beaten eggs. Cook for another minute, stirring constantly. Spread the mixture on a platter to cool. When it is firm, shape it into 8 to 10 cylinders about 7.5 cm (3 inches) long. Roll these croquettes in the other beaten egg, then in breadcrumbs, and deep fry them in fat or oil until they are golden-brown.

NARCISSE AND NARCISSA G. CHAMBERLAIN
THE CHAMBERLAIN SAMPLER OF AMERICAN COOKING

Cornmeal Puffs

To make 10 to 12 large puffs, or 2½ to 3 dozen cocktail-size puffs

100 g	cornmeal	3½ oz
¼ litre	water	8 fl oz
125 g	butter	4 oz
¼ tsp	salt	¼ tsp
90 g	flour	3 oz
4	eggs	4

Preheat the oven to 190°C (375°F or Mark 5). Combine the water, butter and salt in a medium-sized saucepan. Bring to the boil. Add the cornmeal and flour all at once. Stir rapidly over a medium heat until the mixture leaves the sides of the pan and forms a compact ball. Continue to cook for 3 minutes, mashing the dough against the sides of the pan.

Remove from the heat, turn the dough into the small bowl of an electric mixer, and beat for about 1 minute to cool the dough slightly. Or beat with a sturdy wooden spoon to cool it.

Beat in the eggs one at a time. Continue beating until the dough is smooth and has a satiny look.

Drop the dough by tablespoonfuls or teaspoonfuls on to an ungreased baking sheet, swirling the tops to round off the puffs. Space large puffs 5 cm (2 inches) apart, small puffs 4 cm (1½ inches) apart. Bake for 50 minutes.

Slit each puff with a knife point and return to the oven for 10 minutes to crisp the centres. Cool, and fill with chicken, tuna, shrimp or crab salad or cocktail spreads to serve as luncheon entrées or party snacks.

JEANNE A. VOLTZ
THE FLAVOR OF THE SOUTH

Polenta Pie with Salt Cod

Polenta Pastizada di Magro

The technique of making polenta is shown on page 40. If salt cod is not available, use other filleted salt fish. To prepare salt fish for cooking, cut it into pieces and soak for at least 24 hours, changing the water several times.

This recipe comes from the Friuli region of the Italian Alps.

To serve 6

500 g	cornmeal, boiled with 2.5 litres (4 pints) water and a pinch of salt for 30 minutes to make polenta	1 lb
1 kg	salt cod, filleted, cut into small pieces, soaked, washed and dried	2 to 2½ lb
60 g	flour	2 oz
17.5 cl	olive oil	6 fl oz
200 g	onions, sliced and/or 3 garlic cloves, pounded to a paste	7 oz
2 tbsp	puréed tomato	2 tbsp
1 kg	tomatoes, skinned and mashed	2 to 2½ lb
	salt and freshly ground pepper	
30 g	parsley, chopped	1 oz

Turn the polenta out immediately it is cooked on to a wet marble slab or other cold work surface. Flatten it out until it is 1 cm (½ inch) thick, using a knife blade dipped repeatedly into boiling water. Let it cool, and slice it into strips.

Coat the pieces of cod with flour. Brown them in a little hot oil, drain, and set aside. Add more oil to the pan, heat it and fry the onion and/or garlic. Add the puréed tomato and cook for 2 to 3 minutes. Pour in the fresh tomatoes, season with salt and freshly ground pepper and add the parsley. Cook uncovered for about 15 minutes, then add the cod, laying the pieces side by side in the pan. Simmer gently for another 15 minutes.

Butter a 1.5 litre (2½ pint) deep baking dish or baking tin. Cover the bottom with parallel strips of polenta. Cover with pieces of cod and plenty of sauce; add another layer of polenta strips crosswise to the first, and so on, ending with a layer of polenta. Sprinkle the top layer with oil. Bake in an oven preheated to 200°C (400°F or Mark 6) for 20 to 25 minutes or until the top is golden-brown.

LUIGI CARNACINA AND VINCENZO BUONASSISI
IL LIBRO DELLA POLENTA

Layered Polenta with Cheese

Mamaliga cu Brinza

This is the oldest and most popular way to prepare a layered dish of mamaliga—the Romanian word for polenta. The basic technique for preparing polenta is shown on page 40.

For this dish, a Romanian would probably use telemea, the most popular local white salt cheese, similar to the Greek feta. This dish can also be made with 500 g (1 lb) streaky bacon, fried and chopped. If bacon is added, a stronger, yellow cheese such as cascaval, the Romanian equivalent of the Italian caciocavallo, should be used. The English equivalent cheese would be strong Cheddar.

To serve 4

200 g	coarse cornmeal	7 oz
250 g	white salt cheese, crumbled with a fork	8 oz
125 g	butter	4 oz
1 litre	water	1¾ pint
	salt	

Grease a baking dish about 18 cm (7 inches) in diameter and 5 to 10 cm (2 to 4 inches) deep with 15 g (½ oz) of the butter. Cook the cornmeal for 30 minutes in the salted water to make polenta. Take some of the hot polenta and spread it in a layer about 1 cm (½ inch) thick in the dish. Sprinkle generously with some of the crumbled cheese and dot with butter. Pour on another layer of polenta, and so on, ending with a layer of cheese. Bake in an oven preheated to 200°C (400°F or Mark 6), either for about 10 minutes, so that the heat has just penetrated through, or for about 20 to 30 minutes so that the top layer of cheese is golden-brown.

ANISOARA STAN
THE ROMANIAN COOKBOOK

Paduan Polenta Pie

Polenta Pasticciata alla Padovana

This recipe calls for a firm polenta. The making of polenta is shown on page 40. If soppressa *salami is not available, use another highly flavoured Italian salami. Prosciutto is un-smoked ham. If it is not available, gammon can be substituted.*

To serve 6		
500 g	cornmeal boiled in 2.5 litres (4 pints) of water and a pinch of salt for 30 minutes to make polenta	1 lb
200 g	Parmesan cheese, grated	7 oz
60 g	butter, cut into small pieces	2 oz
	Meat sauce	
300 g	lean veal, minced	10 oz
200 g	prosciutto, finely chopped	7 oz
200 g	*soppressa* salami, finely chopped	7 oz
200 g	chicken livers, cleaned and sliced	7 oz
190 g	butter	6½ oz
½	onion, chopped	½
1	small carrot, chopped	1
½	stick celery	½
300 g	mushrooms, sliced	10 oz
12.5 cl	dry white wine	4 fl oz
1 kg	puréed tomatoes	2 to 2½ lb
½ tsp	coarse salt	½ tsp
2 tsp	dried thyme	2 tsp
1	bay leaf, crumbled	1

Make the polenta; as soon as it is cooked turn it out on to a wet marble slab or other smooth work surface. Flatten it out to a thickness of about 2 cm (¾ inch), using a knife blade dipped repeatedly into boiling water. Let the polenta cool.

Melt 150 g (5 oz) of the butter in a saucepan, lightly brown the chopped onion, carrot and celery and add the veal. Cook for 15 minutes over a medium heat, stirring frequently. Add the prosciutto, the *soppressa* and the mushrooms. Cook for another 10 minutes, then pour in the wine, increasing the heat. Cook for another 4 or 5 minutes until the wine is absorbed and the cooking liquid slightly reduced in volume. Then add the tomatoes. Mix the salt with the thyme and bay leaf, and add them to the mixture in the pan. Simmer this sauce, uncovered, for 20 minutes. Brown 40 g (1½ oz) of the butter in a frying pan, stir in the chicken livers, sprinkle lightly with salt and brown. Then add the livers to the sauce.

Butter a 1.75 litre (3 pint) baking dish, put in a layer of polenta, cover with some of the sauce, and sprinkle with Parmesan cheese. Repeat the layers and continue until all the ingredients are used up, ending with a layer of polenta. Dot with butter pieces and sprinkle over all but 60 g (2 oz) of the cheese. Bake in an oven preheated to 200°C (400°F or Mark 6) until the cheese is melted and golden, about 15 minutes. Serve very hot, with the remaining cheese on the side.

LUIGI CARNACINA AND VINCENZO BUONASSISI
IL LIBRO DELLA POLENTA

Polenta with Cabbage

Polenta con Cavoli alla Ligure

The technique of making polenta is demonstrated on page 40.

To serve 6		
300 g	coarse cornmeal, boiled with about 1.5 litres (2½ pints) water, and a pinch of salt, for 30 minutes to make polenta	10 oz
1	Savoy cabbage or other crinkly-leaved winter cabbage, outer leaves and core discarded, chopped	1
	salt	
12.5 cl	olive oil	4 fl oz
200 g	Parmesan cheese, grated	7 oz
	flour	
60 g	lard	2 oz

Boil the cabbage in salted water for 10 minutes. Drain it well, then stew it in the oil until the oil is well absorbed, adding a pinch more salt. Allow to cool.

As soon as the polenta is cooked, spoon it into a big bowl and stir in the cabbage and cheese. Allow it to cool. Turn it out on to a board, and flatten it to a thickness of about 2.5 cm (1 inch). Cut into 2.5 cm (1 inch) cubes and dust lightly with flour.

Just before serving, heat the lard in a frying pan over a medium heat. When it is hot, put in the cubes, a few at a time, and fry them until they are golden-brown. Drain them on absorbent paper and serve them very hot and crisp.

VINCENZO BUONASSISI AND LUIGI CARNACINA
IL LIBRO DELLA POLENTA

Polenta Pie with Wine Pastry

Polenta Pastizada all'Antica

The technique of making polenta is demonstrated on page 40.

	To serve 4	
500 g	cornmeal	1 lb
2.5 litres	boiling salted water	4¼ pints
	salt	
	Wine pastry dough	
About 15 cl	red wine and cold water, mixed	About ¼ pint
300 g	flour	10 oz
100 g	butter, cut into pieces and chilled	3½ oz
4 tbsp	oil	4 tbsp
	salt	
	Pork filling	
200 g	sausage-meat, broken up with a fork	7 oz
500 g	lean pork, boiled and finely chopped	1 lb
150 g	butter	5 oz
12	sage leaves, coarsely chopped	12
300 g	pork belly fat, cut into small pieces	10 oz
	salt and pepper	
	grated nutmeg	

To make the pastry, pour the flour on to a marble slab or other cold work surface and make a well in the centre. Put the butter, oil and a pinch of salt into the well and work them gently into the flour. Then gradually add the wine and water mixture. Mix well, put the dough into a bowl, cover it with a cloth and leave in a cool place for 30 minutes.

To make the pork filling, melt 60 g (2 oz) of the butter in a frying pan, add the chopped sage leaves and pork fat and mix well. Add the sausage-meat, chopped pork, salt and pepper and grated nutmeg. Mix well and cook, stirring frequently, until the pork is lightly browned.

Divide the dough into two pieces. Roll out one piece to fit the bottom and sides of a baking dish about 20 cm (8 inches) in diameter and about 15 cm (6 inches) deep. Butter the dish and line it with the dough, pressing it down well.

Cook the polenta. Fill the pie with alternate layers of polenta and pork filling, ending with a layer of filling.

Roll out the second piece of dough to fit the top of the baking dish. Cover the dish with the pastry, making sure the dough sticks well to the rim of the dish. Brush the pastry with melted butter and bake in an oven preheated to 220°C (425°F or Mark 7) for 20 to 30 minutes or until nicely browned. Let the pie stand for a few minutes before serving.

LUIGI CARNACINA AND VINCENZO BUONASSISSI
IL LIBRO DELLA POLENTA

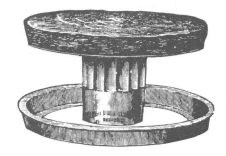

Polenta Balls with Walnut Sauce

Kachamak s Orehov Sos

Kachamak *is the Bulgarian name for polenta and is served in all kinds of shapes. This recipe, from the Smoliyan region of the Rhodope Mountains in Bulgaria, is for the village-style* kachamak, *served as a side dish with sliced cold meats. While still hot,* kachamak *is also pressed into rinsed small porcelain moulds or shaped into balls with an ice-cream scoop; or it can be spread in a layer and, when cold, cut out with biscuit cutters. The technique for making polenta is on page 40.*

	To serve 4 to 6	
200 g	coarse cornmeal, boiled with 1 litre (1¾ pints) water and a pinch of salt for 30 minutes to make polenta	7 oz
	Walnut sauce	
200 g	shelled walnuts	7 oz
1 or 2	garlic cloves, peeled	1 or 2
	salt	
15 cl	olive oil	¼ pint
2 tbsp	wine vinegar	2 tbsp
1 to 2 tbsp	water	1 to 2 tbsp

Using a tablespoon dipped in cold water, shape the fresh hot polenta into 20 balls, the size of eggs, and allow them to cool. To prepare the sauce, pound the garlic cloves together with a pinch of salt in a mortar, until the mixture is reduced to a pulp; add the walnuts and pound to a paste. Blend the paste with the olive oil, vinegar and water until the sauce has the consistency of single cream. Check for seasoning.

Arrange the dumplings on a large serving dish and pour the sauce over them. Keep the dish tightly covered until it is to be brought to the table.

DR. L. PETROV, DR. N. DJELEPOV, DR. E. IORDANOV AND S. UZUNOVA
BULGARSKA NAZIONALNA KUCHNIYA

Semolina with Tomato Sauce

Semoule de Blé Dur Sauce Tomate

To serve 6

150 g	semolina	5 oz
1 litre	water	1¾ pints
	salt and pepper	
2	eggs	2
50 g	butter	2 oz
100 g	Gruyère cheese, grated	3½ oz
½ litre	tomato sauce (*page 166*)	16 fl oz

Bring the water to the boil, add salt, and sprinkle in the semolina, stirring with a wooden spoon. Cook for about 15 minutes, stirring to prevent the semolina from sticking to the pan. Remove from the heat and beat in the eggs, butter and 75 g (2½ oz) cheese. Season with pepper, and more salt if needed. Spread on a flat plate or marble surface and leave to cool. Cut into 5 cm (2 inch) squares. Arrange them on an oiled ovenproof dish and cover with the tomato sauce. Sprinkle the remaining cheese on top and bake in an oven preheated to 200°C (400°F or Mark 6) for 15 to 20 minutes.

CHRISTIANE SCHAPIRA
LA CUISINE CORSE

Semolina Cakes with Cheese Filling

Griessküchlein mit Käse Gefüllt

To serve 4

160 g	semolina	5½ oz
250 g	Gruyère cheese, thinly sliced	8 oz
1 litre	milk	1¾ pints
	salt	
1	egg, lightly beaten	1
1 tbsp	breadcrumbs	1 tbsp
30 g	flour	1 oz
	fat or oil for frying	

Bring the milk to the boil, add a little salt, stir in the semolina and cook for 15 to 20 minutes to a thick paste, stirring well all the time. Spread the hot paste 1 cm (½ inch) thick on a china plate first rinsed in cold water, or on a dampened wooden board and allow to cool. Then stamp out round shapes with an upturned glass or a biscuit cutter. Use the same cutter to stamp rounds from the cheese slices. Place one cheese round between two of paste. Dip the "sandwiches" in beaten egg, then in the breadcrumbs mixed with the flour, and fry in hot fat or oil till golden-brown on both sides.

EVA MARIA BORER
TANTE HEIDI'S SWISS KITCHEN

Couscous with Seven Vegetables

Couscous "Bidaoui" aux Sept Légumes

To serve 8 to 10

1 kg	couscous	2½ lb
1 kg	meat (knuckle of veal or shoulder of mutton) cut into quarters	2½ lb
1 kg	onions, sliced	2½ lb
1	white cabbage, cut into pieces	1
300 g	butter	10 oz
½ tsp	powdered saffron	½ tsp
	salt and pepper	
6 litres	water	10 pints
4 or 5	tomatoes, skinned and quartered	4 or 5
250 g	aubergines, cut into pieces	8 oz
500 g	carrots, sliced	1 lb
250 g	turnips, cut into pieces	8 oz
2	red sweet peppers, seeded and chopped	2
6 tbsp	chopped fresh coriander	6 tbsp
500 g	pumpkin, cut into pieces	1 lb

In the bottom half of a *couscoussier*, put the meat, a quarter of the onions, the cabbage and 150 g (5 oz) of the butter. Season with the saffron, salt and pepper, cover with the water and bring to the boil. Put the couscous into the top half of the *couscoussier*, and seal the two halves together with a band of cheesecloth soaked in flour and water paste. Steam for 30 minutes from the time the steam begins to escape. Remove the top half of the *couscoussier*, cover the bottom half and leave it to simmer for at least 1 hour.

Put the couscous into a large bowl. Crush the grains with a wooden spoon to separate them. Allow the couscous to cool, then sprinkle it with cold water and fluff it again. Continue sprinkling and fluffing until the grains are swollen and saturated. Let the couscous stand for about 30 minutes.

About 1 hour before serving, put all the remaining vegetables except the pumpkin in the bottom half of the *couscoussier* with the meat and cabbage, and simmer for about 30 minutes. Cook the pumpkin separately, in a little of the meat cooking liquid, until soft but still intact, about 15 minutes.

Half an hour before the meal, replace the couscous in the top of the *couscoussier*, reseal the two halves and when the steam begins to rise, pour the couscous into a bowl. Add the remaining butter, mix well, and add as much meat cooking liquid as the couscous will absorb, fluffing it all the time.

Pile the couscous in a mound on a large, flat round dish. Make a well in the centre and fill it with the meat and vegetables. Serve the meat cooking liquid on the side.

LATIFA BENNANI SMIRES
LA CUISINE MAROCAINE

Couscous with Mutton

Kousksi bil Ghalmi

The technique of making harissa *sauce is shown on page 39.*

To serve 10

750 g	couscous	1½ lb
500 g	mutton, diced	1 lb
100 g	mutton fat, diced	3½ oz
	salt	
½ tsp	ground black pepper	½ tsp
¾ tbsp	*harissa*	¾ tbsp
½ tsp	paprika	½ tsp
1	onion, chopped	1
15 cl	olive oil	¼ pint
1.75 litre	water	3 pints
1¾ tbsp	puréed tomato	1¾ tbsp
60 g	dried chick peas, soaked overnight	2 oz
1	head cardoon, stalks only, scraped and chopped into pieces	1
3 or 4	potatoes, peeled, whole	3 or 4
2 or 3	carrots, cut in half	2 or 3
2	small turnips, cut in pieces	2
30 g	salted butter	1 oz
1 tbsp	ground cinnamon	1 tbsp
1 tbsp	ground rose petals (optional)	1 tbsp

Put the mutton and mutton fat into the bottom of the *couscoussier* and season with salt, pepper, *harissa* and paprika. Brown the onion in oil for several minutes. Add ¼ litre (8 fl oz) of water to the onion. Stir in the puréed tomato and chick peas, and cook for 15 to 20 minutes. Add the other vegetables, cover with the rest of the water and bring to the boil.

Moisten the couscous with a little cold water, fill the top half of the *couscoussier* without packing the grains too tightly, and put the two halves of the pot together. Time the cooking from the moment the steam begins to rise through the top half. Cook for 30 to 40 minutes, then remove the top half of the pot, empty the couscous on to a dish, sprinkle with a little cold water, and mash lightly with a wooden spoon. Replace the couscous in the top of the *couscoussier*, put the whole pot back on the heat, and bring to the boil a second time.

Empty the couscous on to a serving dish. Skim the fat from the surface of the stew, then add the butter, cinnamon and rose petals. Pour half of the cooking liquid over the couscous and mix well. Pour out the rest of the cooking liquid to serve as a gravy; arrange the meat and vegetables on a separate serving dish. Allow to rest for a moment, then serve.

MOHAMED KOUKI
LA CUISINE TUNISIENNE D' "OMMOK SANNAFA"

Boiled Pasta

Macaroni with Four Cheeses

Maccheroni ai Quattro Formaggi

Fontina *is a fairly hard, sharp, yellow cheese.* Robiola *is a soft, white cheese; if it is not available, Bel Paese can be substituted.*

To serve 6

500 g	macaroni, *rigatoni* or *penne*	1 lb
80 g each	Gruyère, *fontina,* and *robiola* cheese, cut into very thin strips or coarsely grated	2½ oz each
120 g	Parmesan cheese, grated	4 oz
100 g	butter, melted	3½ oz
	salt and freshly ground pepper	

Boil the pasta, drain it, and return it to the saucepan with most of the butter. Add the Gruyère, *fontina* and *robiola,* 80 g (2½ oz) of the Parmesan and season with salt and pepper. Toss well. Transfer the mixture into a buttered ovenproof dish, sprinkle with the rest of the butter and the Parmesan and place in an oven preheated to 200°C (400°F or Mark 6) for 5 to 10 minutes, or until the cheese has melted but not coloured.

VINCENZO BUONASSISI
THE CLASSIC BOOK OF PASTA

Pasta with Broad Beans

To serve 4

500 g	*tagliatelle*	1 lb
1 kg	fresh broad beans, shelled and skins removed	2 lb
1	onion, chopped	1
3 tbsp	olive oil	3 tbsp
	salt	
50 to 100 g	Parmesan cheese, grated	2 to 3½ oz

Put a large pot of water on to boil. Fry the onion in the oil until soft. Add the beans, a pinch of salt and enough boiling water to barely cover the beans. With the lid slightly ajar, boil the beans rapidly until the water has nearly evaporated. Meanwhile, salt the remaining boiling water and cook the pasta in it. When the pasta is cooked, drain it and put it on a warmed serving dish. Mix in the beans and grated Parmesan.

ROSEMARY CROSSLEY
THE DOLE COOKBOOK

Straw and Hay Pasta

Paglia e Fieno

The techniques for making plain pasta dough and coloured pasta dough are shown on pages 44 and 50 respectively. The cutting of pasta dough is demonstrated on pages 46 to 48.

	To serve 4	
100 g	spinach, stalks discarded, leaves washed, cooked and puréed	3½ oz
430 g	flour	15 oz
3	eggs	3
	salt	
30 g	butter	1 oz
125 g	ham, finely chopped	4 oz
17.5 cl	double cream	6 fl oz
	grated Parmesan cheese	

Make a firm dough with 400 g (14 oz) of flour, the eggs and a pinch of salt, then knead until smooth and elastic and divide it into two pieces, one twice as big as the other. Leave the smaller piece to dry a little.

Roll out the larger piece not too thinly, leave it to dry a little, then cut it into strips about 1 cm (½ inch) wide. Knead the remaining dough with the spinach purée, adding the rest of the flour, then roll it out and cut it into strips the same size as the white pasta. Cook both pastas in plenty of boiling, salted water until they are *al dente*.

In a large pan, melt the butter and lightly brown the diced ham until the fat part is transparent, then stir in the cream. Season with salt and simmer for 2 minutes. Meanwhile, drain the pasta. Put the pasta into the pan with the ham and stir until the pasta is evenly coated. Serve sprinkled with plenty of grated Parmesan cheese.

ANNA MARTINI
PASTA & PIZZA

Noodles with Poppy Seed

If fresh noodles are being used, the cooking time should be reduced to 2 to 3 minutes.

	To serve 4	
250 g	broad noodles	8 oz
2 tbsp	poppy seeds, washed and drained	2 tbsp
60 g	blanched almonds, slivered	2 oz
2 tbsp	rendered chicken fat	2 tbsp
	salt and pepper	

Break the noodles into 5 cm (2 inch) pieces. Cook them in a large amount of boiling salted water for 8 to 10 minutes or until tender, but not mushy. In a frying pan, toast the poppy seeds with the almonds in the fat. Pour over the noodles, dusting with salt and pepper. Toss and serve very hot.

FANNIE ENGLE AND GERTRUDE BLAIR
THE JEWISH FESTIVAL COOKBOOK

Potato Noodles with Poppy Seeds

Zemiakové Rezance s Makom

Ground walnuts can be substituted for the ground poppy seeds if preferred.

	To serve 8	
600 g	potatoes, boiled in their skins and peeled	1¼ lb
90 g	poppy seeds, ground	3 oz
1	egg, beaten	1
300 g	fine semolina	10 oz
	salt	
60 g	butter	2 oz
100 g	castor sugar	3½ oz

Press the potatoes through a sieve. Add the egg, semolina and a pinch of salt and work them into a dough. Cut the dough into short noodles, slightly thicker than matchsticks. Drop the noodles into boiling salted water, and cook for 2 to 3 minutes or until they are soft. Drain the noodles, dot them with butter and sprinkle them with ground poppy seeds and sugar.

VOJTECH SPANKO
SLOVENSKA KUCHARKA

Noodles with Roquefort

Nouilles au Roquefort

	To serve 4	
300 g	noodles	10 oz
125 g	Roquefort cheese	4 oz
	salt	
4 tbsp	double cream	4 tbsp
	freshly ground pepper	

Cook the noodles in plenty of rapidly boiling salted water until just tender. Meanwhile, crush the Roquefort with a fork, then gradually incorporate the cream. Season with pepper. Drain the noodles, add the Roquefort mixture, and mix gently over a low heat for 2 to 3 minutes. Serve very hot.

MYRETTE TIANO
PÂTES ET RIZ

Noodles with Tomato Sauce

Nouilles à la Sauce Tomate Crue

	To serve 4	
300 g	noodles	10 oz
	salt	
	Tomato sauce	
750 g	tomatoes, plunged into boiling water for 1 minute, skinned, seeded and diced	1½ lb
1	bunch basil, washed and chopped	1
6	garlic cloves, peeled and crushed with the back of a knife	6
	salt and pepper	
20 cl	olive oil	7 fl oz

Mix the basil with the tomatoes and add the crushed garlic. Season with salt and pepper, add the olive oil, cover, and put in a cool place. Cook the noodles in plenty of rapidly boiling salted water until just done. Drain, toss with the tomato sauce and serve immediately.

MYRETTE TIANO
PÂTES ET RIZ

Macaroni with Meat Sauce

Maccheroni alla Bolognese

This flavourful dish can be improved by adding a few dried mushrooms or, even better, fresh ones. It is not difficult to prepare, and the sauce can be cooked a few hours in advance.

	To serve 4	
400 g	*rigatoni*	14 oz
About 30 g	Parmesan cheese, grated	About 1 oz
	Meat sauce	
150 g	lean beef, minced	5 oz
1	medium-sized carrot, scraped, and finely chopped	1
1	stick of celery, scraped, and finely chopped	1
1	small onion, finely chopped	1
50 g	green streaky bacon, finely chopped	2 oz
50 g	butter	2 oz
3	chicken hearts, halved (optional)	3
2 tsp	flour	2 tsp
10 cl	stock	3½ fl oz
1	clove	1
	pepper	
	freshly grated nutmeg	
15 g	dried mushrooms, soaked in water and drained, or 150 g (5 oz) fresh mushrooms (optional)	½ oz
About 20 cl	milk	About 7 fl oz
3	chicken livers, trimmed, soaked in abundant cold water for 15 minutes, drained and cut into cubes	3

To prepare the sauce, put the chopped vegetables and bacon into a pan with the butter. Place the pan over a moderate heat and cook until the vegetables have softened. Add the beef and the chicken hearts, if available, and continue cooking, stirring frequently, until the meat has browned. Sprinkle with the flour, and add the stock. Add the clove, a pinch each of pepper and nutmeg, and the mushrooms, if using. Stir well, then cover and cook over a very low heat for about 1 hour, adding a few spoonfuls of milk and stirring from time to time.

When the sauce is almost ready, put plenty of salted water on to boil for the pasta. When the water is boiling, put in the pasta, stir, and cook over a high heat. Add the chicken livers to the sauce and continue cooking it over a moderate heat. Taste and if necessary adjust the seasoning. When the pasta is cooked, drain it. Put the pasta into a warmed bowl, add the cheese and the sauce; mix thoroughly and serve.

FERNANDA GOSETTI
IN CUCINA CON FERNANDA GOSETTI

Batter Noodles

The technique for making these noodles is demonstrated on page 60. A paper cone may be used to replace the piping bag with a nozzle shown in the picture.

Treated as a gratin, these rich, round, tender, eggy noodles are quite astonishing—drowned in cream and sprinkled with grated cheese, or liberally sprinkled with meat or poultry roasting juices and cheese. Served as a garnish, they may also be tossed in butter and seasoned to taste, and a few *fines herbes* may be added; or they may be tossed with fresh breadcrumbs that have first been cooked gently and tossed often in butter until lightly golden and crisp—more butter added the moment the noodles are joined to the crumbs. The noodles may, of course, be combined with other ingredients, either as a gratin or sautéed.

	To serve 3 or 4	
200 g	flour	7 oz
	salt	
1 tbsp	olive oil	1 tbsp
4	eggs	4

Put half of the flour into a mixing bowl and whisk the other ingredients into it. When smooth, add more flour, sprinkling it over the surface a little at a time and whisking it in, to bring the consistency to that of a firm batter.

Bring a pan of salted water to the boil; choose a pan with the largest surface available—a large roasting tin serves well. Reduce the heat and let the water barely simmer. Fill a paper cone or piping bag with batter, squeeze the top firmly closed, snip off the tip of the paper cone, if using, to leave a tiny hole something less than 5 mm (¼ inch) in diameter, and continuing to squeeze and hold the top part in one hand, squeeze the body of the cone with the other, holding the tip just over the surface of the water.

As you squeeze the ribbons of batter, relax the pressure regularly to let them separate, forming 7.5 to 12 cm (3 to 5 inches) lengths. Move the tip over the surface, being careful not to squeeze the batter on to the already formed noodles. Increase the heat, cover and poach for half a minute or so—until the water returns to the boil. Drain immediately.

RICHARD OLNEY
SIMPLE FRENCH FOOD

Thin Pasta with Capers, Olives and Anchovies

Linguine Capperi Olive e Acciughe

Linguine are long, flat strips of pasta, slightly broader than linguettine (page 11). The author recommends using salted capers rather then capers pickled in vinegar.

This recipe may be varied by browning 2 tablespoonfuls of breadcrumbs in the oil before adding the capers and olives.

	To serve 6	
600 g	*linguine* or spaghetti	1¼ lb
100 g	capers, soaked in water for 1 hour	3½ oz
100 g	black olives, stoned	3½ oz
100 g	salt anchovies, soaked, filleted, rinsed, dried and thinly sliced	3½ oz
2	garlic cloves	2
15 cl	oil	¼ pint
2 tbsp	water	2 tbsp
6 tbsp	chopped parsley	6 tbsp
	pepper	

Lightly fry the garlic in the oil. Add the capers, olives, water, parsley and pepper. Cook for 4 to 5 minutes. Remove the pan from the heat. Add the anchovies and stir them into the mixture until they disintegrate.

Bring a pan of lightly salted water to the boil. Throw in the pasta and cook until it is *al dente*. Drain the pasta and serve very hot with the sauce poured over.

JEANNE CARÒLA FRANCESCONI
LA CUCINA NAPOLETANA

Spaghetti with Mussels

Vermicelli alle "Cozze" in Bianco

This classic Neapolitan recipe uses the colloquial name "vermicelli" to mean spaghetti. To prepare mussels for cooking, scrape each of them to remove the beard and any other growths from the shell, then put them in a pan of clean, salted water for several hours. Change the water if it becomes muddied. Pick out and discard any opened shells.

	To serve 6	
600 g	spaghetti, cooked, drained, and kept hot	1¼ lb
1.5 kg	live mussels, scraped and washed	3 lb
2	garlic cloves, whole or chopped	2
3 tbsp	oil	3 tbsp
	freshly ground black pepper	
	chopped parsley	

In a large frying pan, lightly fry the garlic in the oil. If you put the cloves in whole, remove them as soon as they have browned; if you have chopped them, cook them until they sizzle but do not remove them. Add the pepper to taste and the mussels. Stir the mixture. Cover the pan. As the mussels open, remove them one by one from the pan and put them in a bowl. When all the mussels have been removed from the pan, after about 5 minutes, continue simmering the liquid that remains, to reduce it.

Shell the mussels and return them to the pan. Add the parsley and cook on a medium heat for about 2 to 3 minutes.

Moisten the spaghetti with some of the juices from the pan. Serve the mussels with the cooking liquid in a large sauceboat so that each diner can serve himself.

JEANNE CARÒLA FRANCESCONI
LA CUCINA NAPOLETANA

Spaghetti with Clams and Tomato Sauce

Vermicelli alle Vongole con i Pelati

This classic Neapolitan recipe uses the colloquial name "vermicelli" to mean spaghetti.

	To serve 6	
600 g	spaghetti, cooked, drained and kept hot	1¼ lb
1.25 kg	live clams in their shells, washed and drained	2¾ lb
1 kg	tomatoes, skinned, seeded and chopped	2 to 2½ lb
15 cl	olive oil	¼ pint
2	garlic cloves, chopped	2
	pepper	
	chopped parsley	

Pour 6 tablespoons of the oil into a frying pan. Heat the oil and add the clams. When the shells open up, remove the clams from the pan. Discard the shells and put the clams aside. Reduce the clams' cooking liquid over a medium heat, leave it to cool and strain it through a sieve or a piece of muslin.

In a saucepan, heat the remaining oil and fry the garlic in it until it turns golden. Remove the garlic from the pan. Add the tomatoes to the pan and season with pepper. Boil for 3 to 4 minutes over a high heat. Add the clams' cooking liquid and cook until the sauce is thick. Add the clams and some chopped parsley and simmer for 3 to 4 more minutes.

Pour three-quarters of the sauce over the spaghetti and serve the rest in a sauceboat.

JEANNE CARÒLA FRANCESCONI
LA CUCINA NAPOLETANA

Spaghetti with Cuttlefish in its Ink

Pasta cu Niuru di Sicci

To prepare cuttlefish, slice the fish open carefully with a sharp knife; avoid damaging the ink sac. Remove the cuttlebone, cut out the ink sac and reserve it. Remove and discard the beak-like mouth and the viscera. If the cuttlefish is fresh, the ink will be liquid. If frozen, it will have solidified; dissolve it in a tablespoonful of boiling liquid (water, stock or wine).

	To serve 4	
600 g	thin spaghetti, cooked	1¼ lb
	salt	
100 g	mature *pecorino* cheese, grated	3½ oz
	Cuttlefish sauce	
500 g	cuttlefish, boned and sliced into thin strips, ink sacs reserved	1 lb
1	onion, thinly sliced	1
	olive oil for frying	
4 tbsp	chopped parsley	4 tbsp
300 g	tomatoes, skinned and roughly chopped	10 oz
	salt and pepper	

Open the ink sacs and carefully pour the ink into a bowl. Brown the onion in hot oil with the parsley, then add the tomatoes and cuttlefish. Stir the mixture constantly, and cook over a medium heat for about 15 minutes or until the liquid is reduced slightly. Then add the ink from the bowl and seasoning. The sauce will take on a brownish hue with topaz reflections, due to the mingling of the oil and the tomato with the ink. Pour this dark, savoury sauce over the cooked spaghetti and sprinkle with grated cheese.

PINO CORRENTI
IL LIBRO D'ORO DELLA CUCINA E DEI VINI DI SICILIA

Spaghetti with Courgettes

Pâtes aux Courgettes

	To serve 4	
300 g	thin spaghetti	10 oz
3	courgettes, thinly sliced into rounds	3
5 tbsp	olive oil	5 tbsp
	salt and freshly ground pepper	
6	basil leaves, finely chopped	6
80 g	Gruyère or Parmesan cheese, grated	2½ oz

Sauté the courgettes in 2 tablespoons of the oil over a high heat for 8 to 10 minutes. Season with salt and pepper.

Cook the spaghetti for 7 minutes in plenty of rapidly boiling salted water. Drain. Add the courgettes with their cooking juices, the rest of the oil and the chopped basil. Season with freshly ground pepper. Mix well. Serve hot, with the grated cheese in a separate dish.

MYRETTE TIANO
PÂTES ET RIZ

Pasta with Fried Courgettes

Pasta chi Cucuzzeddi Fritti

Salted ricotta *cheese has better keeping qualities than fresh* ricotta *and when left to age becomes drier and more compact.*

To serve 6		
600 g	thin spaghetti	1¼ lb
600 g	courgettes, sliced into rounds	1¼ lb
2	garlic cloves, crushed	2
6 tbsp	olive oil	6 tbsp
	salt and freshly ground black pepper	
100 g	peppered *pecorino*, grated, or salted *ricotta* cheese, crumbled	3½ oz

Soften the garlic cloves for a moment in the smoking oil, then remove the garlic and fry the courgettes. Drain, reserving the oil. Season the courgettes then transfer them to a plate, and keep them hot. Cook the spaghetti until *al dente* in boiling, salted water, then drain the spaghetti and add to it the cheese, courgettes and oil. Serve with freshly ground black pepper.

PINO CORRENTI
IL LIBRO D'ORO DELLA CUCINA E DEI VINI DI SICILIA

Pasta with Cauliflower, Sardine and Anchovy Sauce

Pasta Palina o a la Paulota

To serve 6		
600 g	*ziti*	1¼ lb
1	large cauliflower, about 1 kg (2 lb), separated into florets	1
100 g	fresh sardines or anchovies, filleted	3½ oz
50 g	salt anchovies, soaked, filleted, rinsed and dried	2 oz
	salt	
	olive oil	
50 g	onion, sliced	2 oz
1	garlic clove	1
4	cloves, crushed	4
	ground cinnamon	
250 g	puréed tomato	8 oz
	freshly ground black pepper	

Boil the cauliflower florets in salted water for about 5 minutes. Drain, reserving the cooking liquid. Lightly fry the florets in oil, together with the fresh sardine or anchovy fillets, onion and garlic. Add the cloves, a pinch of cinnamon

and the tomato purée. Simmer for 10 to 15 minutes, then add the salt anchovy fillets, and cook until these disintegrate into the mixture—about 5 minutes.

Boil the pasta in the cauliflower water until firm to the bite. Drain, and stir the pasta into the pan with the sauce. Add freshly ground pepper at the moment of serving.

PINO CORRENTI
IL LIBRO D'ORO DELLA CUCINA E DEI VINI DI SICILIA

Pasta with Seafood

Fedelini alla Teodolinda

Fedelini **are a type of long, cylindrical pasta, similar to spaghetti but thinner.**

To serve 6 to 8		
1 kg	*fedelini* or spaghetti	2 to 2½ lb
150 g	live mussels, washed, beards removed	5 oz
250 g	live clams, washed	8 oz
50 g	fresh uncooked prawns	2 oz
50 g	tuna, finely chopped	2 oz
50 g	salt anchovies, soaked, filleted, rinsed, dried and finely chopped	2 oz
100 g	squid, cleaned and skinned; head, viscera and bone removed; flesh chopped	3½ oz
20 cl	oil	7 fl oz
4	garlic cloves	4
4 tbsp	chopped parsley	4 tbsp
4 or 5	basil leaves, chopped	4 or 5
½	small, sweet green pepper, seeded	½
8 cl	dry white wine	3 fl oz
500 g	tomatoes, skinned, seeded and chopped	1 lb
	salt	

Cook the mussels, clams and prawns with water to cover in a heavy frying pan. When the mussel and clam shells have opened, turn off the heat, shell them and place them in a dish. Shell the prawns, cut them into small pieces and add to the mussels and clams. Reserve the liquid left in the pan, taking care to remove the sediment of sand by straining the liquid through cheesecloth.

Put the oil, garlic, parsley, the basil leaves, green pepper, tuna and anchovies in a deep saucepan and fry for 2 minutes. Chop the clams into small pieces, and add them with the squid to the pan. Brown, then gradually pour in the wine. Turn up the heat and allow the wine to evaporate. Then add the tomatoes and reserved cooking liquid and cook, uncovered, over a medium heat for about 15 minutes. Add the mussels and prawns and simmer gently for 5 to 10 minutes. Season.

Cook the pasta in plenty of boiling, salted water until tender but still firm. Drain well, pile into a serving dish and pour on the shellfish in their sauce. Serve immediately.

LUIGI VOLPICELLI AND SECONDINO FREDA
L'ANTIARTUSI: 1000 RICETTE

Swabian Beef Stew with Cut Noodles

Gaisburger Marsch mit Spätzle

To serve 4

400 g	boiled beef, cubed	14 oz
400 g	potatoes, diced	14 oz
	salt	
1.5 litres	meat stock (*page 165*)	2½ pints
	freshly grated nutmeg	
50 g	butter or lard	2 oz
8 tbsp	chopped onion	8 tbsp
2 tbsp	finely sliced chives	2 tbsp
	fried bread cubes (optional)	
	Cut-noodle dough	
500 g	flour	1 lb
4	large eggs	4
1 tsp	salt	1 tsp

Boil the potatoes in slightly salted water for 10 minutes. Do not overcook or they will become floury. Drain the potatoes, reserving the cooking liquid.

To make the noodles, beat the flour, eggs and salt together vigorously in a bowl until they form a dough containing bubbles. If the dough is too stiff to roll out, add 1 to 2 tablespoons of cold water. Bring a pan of water to the boil. Spoon approximately 100 g (3½ oz) of dough on to a board. Roll it out thinly so that a strip 5mm (¼ inch) wide hangs over the edge of the board. Cut off this strip and drop it into the boiling water. Repeat this procedure until all the dough is cut into strips, dipping the knife frequently into cold water to prevent it sticking to the dough.

Bring the water gently back to the boil and cook the noodles until they float on the surface. As they come to the surface, remove the noodles with a skimmer and dip them into cold water. When all the noodles are ready, empty them into a colander and rinse under cold running water.

Put the cooked potatoes and the beef cubes in the meat stock with 15 cl (¼ pint) of the potato cooking liquid. Season to taste and add a pinch of nutmeg. Heat the butter in a frying pan and gently fry the onions until they turn golden.

Add the noodles to the stew and cook for a further 5 minutes to heat them thoroughly. Before serving, add the fried onions and sprinkle the stew with the chives. Cubes of fried bread can be used as a garnish.

HANS KARL ADAM
DAS KOCHBUCH AUS SCHWABEN

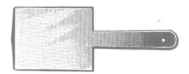

Trahana with Cheese

Liuta Trahana

Trahana, *a leavened pasta, with a pleasantly sour flavour, is one of the most ancient grain products. It is eaten throughout the Balkans and the countries of the former Ottoman Empire. Trahana takes at least two weeks—and a dry, sunny climate—to prepare. A purée made from vegetables, such as courgettes, sweet chili peppers and sometimes hot chili peppers is mixed with flour into a dough. A mixture of ground sesame seeds and sour dough (flour and water left for a few days in a warm place to ferment naturally) is added to the dough, which is then set in a warm place for a few days. When it has doubled in bulk, the dough mixture is sieved or chopped into small pieces the size of peas and left to dry out until completely hard and dry—at least a week. Fortunately,* trahana *can be bought commercially from Greek, Cypriot or Turkish grocers. It is best stored in linen bags, to aerate it and keep it fresh and dry. It can be cooked and served like any pasta as an accompaniment to meat, fish or cheese. The* sirene *cheese given in this recipe is a salty white cheese similar to the Greek* feta.

To serve 4

280 g	*trahana*	9 oz
60 g	onion, sliced	2 oz
60 g	butter	2 oz
1 tsp	paprika	1 tsp
2½ litres	boiling water	4½ pints
4 tsp	salt	4 tsp
125 g	*sirene* cheese, crumbled with a fork	4 oz

Fry the onion in the butter until brown. Remove the pan from the heat and stir in the paprika.

Add the salt to the boiling water and drop in the *trahana*. Boil briskly, uncovered, for 3 minutes, or until the *trahana* is just soft on the outside. Drain immediately and serve on hot plates. Spoon the onion mixture over the *trahana*; sprinkle with the cheese, and serve.

DR. L. PETROV, DR. N. DJELEPOV, DR. E. IORDANOV AND S. UZUNOVA
BULGARSKA NAZIONALNA KUCHNIYA

"The Stew that is Always Good"

Minestra Sempre Buona

"Paternostri" and "avemarie" are two types of pasta; the former are small, perforated and ridged; the latter are smaller and have no ridges. Any medium-sized pasta, such as conchiglie, fusili or ruote (page 10) can be used. If bean broth (the cooking liquid from dried beans) is not available, use a well-flavoured meat stock (recipe, page 165).

This very ancient and unusual recipe comes from Camaiore, a small town in northern Tuscany, Italy, near Viareggio. The dish is prepared like a risotto, but pasta replaces the rice.

To serve 4		
350 g	*paternostri* or *avemarie* or other medium-sized pasta	12 oz
6 tbsp	oil	6 tbsp
1	onion, finely chopped	1
1	carrot, finely chopped	1
3 or 4	celery leaves, finely chopped	3 or 4
1	garlic clove, finely chopped	1
	grated nutmeg (optional)	
1.25 litres	bean broth, brought to boiling point	2 pints

Pour the oil into a risotto pan, heat and add the onion, carrot, celery, garlic and nutmeg, if desired. Fry slowly. This mixture is known as a *battuto*. When the *battuto* is nicely browned, add the pasta and stir until it begins to brown. Then gradually pour in the bean broth, stirring constantly until the pasta is cooked. The result should resemble a risotto in consistency.

MARIÙ SALVATORI DE ZULIANI
LA CUCINA DI VERSILIA E GARFAGNANA

Tagliatelle with Prosciutto

Tagliatelle al Prosciutto

To serve 6		
750 g	tagliatelle	1½ lb
150 g	prosciutto, thinly sliced and cut into strips 5 mm (¼ inch) wide	5 oz
	salt	
125 g	butter	4 oz
60 g	Parmesan cheese, freshly grated	2 oz
	freshly ground black pepper	

Bring a pan of lightly salted water to the boil, and add the *tagliatelle*. Meanwhile, put the butter in a small saucepan over a very low heat. As soon as the butter is just melted add the strips of prosciutto. The prosciutto must simply be heated—it must not fry.

When the *tagliatelle* are cooked, drain them and place them on a warmed serving dish. Pour over the grated Parmesan cheese, grind over a fair amount of pepper, add the prosciutto, mix, and send to the table.

ENRICA AND VERNON JARRATT
THE COMPLETE BOOK OF PASTA

Trenette with Pesto

Pesto is more an unguent than a sauce and, as its name suggests (*pestare:* to pound), it is made by pounding all the ingredients in a mortar. One tablespoon of pine-nuts may be added to the *pesto* at the beginning, or several tablespoons of curdled milk or *prescinseau* (a soft whey obtained from curdled milk). A little Parmesan cheese may be combined with the *pecorino* cheese.

To serve 4 to 6		
500 g	*trenette*	1 lb
3	medium-sized potatoes, peeled and cut into pieces	3
90 g	green beans, sliced	3 oz
	salt	
About 30 g	Parmesan cheese, grated	About 1 oz
	Pesto	
36	basil leaves, washed and torn into pieces	36
3	garlic cloves, chopped	3
	coarse salt	
90 g	*pecorino* cheese, grated	3 oz
1 tbsp	olive oil	1 tbsp

To make the *pesto*, pound a little of the garlic and some of the basil leaves together in a mortar, gradually adding more garlic and basil and a little coarse salt. Only add more when you have obtained a good pulp. When all of the garlic and basil are incorporated, continue pounding with a circular movement and start to add the grated *pecorino* so all the ingredients blend to form a fairly thick sauce. Dilute with a little olive oil (preferably a clear, light variety).

Cook the potatoes in plenty of boiling, salted water for 10 minutes. Add the *trenette*, and about 5 minutes later add the green beans (which should be very young). When the *trenette* are cooked *al dente*, after about 10 minutes, drain everything. Mix the potatoes, *trenette* and beans with the *pesto* and serve with grated Parmesan passed separately.

VINCENZO BUONASSISI
THE CLASSIC BOOK OF PASTA

Fried, Moulded and Baked Pasta

Two-Sides Browned Noodles
Liang Mien Huang

To serve 2 to 4

250 g	fresh egg noodles	8 oz
6	large dried mushrooms	6
90 g	dried flat-tip bamboo shoots	3 oz
35 cl	warm water	12 fl oz
180 g	shredded Chinese cabbage or other crisp green cabbage	6 oz
5 tbsp	peanut or corn oil	5 tbsp
1 tbsp	soy sauce	1 tbsp
$\frac{1}{2}$ tsp	sugar	$\frac{1}{2}$ tsp
2 tsp	cornflour	2 tsp
1 tsp	sesame-seed oil	1 tsp

Wash the mushrooms and bamboo shoots and soak them in the warm water for 1 hour. Squeeze the water out of the vegetables, reserving the water for later use. Finely shred the mushrooms and bamboo shoots and set them aside on a plate with the shredded cabbage.

Cook the egg noodles in about 2 litres (3½ pints) of boiling water for 2 to 3 minutes. Drain and mix in 1 tablespoon of the peanut or corn oil. Spread the noodles on a plate to cool.

Heat a large frying pan until very hot. Add 1 tablespoon of the oil to coat the pan. Spread the cooked egg noodles in the pan, side to side, for about 5 minutes, so that the noodles will shift along the bottom surface of the pan. The noodles will start to brown. Swirl for another 2 minutes, then flip the noodle patty over. Add 1 more tablespoon of oil and brown. Transfer to a platter and keep the patty warm in the oven.

Heat a *wok* or pan, and add the remaining 2 tablespoons of peanut or corn oil. Stir-fry the mushrooms, bamboo shoots, and cabbage together for 2 minutes, or until the vegetables wilt. Add the soy sauce and sugar. Stir to mix.

Strain the reserved mushroom-bamboo shoot water and slowly pour about 12.5 cl (4 fl oz) of it into the *wok*. In a cup, combine 4 tablespoons of the soaking water with the cornflour. Discard the remaining soaking water. When the liquid in the *wok* begins to boil slowly, stir in the well-blended cornflour mixture. When the ingredients are coated with a light glaze, add the sesame-seed oil and mix well. Pour the vegetables and sauce on top of the patty and serve hot.

FLORENCE LIN
FLORENCE LIN'S CHINESE VEGETARIAN COOKBOOK

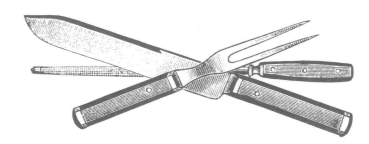

Special Fried Fresh Egg Noodles with Chicken
Chow San Min

To serve 4

500 g	fresh egg noodles	1 lb
175 g	boneless chicken breast, skinned and thinly sliced	6 oz
3 to 4 tbsp	groundnut oil	3 to 4 tbsp
60 g	bamboo shoots, thinly sliced	2 oz
60 g	mushrooms, thinly sliced	2 oz
	salt	
1 tsp	cornflour, mixed with a little water	1 tsp
	sesame-seed oil	
2 or 3	spring onions, finely chopped	2 or 3

Place the noodles in a saucepan of boiling water for half a minute, then drain them through a sieve and hold them under cold running water for 10 seconds. Put the noodles in a hot oiled pan and cook for 1 minute, turning occasionally. Place the noodles in a warmed serving dish.

Put the chicken into the oiled pan and cook over a high heat for half a minute. Add the bamboo shoots and the mushrooms and cook for another minute. Add salt to taste. Add the cornflour dissolved in water and a few drops of sesame-seed oil and cook for 1 minute more.

Place this mixture on top of the noodles and garnish with finely sliced spring onions.

S. K. CHENG (EDITOR)
SHANGHAI RESTAURANT CHINESE COOKERY BOOK

Fried Chinese Egg Noodles

Tch'ao Mienn

The technique of frying noodles is demonstrated on page 66.

To serve 4

250 g	Chinese egg noodles	8 oz
200 g	lard	7 oz
250 g	large shrimps or prawns, shelled	8 oz
175 g	pork, minced	6 oz
1	boiled crab, meat extracted	1
	salt	
2 tbsp	sesame-seed oil	2 tbsp
1 tbsp	vinegar	1 tbsp

Cook the egg noodles in boiling water for 3 minutes or until barely tender. Drain, rinse in cold water and drain again. Melt 30 g (1 oz) of the lard and fry the shrimps or prawns in it for 1 minute. Set them aside. Fry the pork in the same lard until it begins to brown; set aside. Fry the crab meat in the same pan for 1 minute; set aside. Melt the remaining lard in a large frying pan, add the cooked noodles, and fry them until they are golden. Add the shrimps or prawns, pork and crab, season with salt, and pour on the sesame-seed oil and vinegar.

H. LECOURT
LA CUISINE CHINOISE

Spaghetti with Bacon and Eggs

Spaghetti alla Carbonara

If you want a slightly stronger, even pungent taste, some ingredients may be varied: for example, use smoked bacon instead of green bacon, and 1 or 2 tablespoons of *pecorino* in addition to the Parmesan.

To serve 4

350 g	spaghetti	12 oz
100 g	green streaky bacon, cut into small strips	3½ oz
4	egg yolks	4
1 tbsp	olive oil, or 15 g (½ oz) butter	1 tbsp
2 tbsp	single cream	2 tbsp
50 g	Parmesan cheese, grated	2 oz
	freshly ground black pepper	

Put the oil or butter into a fairly large frying pan, add the strips of bacon and fry them lightly over moderate heat until the bacon fat has melted. Remove the pan from the heat and

set aside, keeping the pan warm.

Cook the spaghetti in plenty of boiling, salted water. Meanwhile, beat the egg yolks in a bowl with a whisk; then whisk in the cream and half of the Parmesan, and add a generous amount of black pepper (you can vary the amount to taste). When the spaghetti is still very firm to the bite, drain it; transfer it to the pan with the bacon, and place over a medium heat. Stir the spaghetti so that it absorbs the flavour of the bacon, then remove from the heat and pour the egg mixture over it. Stir quickly and serve straight away. Serve the remaining Parmesan separately.

ANNA MARTINI (EDITOR)
PASTA & PIZZA

Vermicelli Catalan-Style

Fideos a la Catalana

To serve 4

500 g	thick vermicelli	1 lb
300 g	pork spare ribs, chopped into 5 cm (2 inch) pieces with a cleaver	10 oz
30 g	lard	1 oz
1	onion, chopped	1
200 g	tomatoes, skinned, seeded and chopped	7 oz
2 tbsp	chopped parsley	2 tbsp
100 g	*chorizo* or other spicy garlic-flavoured frying sausages, cut in pieces	3½ oz
1 litre	boiling water	1¾ pints
	salt	

In a large saucepan, fry the spare ribs in the lard over a moderate heat. When the spare ribs are lightly browned, add the onion. When the onion begins to brown, add the tomatoes and parsley. Add the sausages and brown them evenly.

Break the vermicelli into lengths to fit the saucepan. Brown them evenly, then pour in the boiling water. Season with salt, cover and simmer for 10 minutes or until the pasta is cooked and most of the water absorbed.

VICTORIA SERRA
TIA VICTORIA'S SPANISH KITCHEN

Fried Rice Noodles

Chao Mifen

Since fried noodles are traditionally considered an economy dish, you can, if you wish, use less meat than the recipe calls for. "Tree ears" or "cloud ears" (auricularia polytricha) are small, crinkly, gelatinous dried black fungi. They are sold by weight in Chinese provision stores.

	To serve 4 or 5	
500 g	dried rice noodles	1 lb
1.25 litres	boiling water	2 pints
60 g	tree ears	2 oz
2 or 3	pork chops, for a yield of 250 to 350 g ($\frac{1}{2}$ to $\frac{3}{4}$ lb) meat	2 or 3
4 tbsp	soy sauce	4 tbsp
1 tsp	cornflour	1 tsp
5	spring onions, trimmed	5
8 cl	peanut oil	3 fl oz
2 tsp	salt	2 tsp
4 tsp	sesame-seed oil	4 tsp

Put the dry noodles in a large bowl and pour 1 litre (1$\frac{3}{4}$ pints) of the boiling water over them. Let them soak for 15 minutes, then drain them and rinse them twice in cold running water.

Put the tree ears in a small bowl, cover them with the remaining water, and soak for 10 minutes. Drain and rinse them thoroughly, picking them over carefully for any impurities, such as tiny pieces of wood that might still be embedded.

To make it easier to slice the pork thinly, place it in the freezer for about 10 minutes, until it becomes slightly stiff but not frozen. Then cut it into wafer-thin strips, about 7.5 cm (3 inches) long and 5 mm ($\frac{1}{4}$ inch) wide. Add 3 tablespoons soy sauce and the cornflour to the pork and mix thoroughly.

Cut 2 of the spring onions, both white part and green, in half and slice lengthwise into thin shreds; add these to the meat. Chop the remaining spring onions into 5 cm (2 inch) lengths and shred them very finely. Set these aside.

Heat your *wok* or pan over a high heat for 15 seconds, then pour in the peanut oil. It will be ready when the first tiny bubbles form and a few small wisps of smoke appear. Add the meat mixture to the pan and stir-fry vigorously for 15 seconds, using your spoon or a fish slice in a continuous scooping motion to toss the meat shreds around in the pan.

Add the tree ears and stir-fry for 1 minute more before removing all but a few tablespoons of the pork and tree ears.

Add the noodles and shredded spring onions to the pan, along with the salt and sesame-seed oil. Stir-fry the noodles, vigorously enough to keep them from sticking to the side of the pan, for 2 minutes. Return the partially cooked pork and tree ears to the pan and add the remaining soy sauce. Let the noodles cook over a fairly high heat, for 10 more minutes, stirring them regularly to make sure that they do not stick to the pan and that all of the ingredients cook evenly. At this point the noodles will be rather soft. If you like really crunchy noodles, cook them longer. The longer you cook them, the crisper they will become.

ELLEN AND JOHN SCHRECKER
MRS. CHIANG'S SZECHWAN COOKBOOK

Green Lasagne with Meat Sauce

Lasagne Verdi alla Bolognese

The preparation of spinach pasta is shown on page 50.

	To serve 6	
1 kg	spinach pasta *(page 167)*	2 to 2$\frac{1}{2}$ lb
$\frac{1}{2}$ litre	white sauce *(page 165)*	16 fl oz
100 g	Parmesan cheese, grated	3$\frac{1}{2}$ oz
	Meat sauce	
200 g	*pancetta*, or green streaky bacon or gammon, finely chopped	7 oz
500 g	lean beef, minced	1 lb
60 g each	celery and onion, finely chopped	2 oz each
1	carrot, finely chopped	1
3	chicken giblets, minced	3
1 litre	chicken stock *(page 165)*	1$\frac{3}{4}$ pints
	salt	
1 kg	tomatoes, skinned, seeded and chopped	2 to 2$\frac{1}{2}$ lb
200 g	butter	7 oz

Roll the spinach pasta out into a thin sheet, and cut it into at least 10 rounds or rectangles, to fit the shape of the 1.5 litre (2$\frac{1}{2}$ pint) oven dish that is to be used for the lasagne.

Brown the *pancetta*, bacon or ham in a saucepan for about 5 minutes. Add the minced beef, celery, onion, carrot and the giblets. Cook over a fairly brisk heat, stirring frequently, for 20 minutes. Then pour in 30 cl ($\frac{1}{2}$ pint) of the stock and add a pinch of salt. Increase the heat a little and, continuing to stir, cook until the liquid is absorbed, about a further 20 minutes. Then add the tomatoes and butter and the remainder of the stock. Simmer for at least 90 minutes, or until the mixture is the consistency of a thick sauce.

In fast-boiling, salted water, cook the rounds or rectangles of pasta one at a time, until tender but still quite firm. Drain the pasta on tea towels.

Moisten the oven dish with a little of the meat sauce, place a piece of pasta in the bottom and add more meat sauce, a layer of white sauce, then a layer of grated cheese. Cover with another piece of pasta and repeat the process until all of the ingredients are used up, ending with a layer of white sauce. Place the dish in an oven preheated to 200°C (400°F or Mark 6) and bake for 15 to 20 minutes or until the top is golden-brown. Serve hot.

LUIGI VOLPICELLI AND SECONDINO FREDA
L'ANTIARTUSI: 1000 RICETTE

Lasagne with Veal and Mozzarella

Lasagne all'Abruzzese

The technique of making pasta dough is shown on page 44.

To serve 4

350 g	pasta dough (*page 167*)	12 oz
200 g	*mozzarella* cheese, diced	7 oz
2	eggs, hard-boiled and diced	2
75 g	butter, melted	2½ oz
	Veal sauce	
250 g	veal, minced	8 oz
15 g	butter	½ oz
4 tbsp	dry white wine	4 tbsp
350 g	puréed tomatoes	12 oz
	salt and pepper	
125 g	Parmesan cheese, grated	4 oz
1	egg	1

Roll out the pasta dough thinly and slice it into strips to fit the bottom and sides of your baking dish. Cook the fresh pasta for about 1 minute in boiling, salted water, drain and put the strips on a tea towel to dry.

To make the meat sauce, heat the butter and when it starts to foam, add the minced veal and brown thoroughly. Add the wine and cook rapidly until the smell of the wine disappears. Add the puréed tomatoes and bring to the boil. Season with salt and pepper. Reduce the heat and simmer. Mix the Parmesan cheese and the egg in a bowl, then stir them gradually into the meat sauce. Simmer until the sauce thickens.

Butter an ovenproof dish and line the bottom and sides with the pasta strips. Cover with meat sauce, then sprinkle evenly with some of the diced hard-boiled egg and *mozzarella* cheese. Cover with another layer of pasta and continue in the same way, ending with a layer of pasta. Pour the melted butter over the lasagne and bake in an oven preheated to 180°C (350°F or Mark 4) for about 15 minutes or until the top is just beginning to brown. Serve very hot.

ANNA MARTINI
PASTA & PIZZA

Lasagne with Four Cheeses

Lasagne di Meluzza Comasca

Provolone *is a smoked cheese. Any smoked cheese can be substituted.* Caciocavallo *can be found under the name* cachkeval *in Greek or Cypriot grocers; if it is not available,* Gruyère *can be used.* Gruyère *can also be substituted for* mozzarella, *a buffalo milk cheese from southern Italy.*

To serve 4

350 g	lasagne	12 oz
50 g	*provolone* cheese, thinly sliced	2 oz
50 g	*caciocavallo* cheese, grated	2 oz
100 g	*mozzarella* cheese, thinly sliced	3½ oz
50 g	Parmesan cheese, grated	2 oz
	salt	
75 g	butter	2½ oz
1 tbsp	sugar, mixed with 1 tsp ground cinnamon	1 tbsp

Cook the lasagne in boiling, salted water until they are *al dente,* and spread them out on a towel to dry. Take care not to let them dry out completely.

Butter a 1.5 litre (2½ pint) pie dish, and line the bottom with a layer of lasagne. Cover this with half of the sliced *provolone* and half of the grated *caciocavallo.* Add a second layer of lasagne and cover with half of the *mozzarella,* then half of the Parmesan. Make another layer of lasagne, dot with butter, and sprinkle with half of the sugar and cinnamon. Repeat the layers, ending with a layer dotted with butter and sprinkled with cinnamon sugar. Bake in an oven preheated to 180°C (350°F or Mark 4) for 20 minutes or until lightly browned.

MASSIMO ALBERINI
CENTO RICETTE STORICHE

Czech Curd Cheese and Noodle Pudding

Topfen-Nudel-Auflauf

To serve 4

250 g	broad noodles or *tagliatelle*	8 oz
375 g	curd cheese	13 oz
¼ litre	soured cream or soured milk	8 fl oz
	salt	
125 g	bacon, diced	4 oz
1	onion, finely chopped	1
15 g	butter	½ oz
3	eggs	3

Boil the pasta in salted water until done, pour it into a strainer, rinse with cold water and leave to drain. Pass the curd cheese through a fine sieve, stir in 6 tablespoons of the soured cream or milk and season with salt. Fry the diced bacon with the onion in a frying pan until the bacon is crisp.

Grease a deep ovenproof dish with the butter. Place a layer of pasta in the bottom, cover with a layer of the bacon and onion mixture, followed by a layer of curd cheese. Continue in this way until all of the ingredients are used up, finishing with a layer of cheese.

Mix the eggs with the remaining soured cream or milk and pour the mixture over the contents of the dish. Cook in an oven preheated to 180°C (350°F or Mark 4) for about 45 minutes or until the top is brown. Serve with a green salad.

GRETE WILLINSKY
KOCHBUCH DER BÜCHERGILDE

━━━━━◆━━━━━

Gratin of Stuffed Pasta Rolls

Cannelloni Laziali

The technique of making pasta dough is demonstrated on page 44; the technique of rolling up the filled cannelloni is shown on page 65.

To serve 6

350 g	flour	12 oz
4	eggs	4
	salt	
	olive oil	
20 cl	meat sauce (*page 167*)	7 fl oz
120 g	Parmesan cheese, grated	4 oz
50 g	butter	2 oz
	Meat filling	
50 g	butter	2 oz
1	small onion, chopped	1
1	small carrot, chopped	1
1	stick celery, chopped	1
1 tbsp	chopped parsley	1 tbsp
300 g	boneless pork loin, chopped	10 oz
50 g	prosciutto, chopped	2 oz
30 g	dried mushrooms, soaked in warm water until softened, drained and chopped	1 oz
1	lamb's brain, blanched, cleaned and cut into small pieces	1
	salt and pepper	
	grated nutmeg	
10 cl	white wine	3½ fl oz
2 tsp	flour	2 tsp
300 g	puréed tomato	10 oz

Make the pasta dough with the flour, eggs, a pinch of salt and a drop of oil. Roll out the dough 3 mm (⅛ inch) thick and cut it into 7.5 by 10 cm (3 by 4 inch) rectangles. Parboil these rectangles for about 1 minute; remove them with a skimmer and leave to cool on a towel.

In a pan, heat half of the butter, and add the onion, carrot, celery and parsley. Lightly colour these ingredients over a low heat; then add the pork, prosciutto and mushrooms. Stir, allow the flavours to blend, and add the brain. Cook for another few minutes, stirring occasionally, then season with a little salt and pepper and add a small pinch of nutmeg. Pour on the wine, and cook over a high heat until most of the wine has evaporated. Sprinkle over the flour to bind the filling mixture, and finally add the puréed tomato. Cook over a moderate heat until the mixture has the consistency of a very thick sauce. Remove the pan from the heat, put the entire mixture into a bowl, and let it cool, so that it becomes even thicker.

Portion out the filling on to the rectangles of pasta, roll them up, and line them up in a buttered baking dish. Cover them with the meat sauce, the grated Parmesan and the remaining butter, cut into slivers. Put the dish in an oven preheated to 180°C (350°F or Mark 4) for about 20 minutes, or until the top is golden-brown.

VINCENZO BUONASSISI
IL CODICE DELLA PASTA

━━━━━◆━━━━━

Pasta Squares with Ham

Łazanki z Szynką

The preparation of small pasta squares is shown on page 48; the technique of layering them is demonstrated on page 63.

Łazanki, from Poland, can also be served mixed with cooked cabbage or mushrooms, or with grated Parmesan cheese.

To serve 4

6	eggs, 3 lightly beaten, 3 with yolks separated from whites, whites stiffly beaten	6
250 g	flour	8 oz
	salt	
75 g	butter, softened	2½ oz
12.5 cl	soured cream	4 fl oz
250 g	ham, chopped	8 oz

Mix the beaten eggs with the flour and knead the mixture to form a dough. Roll out the dough thinly and leave it to dry for about 30 minutes. Then cut it into 1 cm (½ inch) squares. Boil these *łazanki* in a pan of salted water for 3 to 5 minutes or until tender. Drain.

Mix the butter with the egg yolks and cream and then stir in the *łazanki*. Fold in the beaten egg whites. Butter a 90 cl (1½ pint) baking dish and put in alternate layers of *łazanki* and pieces of chopped ham, ending with *łazanki*. Bake for 1 hour in an oven preheated to 180°C (350°F or Mark 4). The top should be golden-brown.

MARIA DISSLOWA
JAK GOTOWAC

Baked Pasta Pudding with Meat Sauce

Sfurmatu d'Anilletti 'O Furnu

Anelletti (anilletti *in Sicilian dialect*) *are small ring-shaped pasta. Ruote* (shown on page 10) *or pasta of a similar size can be substituted. Tuma* is a Sicilian sheep's milk cheese similar to ricotta, *which could be used instead.*

To serve 6

500 g	*anelletti*	1 lb
	salt	
50 g	*tuma* cheese, sliced	2 oz
100 g	*caciocavallo* cheese, grated	3½ oz
80 g	butter, cut into small pieces	2½ oz
80 g	dry breadcrumbs	2½ oz
1	aubergine, sliced and fried in 2 tbsp oil (optional)	1
2	eggs, hard-boiled and sliced (optional)	2
	Meat sauce	
350 g	lean beef, minced	12 oz
¼ litre	red wine	8 fl oz
1	bay leaf	1
3	cloves	3
1	onion, sliced	1
2 tbsp	chopped fresh parsley	2 tbsp
2 tbsp	oil	2 tbsp
300 g	tomatoes, skinned, seeded and roughly chopped	10 oz
5	walnuts, pounded or ground	5
	ground cinnamon	
	salt and pepper	
1	aubergine, sliced and fried in 2 tbsp of oil	1

For the sauce, first marinate the minced beef in the red wine with the bay leaf and cloves for 2 hours. Drain the beef, and discard the marinade.

Brown the onion and parsley in oil, then add the beef. Cook it for about 10 minutes, stirring frequently, then add the tomatoes, walnuts and a pinch of cinnamon. Season with salt and pepper and add the fried aubergine. Mix well. Remove the mixture from the pan and chop thoroughly with a *mezzaluna* or other chopping knife.

Cook the pasta in boiling, salted water until it is *al dente*. Drain the pasta and mix it with the meat sauce. Add the sliced *tuma* cheese to the mixture, and stir in the *caciocavallo* cheese. Butter a 1.75 litre (3 pint) soufflé dish and dust it with some of the breadcrumbs. The dish can be lined with slices of

aubergine and hard-boiled egg slices to make an attractive design on the outside of the pudding. Pour the mixture into the dish, top with the remaining breadcrumbs and the pieces of butter, and bake in an oven preheated to 180°C (350°F or Mark 4) for 15 minutes. Allow the pudding to rest for 10 minutes, then unmould on to a warmed serving dish.

PINO CORRENTI
IL LIBRO D'ORO DELLA CUCINA E DEI VINI DI SICILIA

Baked Pasta with Aubergine

Timballo di Maccheroni al Forno

To serve 4

250 g	cooked, drained *penne*	8 oz
4	aubergines, cut lengthwise into 5 mm (¼ inch) slices	4
	oil	
	flour	
2	eggs, beaten with 3 tbsp grated Parmesan cheese, and seasoned with salt and pepper	2
	lard	
About 90 cl	tomato sauce (*page 166*)	About 1½ pints
2	Italian pork sausages, fried and crumbled	2
1	chicken liver, sautéed and chopped	1
1	slice cooked tongue, cut into strips	1
30 g	cooked white chicken meat, sliced	1 oz
60 g	parboiled peas	2 oz
1	egg, hard-boiled and chopped	1
30 g	*mozzarella* cheese, chopped	1 oz
3 to 4 tbsp	grated Parmesan cheese	3 to 4 tbsp

Fry the aubergine slices in oil on both sides until golden. Drain and dry well on absorbent paper, and then flour and dip them in the seasoned mixture of beaten eggs and grated Parmesan cheese. Fry the slices again until they are well coloured; drain them. Grease four individual baking dishes with lard and line them with aubergine slices. Reserve the rest of the slices for the top.

Mix the cooked *penne* with most of the tomato sauce, reserving a little of the sauce for garnish. Mix in the sausages, chicken liver, tongue, chicken, peas, egg, *mozzarella* and 2 tablespoons of the Parmesan cheese.

Fill the lined dishes with the mixture. Cover them with the remaining aubergine slices. Spread the tops with a little tomato sauce and strew with the remaining grated Parmesan. Cover with foil and bake in an oven preheated to 190°C (375°F or Mark 5) for 25 minutes. Turn them out and serve as individual portions.

FRANCO LAGATTOLLA
THE RECIPES THAT MADE A MILLION

Marvellous Macaroni and Cheese

To serve 4

250 g	elbow macaroni	8 oz
250 g	mature Cheddar cheese, grated	8 oz
40 g	butter	1½ oz
30 g	onion, chopped	1 oz
30 g	flour	1 oz
½ tsp	salt	½ tsp
⅛ tsp	pepper	⅛ tsp
¼ litre	double cream	8 fl oz
12.5 cl	dry white wine	4 fl oz

Cook the macaroni until just tender. Drain. Heat the butter and cook the onion in it until soft, about 10 minutes. Stir in the flour, salt and pepper. Slowly add the cream and wine and cook over a low heat, stirring constantly, until this sauce is thickened. Add the cheese and stir until melted. Mix together the macaroni and cheese sauce. Put into a greased 1.5 litre (2½ pint) casserole. Bake in an oven preheated to 180°C (350°F or Mark 4) for 15 minutes or until thoroughly heated through. Serve with buttered fresh leaf spinach.

JOSÉ WILSON (EDITOR)
HOUSE AND GARDEN'S NEW COOKBOOK

Macaroni Pie

Timpalle di Maccheroni al Latte

To serve 6

500 g	macaroni	1 lb
500 g	shortcrust pastry dough (*page 166*)	1 lb
1 litre	milk	1¾ pints
90 g	Parmesan cheese, grated	3 oz
60 g	butter	2 oz
150 g	*mozzarella* cheese, thinly sliced	5 oz
3	eggs, hard-boiled and quartered	3
	salt and freshly ground pepper	

Roll out the shortcrust dough and use it to line a large casserole or deep pie dish, reserving about one-third of the dough for the pastry lid.

Meanwhile, bring the milk to the boil in one pan, and half cook the macaroni in boiling salted water in another pan.

Drain the macaroni and finish cooking it in the milk, but take care not to overcook it. Drain away the excess milk, leaving the macaroni very moist, and mix it with the Parmesan cheese and butter. Then spread out the macaroni in the pastry-lined casserole or dish, arranging it in layers seasoned with salt and pepper and separated by slices of *mozzarella* cheese and the quartered hard-boiled eggs. Take care that the layers are all packed well together. Put on the pastry lid, folding it over all the way round to effect a good seal between the lid and the pastry lining.

Cook in an oven preheated to 190°C (375°F or Mark 5) for 40 minutes, or until the pastry is crisp and nicely coloured.

IPPOLITO CAVALCANTI, DUCA DI BUONVICINO
CUCINA TEORICO-PRATICA

Macaroni Gratin

Le Macaroni au Gratin

To serve 4 to 6

500 g	long macaroni	1 lb
2 litres	water	3½ pints
	salt	
1 litre	milk	1¾ pints
¼ tsp	mixed spice	¼ tsp
	freshly ground black pepper	
	nutmeg	
60 g	butter, softened and cut into small pieces	2 oz
100 g	Gruyère cheese, grated	3½ oz
50 g	Parmesan cheese, grated	2 oz
50 g	dry breadcrumbs	2 oz

Bring the water to the boil in a large pan, with a good pinch of salt. Add the macaroni and cook until it is *al dente*. Drain the macaroni and keep it hot. Heat the milk to boiling point, add a pinch of salt, the mixed spice and a little pepper, and grate in some nutmeg. Simmer for 5 minutes.

Mix the butter and Gruyère cheese with the hot macaroni, stirring well to prevent the grated cheese from forming lumps. Put the macaroni in an ovenproof dish and cover with all but ¼ litre (8 fl oz) of the milk. Bake in an oven preheated to 220°C (425°F or Mark 7) for 15 minutes. Remove from the oven; if the macaroni seems dry, add a little of the remaining milk. Sprinkle the macaroni with the Parmesan cheese mixed with the breadcrumbs. Return to the oven and bake at 230 to 240°C (450 to 475°F or Mark 8 or 9) for 10 minutes, or until well browned—or place the macaroni under a hot grill.

Serve in the baking dish. If the macaroni is not to be served at once, keep it warm in the oven with the heat turned off.

ALBIN MARTY
FOURMIGUETTO: SOUVENIRS, CONTES ET RECETTES DU LANGUEDOC

Sicilian Macaroni and Sardine Pie

Pasta con le Sarde

To serve 6

500 g	small or elbow macaroni	1 lb
500 g	fresh sardines, filleted	1 lb
500 g	fennel bulbs, trimmed	1 lb
	flour	
¼ litre	olive oil	8 fl oz
3 or 4	shallots, finely chopped	3 or 4
3	salt anchovies, soaked, filleted, rinsed and dried	3
¼ tsp	powdered saffron, mixed with a little hot water	¼ tsp
50 g	sultanas, soaked in warm water for 15 minutes and drained	2 oz
100 g	pine-nuts	3½ oz
	salt and freshly ground pepper	

Boil the fennel bulbs for 10 minutes in water. Take them out, drain them, and cut them into very small pieces. Save the fennel's cooking liquid.

Take one-third of the sardines and cut them up very small to go in the sauce. Flour the remaining sardines and fry them lightly in about half of the olive oil. Drain and set them aside.

Heat about 4 tablespoons of olive oil and let the shallots take colour in this. Add the chopped sardines and crush them in the pan with a spoon. Add the chopped fennel and let the whole cook for a little (about 10 minutes), adding, if necessary, a small amount of the fennel's cooking liquid.

Heat the remainder of the olive oil, then add the anchovies. Place the pan on a fireproof mat over a very low heat, and help the anchovies to "melt" by using a fork.

Add to the shallot, sardine and fennel mixture the melted anchovies, the saffron, sultanas, pine-nuts and a little salt and pepper, and let it all go on cooking for a few minutes.

Meanwhile, cook the pasta: bring the fennel's cooking liquid to the boil, supplement it if necessary with water, and cook the pasta in this with a little salt. Drain.

Combine the pasta with the sauce. Finally, place a layer of the pasta in an oven dish, with the fried sardines on top and more pasta on top of them, and so on, finishing with a layer of pasta. Bake this dish in an oven preheated to 190°C (375°F or Mark 5) for about 15 minutes.

ALAN DAVIDSON
MEDITERRANEAN SEAFOOD

Baked Macaroni with Minced Meat

Pasticcio Macaronia

To serve 6 to 8

500 g	macaroni	1 lb
1 kg	lamb, minced	2 lb
60 g	butter	2 oz
1	small onion, finely chopped	1
1	garlic clove, chopped	1
2 tsp	salt	2 tsp
½ tsp	pepper	½ tsp
4 tbsp	chopped parsley	4 tbsp
12.5 cl	dry white wine	4 fl oz
350 g	tomatoes, skinned, seeded and diced	12 oz
4	eggs, 2 of them separated	4
1 litre	white sauce (*page 165*) made with nutmeg	1¾ pints
500 g	Gruyère cheese, grated	1 lb

Heat 30 g (1 oz) of the butter in a large frying pan and sauté the minced meat and onion—stirring frequently—until slightly browned. Add the garlic, salt and pepper, parsley, wine and tomatoes. Cover and cook over a medium heat until the meat is cooked and the tomatoes are reduced to a purée, about 15 minutes. Cool and add the two egg whites.

Make the white sauce. Stir into it half of the grated cheese, the two whole eggs and the two egg yolks. Set the sauce aside.

Cook the macaroni in boiling, salted water until soft but firm. Drain the macaroni, and return to the pan. Add the rest of the butter in small pieces.

Butter a 35 by 25 cm (14 by 10 inch) baking dish about 5 cm (2 inches) deep and put half of the macaroni into it. Sprinkle with 125 g (4 oz) cheese and cover with the meat. Top with the remaining macaroni. Sprinkle with some cheese and cover with the sauce. Top with the rest of the cheese and bake in an oven preheated to 180°C (350°F or Mark 4) for 45 minutes or until golden-brown. Leave in a warm place for about 20 minutes, then cut into small squares and serve.

CHRISSA PARADISSIS
THE BEST BOOK OF GREEK COOKERY

Cannelloni with Spinach and Cheese

Panzerotti

The technique of preparing pasta dough is demonstrated on page 44; that of filling pasta rolls is shown on page 65. Mascarpone and crescenza are types of cream cheese.

This exquisite preparation, a speciality of Piacenza cookery, can be made with commercial cannelloni or with cannelloni made from freshly prepared pasta. If desired, the dish can be sauced with double cream instead of the white sauce.

	To serve 4	
16	large cannelloni	16
	salt	
About ½ litre	white sauce (*page 165*)	About 16 fl oz
	Spinach and cheese filling	
500 g	spinach, stems removed, parboiled for 2 minutes, squeezed and chopped	1 lb
	salt	
300 g	*ricotta* cheese	10 oz
200 g	Parmesan cheese, grated	7 oz
150 g	Mascarpone or *crescenza* cheese	5 oz
	freshly ground pepper	
	freshly grated nutmeg	

Put plenty of salted water on to boil for the pasta. When the water boils, put in the cannelloni, one at a time, stir, and cook over a moderate heat. When the cannelloni are half cooked, after 5 to 6 minutes for commercial pasta or 2 minutes for fresh pasta, remove them and plunge them into cold water. Then drain them and spread them out on napkins.

While the pasta is cooking, put the chopped spinach into a bowl with the *ricotta*, about half of the Parmesan, the Mascarpone or *crescenza,* and a pinch each of salt, pepper and nutmeg. Mix together well.

Thoroughly butter an ovenproof dish large enough to hold the cannelloni in a single layer. Preheat the oven to 180°C (350°F or Mark 4). Fill the cannelloni with the prepared spinach and cheese mixture and arrange them in the dish. Sprinkle with the rest of the Parmesan, and cover the cannelloni with the white sauce. Place in the oven for about 20 minutes, or until the sauce is bubbling and the surface is lightly coloured. Serve.

FERNANDA GOSETTI
IN CUCINA CON FERNANDA GOSETTI

Noodles Baked Like a Cake

This dish can be prepared a few hours in advance and refrigerated until baking time.

	To serve 6 to 10	
500	*ziti* or *rigatoni*, cooked and drained	1 lb
40 g	butter, cut into pieces	1½ oz
60 g	Parmesan cheese, grated	2 oz
4 tbsp	breadcrumbs	4 tbsp
1	large egg, lightly beaten	1
250 g	*mozzarella* cheese, coarsely grated	8 oz
125 g	prosciutto, thinly sliced and cut into strips	4 oz
	soured cream (optional)	

Return the pasta to the pot in which it was cooked. Add the butter and half of the Parmesan cheese and toss a few times to coat the pasta well. Set aside.

Butter a round baking dish or a 3 litre (5 pint) soufflé dish. Combine the breadcrumbs and the remaining Parmesan cheese in a measuring cup. Add about a quarter of this mixture to the dish and shake the dish to coat it evenly. Shake the excess crumbs back into the cup. Pour the beaten egg into the dish. Tilt the dish to coat evenly with the egg. Add about a quarter of the breadcrumb and cheese mixture; shake again to coat evenly and pour the excess back into the cup.

Layer about one-third of the pasta into the prepared dish; sprinkle with one-third of the *mozzarella*, half of the prosciutto strips and one-third of the remaining breadcrumb and cheese mixture. Again layer with one-third of the pasta, one-third of the *mozzarella*, half of the prosciutto, and one-third of the breadcrumbs and cheese. Lastly, layer the remaining pasta and *mozzarella*, and top with the remaining breadcrumb and cheese mixture.

Bake in an oven preheated to 180°C (350°F or Mark 4) for 20 to 30 minutes if freshly made, or for 30 to 45 minutes if the dish has been refrigerated. Allow the cake to cool for 10 minutes, then insert a sharp knife around the edges to loosen them slightly. Carefully turn out the cake on to a warmed serving platter. If you wish, you can top the cake with a dollop of soured cream as a garnish. Cut the cake into slices and serve.

KAREN GREEN
THE GREAT INTERNATIONAL NOODLE EXPERIENCE

Timbale of Sweetbreads and Macaroni

Timbale de Macaroni aux Ris de Veau

The technique for making a macaroni timbale is demonstrated on page 68. You can use a food processor instead of the mortar and pestle.

To serve 6 to 8

250 g	long macaroni	8 oz
1 kg	veal sweetbreads, soaked in cold water for 1 hour, blanched for 2 minutes in boiling water, drained, plunged into cold water, tubes, fat and superficial membranes removed	2 lb
6 tbsp	dry white wine	6 tbsp
60 cl	rich gelatinous veal stock (*page 165*)	1 pint
3 or 4	large fresh black truffles	3 or 4
50 g	butter	2 oz
	Mirepoix	
2	medium-sized carrots, finely chopped	2
1	medium-sized onion, finely chopped	1
2 tbsp	butter	2 tbsp
$\frac{1}{2}$	bay leaf, crumbled	$\frac{1}{2}$
$\frac{1}{2}$ tsp	thyme	$\frac{1}{2}$ tsp
	Mousseline forcemeat	
1	large chicken breast, skin and fat removed, scraped free of tendons, and chopped	1
	salt and pepper	
	grated nutmeg	
1	egg white	1
30 cl	double cream, well chilled	$\frac{1}{2}$ pint

Place the sweetbreads side by side on a tea towel in such a way that they form a neat, even-surfaced mass. Place another tea towel over them and a board on top, with approximately a 1 kg (2 lb) weight on the board (a medium-sized tin of preserves does well). Leave the sweatbreads under this weight until well cooled and firm (a couple of hours).

To make the *mirepoix*, melt the butter in a heavy saucepan, add all of the ingredients and cook very gently, stirring regularly for 10 minutes. At the end of this time, the *mirepoix* should be thoroughly cooked but not browned.

Spread the *mirepoix* over the bottom of a heavy earthenware casserole of just the right size to hold the sweetbreads in one layer. Place them side by side on the bed of *mirepoix*. Pour in the white wine and over a high heat (using an heatproof mat for protection), reduce it almost completely, gently shaking the receptacle from time to time to discourage anything sticking to the bottom. Add the stock (enough to cover the sweetbreads generously), bring it to the boiling point, and reduce the heat so that, covered, a near simmer is maintained. Count about 40 minutes of braising time from the time the simmer is reached. Remove the sweetbreads from the sauce, slice them in regular 1 cm ($\frac{1}{2}$ inch) slices, and pass the cooking liquid and the *mirepoix* through a fine sieve. If the sauce remains plentiful and liquid, reduce it over a high heat for a few minutes, stirring constantly. Taste for seasoning; add pepper and salt if necessary. Pour the sauce over the sweetbreads, leave to cool, and stir in the truffles, thickly sliced.

Cook the macaroni in a large pot of boiling salted water and, when nearly cooked but still quite firm, remove the pot from the heat and leave the macaroni to swell for 2 to 3 minutes in the hot water. The strands should remain somewhat firm. Drain them without rinsing and spread the strands of macaroni out, without touching one another, on a tea towel. Generously butter a 2.5 litre (4 pint) dome mould or dome-shaped metal mixing bowl. Beginning with a strand of macaroni which has first been fashioned into a compact, flatly spiralled circle or disc and pressed into the central point at the bottom of the mould, continue twining the strands of macaroni end to end in a close-fitting spiral until the entire mould is lined in this manner. Chill the mould in the refrigerator until the butter is set firmly enough to hold the macaroni in place. Cut the remaining macaroni into short lengths and stir it into the sweetbreads.

To prepare the mousseline forcemeat, pound the chicken breast in a mortar, adding salt, pepper and a small pinch of nutmeg. Gradually add the egg white little by little. Force the mixture a little at a time through a fine nylon drum sieve, removing any debris (nerves or membrane) after each passage. Flatten the surface of the forcemeat, and press a sheet of plastic film over it. Refrigerate until needed. Before using, beat in the cream little by little.

Remove the macaroni mould from the refrigerator. Spread three-quarters of the mixture evenly over the entire surface of the macaroni lining. Fill the mould with the sweetbread, truffle and macaroni mixture, pressing it gently into place so as to leave no air pockets, and spread the remainder of the mousseline over the surface. Press a circle of buttered greaseproof paper over the surface and put the mould to poach in a bain-marie in an oven preheated to 170°C (325°F or Mark 3) for 30 to 40 minutes. (A small trivet such as a metal biscuit-cutter should be used to support the round-bottomed mould in the larger utensil. The mould should be immersed by about three-quarters in nearly boiling water.) If oven space does not permit, the poaching may equally well be done on top of the stove in a large, covered saucepan. The heat should be kept very low to prevent the water returning to a boil. Remove the mould from the bain-marie, lift off the buttered paper and allow the timbale to settle for 7 to 8 minutes before unmoulding it on to a round, preheated serving dish. The bit of liquid that drains on to the serving dish can be sponged up with a paper towel. Cut the timbale into pie-like wedges at table.

RICHARD OLNEY
THE FRENCH MENU COOKBOOK

Moulded Macaroni Pudding

Timbale de Macaroni

To make the mousseline forcemeat called for in this recipe, purée 250 g (8 oz) boned, raw chicken breast with 1 egg white; season with salt, pepper and nutmeg, and incorporate ¼ litre (8 fl oz) double cream. The techniques of preparing a mousseline and lining the mould with macaroni are shown on page 68. To make the velouté sauce, heat 30 g (1 oz) butter, add 2 tablespoons of flour and stir for 2 to 3 minutes; then add 60 cl (1 pint) stock, bring the mixture to the boil over a low heat, stirring constantly. Set the pan half off the heat and simmer for about 40 minutes, skimming off the skin that will form on the side that is off the heat.

To serve 4

200 g	long macaroni	7 oz
500 g	mousseline forcemeat	1 lb
6	large chicken livers, trimmed and halved	6
30 g	butter	1 oz
	salt and pepper	
10 cl	white wine	3½ fl oz
¼ litre	velouté sauce	8 fl oz
2 tbsp	tomato sauce (*page 166*)	2 tbsp
2	slices cured cooked tongue, cut into small rounds	2
100 g	mushrooms, sliced and rapidly sautéed in butter	3½ oz
1	truffle, sliced	1

Cook the macaroni in boiling, salted water until soft but firm to the bite. Drain it without rinsing. Spread the macaroni out on a towel. When the macaroni is cold, take the longest strands and arrange them in a spiral pattern coiling around the base and against the sides of a buttered domed mould. Cover the macaroni with a layer of mousseline forcemeat.

Heat the butter in a pan, add the chicken livers. Season with salt and a little pepper and sauté rapidly. Sprinkle the livers with the white wine. Reduce the liquid by boiling it fast, then moisten the mixture with about 10 cl (3½ fl oz) of the velouté sauce and all of the tomato sauce. Remove from the heat. Add the pieces of tongue, the mushrooms, truffle and the rest of the macaroni, cut into sections. Allow to cool, then use the mixture to fill the interior of the mould. Cover the top of the mould with a layer of forcemeat. Place the mould in a deep pan, on a small trivet, add hot water to the depth of the mould, cover the pan and poach the pudding, covered, over a low heat for 45 minutes. To serve, unmould the pudding on to a serving dish and pour the remaining velouté sauce around the unmoulded pudding.

URBAN DUBOIS
ÉCOLE DES CUISINIÈRES

Grated Noodles with Calf's-Lung Filling

Hortobágyi Reszelt Tészta Tüdővel

This dish is a kind of soufflé, with grated pasta as its starchy base. The technique of preparing and grating the dough is demonstrated on page 45, and the technique of making this type of pasta soufflé is shown on page 74.

This 18th-century recipe seems to have no close parallel in other nations' recipes.

To serve 8

7	eggs	7
About 125 g	flour	About 4 oz
500 g	calf's lung	1 lb
1	small onion, finely chopped	1
30 g	lard	1 oz
	salt and pepper	
1 litre	milk	1¾ pints
1 tbsp	chopped flat-leafed parsley	1 tbsp
12.5 cl	soured cream	4 fl oz

Knead two of the eggs with enough of the flour to make a very, very, hard dough. Grate the dough. Cook the calf's lung in boiling, salted water for 30 minutes. Drain, and put it through a mincer. Sauté the onion in half of the lard for about 10 minutes. Mix the onion with the minced lung. Add a pinch of pepper and salt to taste. Set aside to cool.

Bring the milk to the boil and simmer the grated noodles in it over a low heat, stirring. Cook until the milk is absorbed. Add more milk if necessary. Add a little salt and pepper and mix in the chopped parsley. Cool the noodles to lukewarm.

Mix the cooled noodles with three of the remaining egg yolks, then fold in the stiffly beaten whites of three of the eggs. Grease a heavy 3 litre (5 pint) casserole, 7.5 to 10 cm (3 to 4 inches) deep, with the remaining lard. Pour the noodle and egg mixture into the casserole and pat it down evenly.

Beat the remaining two eggs, and add them to the calf's lung mixture. Make a hole in the middle of the cooked noodle mixture in the casserole and pour in the lung mixture. Spread the entire top with the soured cream. Bake in an oven preheated to 190°C (375°F or Mark 5) for 45 minutes.

GEORGE LANG
THE CUISINE OF HUNGARY

Green Pasta Soufflé

Sformato di Tagliatelle Verdi

The technique of making tagliatelle from fresh pasta dough is shown on page 48. Coloured pasta techniques are on page 50.

To serve 4

3	egg yolks	3
30 cl	white sauce (*page 165*)	½ pint
4	egg whites	4
2 tbsp	freshly grated Parmesan cheese	2 tbsp
125 g	boiled ham, coarsely chopped	4 oz
	salt and freshly ground white pepper	
	freshly grated nutmeg	
	butter	
½ tsp	salt	½ tsp
2.5 litres	water	4½ pints
1 tbsp	vegetable oil	1 tbsp
	Green pasta dough	
250 g	flour, preferably unbleached	8 oz
1	large egg	1
1 tsp	olive oil	1 tsp
125 g	spinach, cooked, drained, squeezed dry and finely chopped	4 oz

Make the pasta by kneading the flour, egg, olive oil and spinach together. Roll out the dough and cut it into *tagliatelle*. Set the pasta aside, covered with a tea towel.

Place a stock-pot containing a large quantity of salted water on the heat. While the water is heating, put the measured water and the vegetable oil together in a large bowl.

When the water reaches boiling point, put in the *tagliatelle* and cook for about 20 seconds or until *al dente*. Drain them, and dip them in the cold water and oil. Wet a tea towel with cold water and spread it out on a pastry board. Lift out the *tagliatelle* very gently and place them on the damp towel.

To make the soufflé, beat the egg yolks in a large bowl. Add the cooled white sauce and grated Parmesan. Mix well, then fold in the ham and seasonings very gently. Let the mixture rest for 15 minutes. Meanwhile, beat the whites until stiff.

Add the *tagliatelle* to the bowl containing the ham mixture, then fold in the egg whites. Toss very gently, taking care not to break the *tagliatelle*. Pour carefully into a soufflé dish well-greased with a little butter, and bake in an oven preheated to 200°C (400°F or Mark 6) for 40 minutes or until the soufflé is risen and golden.

GIULIANO BUGIALLI
THE FINE ART OF ITALIAN COOKING

Timballo of Vermicelli and Fish

Vermicelli is the colloquial name for spaghetti in Naples. The techniques of cooking clams and of cleaning and cooking squid are demonstrated on page 28; mussels may be treated in the same way as clams. The technique of baking a pastry case and lid blind is demonstrated on page 72.

To serve 10 to 12

500 g	spaghetti	1 lb
500 g	white fish fillets	1 lb
90 g	black olives, stoned	3 oz
1 tbsp	capers, washed	1 tbsp
1 tbsp	pine-nuts	1 tbsp
4 tbsp	chopped parsley	4 tbsp
About 30 cl	olive oil	About ½ pint
About 90 g	breadcrumbs	About 3 oz
	Tomato sauce	
750 g	tomatoes, skinned, seeded and puréed	1½ lb
1 tbsp	olive oil	1 tbsp
90 g	shelled young peas	3 oz
90 g	button mushrooms, lightly sautéed	3 oz
500 g	cooked seafood (clams, mussels or squid), cooking juices reserved	1 lb
2 tsp	flour	2 tsp
	Anchovy sauce	
3	salt anchovies, soaked, filleted, rinsed and dried	3
3 tbsp	olive oil	3 tbsp
1	garlic clove, crushed	1
	pepper	
2 tbsp	chopped parsley	2 tbsp
	Pastry dough	
250 g	butter, softened	8 oz
500 g	flour	1 lb
2	eggs, beaten	2
1 tsp	salt	1 tsp

To make the pastry dough, rub the butter with the flour, then gradually add the eggs and salt until the mixture resembles fine breadcrumbs. Form into a ball, wrap in a cloth or plastic film and leave for about an hour in a cool place.

Roll the dough out into two sheets, one larger than the other, about 1 cm (½ inch) thick. Line a very large, round deep pie dish with the larger sheet so that it comes up the sides to form a pastry case, then put a piece of greaseproof paper on the bottom and weight it down with dried peas or beans. Cut the smaller piece of dough into a disc of the same diameter as the pie dish and put it on a greased baking sheet. Bake both in an oven preheated to 180°C (350°F or Mark 4) until firm and golden (about 15 minutes). Remove the paper and dried peas and return the case to the oven for about 5 minutes to dry out. Set aside to cool.

Pound the fish fillets in a mortar with the olives, capers, pine-nuts and parsley to make a firm paste. Soften with 2 tablespoons of the oil and add enough breadcrumbs to bind the mixture. Form little walnut-sized balls, roll them in breadcrumbs and fry in very hot oil until golden-brown.

For the tomato sauce, heat the oil and add the tomatoes and fish balls, then the peas, mushrooms and the cooked seafood and cooking juices. Cook until all the ingredients are tender, then add the flour to thicken the sauce.

To make the anchovy sauce, heat the oil with the crushed garlic until it is brown. Discard the garlic, add the anchovy fillets and cook over a low heat until the anchovies melt into a purée. Add some pepper and the chopped parsley.

Cook the spaghetti, keeping it firm, drain and toss it with the anchovy sauce. Fill the pastry case with a layer of pasta, then fish balls and tomato sauce, ending with pasta. Cover with the pastry lid and bake in an oven preheated to 180°C (350°F or Mark 4) for 45 minutes.

VINCENZO BUONASSISI
THE CLASSIC BOOK OF PASTA

Lasagne Pie with Sole and Crayfish

Torta di Lasagne di Magro con Gamberi

The making of pasta dough is shown on page 44. Cutting the dough is shown on page 48.

This is a modern combination of two 16th-century Italian recipes: Fast-Day Pasta and Crayfish Pie. This version was created by Franco Danielli, head chef of the luxury liner *Raffaello,* in 1973.

To serve 6 to 8

500 g	pasta dough (*page 167*), rolled out and cut into rectangles 5 by 20 cm (2 by 8 inches)	1 lb
12	small sole fillets	12
500 g	live crayfish	1 lb
200 g	butter	7 oz
¼ litre	dry white wine	8 fl oz
	salt and pepper	
25 g	flour	1 oz
100 g	Parmesan cheese, grated	3½ oz
8 cl	brandy	3 fl oz
1 tsp	curry powder	1 tsp

Court-bouillon

½ litre	water	16 fl oz
1	small onion	1
	salt	
5	whole peppercorns	5
2	bay leaves	2
¼ litre	dry white wine	8 fl oz

Boil the court-bouillon ingredients together for 15 minutes. Add the crayfish, and cook, covered, for 7 to 8 minutes or until they are red all over. Peel the crayfish, reserve the tails and put the shells into a food processor or mortar. Add a little broth and grind the shells as finely as possible. Add the rest of the broth, strain through a fine sieve and reserve the mixture.

Cook the fillets of sole in a large frying pan over a medium heat in 50 g (2 oz) of the butter and, when they begin to brown, add the white wine, a pinch of ground pepper and salt to taste. Bring the wine to the boil, simmer for 1 minute and take the frying pan from the heat.

In a saucepan, melt 70 g (2½ oz) of the butter and stir in all but 1 teaspoonful of the flour. Cook for 1 minute, stirring constantly, then whisk in all but 10 cl (3½ fl oz) of the crayfish cooking juices. Bring to the boil. Remove from the heat and stir in the grated cheese. Keep the cheese sauce warm, stirring occasionally to prevent a skin from forming.

Cook the rectangles of dough in boiling water, two or three at a time, until they are *al dente*. Drain them and lay them side by side on a tea towel.

Butter a 25 by 20 cm (10 by 8 inch) square or rectangular ovenproof dish and cover the bottom with a layer of lasagne. Pour on a thin coating of the cheese sauce. Add a layer of sole fillets with a little of their cooking juices. Cover with another bed of lasagne, coat with cheese sauce, more sole and so on, until all the ingredients are used up. The last layer should be of pasta, with cheese sauce poured over. Bake in an oven preheated to 220°C (425°F or Mark 7) for about 10 minutes, but do not allow the pie to brown.

Meanwhile melt the remaining butter. When it begins to brown, add the crayfish tails, sauté them for a few minutes, then add the brandy and flame it. Reduce the heat. Dissolve the curry powder and the teaspoonful of the flour in the remaining crayfish cooking juices and add this to the pan to cook for a few minutes. The sauce should not be too thick.

Serve the pie hot, with the crayfish in their sauce.

MASSIMO ALBERINI
CENTO RICETTE STORICHE

Filled Pasta

Stuffed Wine Pasta with Walnut Sauce

Pansoti con la Salsa di Noci alla Ligure

To serve 4

325 g	flour, sifted	11 oz
6 tbsp	dry white wine	6 tbsp
	salt	
4 tbsp	water	4 tbsp
30 g	Parmesan cheese, grated	1 oz
	Green filling	
350 g	Swiss chard, stalks discarded	12 oz
125 g	borage, stalks discarded	4 oz
1	garlic clove, chopped	1
1	egg	1
125 g	*ricotta* cheese	4 oz
30 g	Parmesan cheese, grated	1 oz
	salt	
	freshly ground pepper	
	Walnut sauce	
150 g	walnuts, shelled and blanched	5 oz
40 g	breadcrumbs, soaked in water and squeezed dry	1½ oz
	salt	
4 tbsp	olive oil	4 tbsp
4 tbsp	soured milk (optional)	4 tbsp

To make the filling, cook the chard and borage in a very little salted water for about 5 minutes, then squeeze dry and put the leaves through a food mill. Add the garlic, egg, *ricotta* and grated Parmesan cheese. Season with salt and pepper, and mix until well blended.

Make the pasta dough by mixing the flour with the wine, a pinch of salt, and the water. Knead until it is smooth and firm. Roll out the dough—not too thin—and cut it into 8 cm (3 inch) triangles. Put a little of the filling in the centre of each triangle, fold the triangle in half and press the edges well together to make the *pansoti*.

Pound the walnuts in a mortar with the breadcrumbs and a little salt to produce a smooth, thick sauce. Stir in the olive oil and the soured milk, if using.

Cook the *pansoti* in plenty of boiling salted water until *al dente*. Drain well and mix the *pansoti* with the walnut sauce, in a heated serving dish. Serve hot with the remainder of the grated Parmesan cheese.

ANNA MARTINI (EDITOR)
PASTA & PIZZA

Ravioli in Broth

Ravioli al Brodo

The techniques of making pasta dough and forming ravioli are shown on pages 44 and 53 respectively. If calf's udder and spinal marrow are unobtainable, increase the quantity of veal to 280 g (9 oz). In this recipe the veal and offal are chopped with a mezzaluna, *a half-moon shaped chopping blade.*

To serve 4

350 g	pasta dough (*page 167*)	12 oz
1 litre	meat stock (*page 165*)	1¾ pints
	Parmesan cheese, grated	
	Filling	
1	Batavian endive, hard or bruised outer leaves removed	1
60 g	borage leaves	2 oz
	salt	
125 g	lean veal	4 oz
	unsalted butter	
125 g	calf's udder	4 oz
125 g	calf's brain, blanched for 5 minutes, membrane removed	4 oz
30 g	spinal marrow, blanched for 5 minutes, membrane removed	1 oz
60 g	sweetbread, blanched for 5 minutes, membrane removed	2 oz
1	egg	1
2	egg yolks	2
30 g	crustless bread, soaked in stock	1 oz
15 g	Parmesan cheese, grated	½ oz
½ tsp	ground mace	½ tsp
½ tsp	ground allspice	½ tsp
	freshly ground black pepper	

Blanch the endive and borage leaves in lightly salted boiling water for 5 minutes; drain, then squeeze the leaves free of excess moisture. Brown the veal very lightly in a little butter. Put the udder into boiling water, bring the water back to the boil and cook for 10 minutes, then drain. Using a *mezzaluna*, chop the veal, udder, brain, marrow, sweetbread, borage and endive as finely as possible. Then pound the mixture in a mortar, a little at a time, until it is reduced to a paste.

Put the paste into a bowl, add the egg and egg yolks, the soaked bread, 15 g (½ oz) of the Parmesan cheese, and the spices. Season to taste. Mix very thoroughly until a smooth paste is obtained. This paste is the filling for the ravioli.

Take a fist-sized lump of pasta dough and roll it out as thinly as possible, flouring the rolling pin and the table to prevent the dough sticking. Cover the remaining dough with a damp tea towel to prevent it drying out. Arrange teaspoonfuls of filling 3 cm (1½ inches) apart in parallel rows on one half of the pasta; fold the other half of the pasta sheet over and press firmly round the edges to seal them together. Press around the fillings of each row to form small cushions. Separate the cushions with a fluted pastry wheel. Repeat, using another lump of pasta dough, and so on until the dough and filling are used up. Place the finished ravioli on a dry cloth, and leave them to dry for at least half an hour before cooking.

Bring the stock to a brisk boil and toss in the ravioli a few at a time, making sure the stock continues to boil. Remove the ravioli with a skimmer as soon as they surface, and put them in a heated soup tureen. When all have been cooked, pour the boiling stock over them and serve with Parmesan cheese.

EMANUELE ROSSI
LA VERA CUCINIERA GENOVESE

Lenten Ravioli

Ravioli di Magro

The basic technique of making ravioli is shown on page 53. Mascarpone is a cream cheese. Any other similar cream cheese can be substituted.

This is an excellent dish, and one which can also be prepared using leftover cooked fish.

To serve 6		
300 g	flour	10 oz
3	eggs	3
	salt	
100 g	butter	3½ oz
2 tsp	dried sage (optional)	2 tsp
6 tbsp	grated Parmesan cheese	6 tbsp

Cheese and fish filling		
100 g	Mascarpone cheese	3½ oz
500 g	white fish such as mullet, bream or hake	1 lb
17.5 cl	white wine	6 fl oz
1	onion, thinly sliced	1
½	lemon, juice strained	½
	salt	
300 g	spinach	10 oz
30 g	butter	1 oz
	pepper	
1	egg	1
2 tbsp	grated Parmesan cheese	2 tbsp

Into a wide oval pan or fish kettle, put the white wine, half of the onion, the lemon juice, just enough water to cover the fish and a pinch of salt. When the liquid begins to boil, put in the fish and simmer, uncovered, for 10 minutes. Remove the pan from the heat and leave the fish to cool in the stock.

Meanwhile, cook the spinach—in the water remaining on the leaves after washing—for about 5 minutes or until soft. Drain it, squeeze it thoroughly and chop it. Put the rest of the onion into a frying pan, add 30 g (1 oz) butter and fry gently over a very low heat, until the onion is transparent but not brown; a few drops of water can be added if needed. Drain the fish, bone and skin it, then flake it. Add the fish to the fried onion, stir, then add the spinach. Season to taste, stir and allow the flavours to mingle, keeping the heat low, for about 10 minutes. Then tip the mixture into a bowl before adding the Mascarpone cheese, 1 egg and 2 tablespoons of Parmesan cheese; mix well and adjust the seasoning if necessary.

To make the ravioli, tip the flour on to a board, making a well in the centre. Break the eggs into the well and work them into the flour. Roll out the dough with a rolling pin, cut and shape the ravioli and stuff them with the fish mixture. Melt the butter in a small frying pan. Add the sage at this stage. Bring a large saucepan of salted water to the boil. Cook the ravioli quickly in the rapidly boiling water until they are soft. Remove them from the saucepan with a slotted spoon. Arrange the ravioli in a deep heatproof dish or bowl, moisten them with a little of the melted butter, and sprinkle with grated Parmesan cheese. Arrange a second layer of ravioli on top, and so on, until all of the ingredients have been used up.

Stand the dish in the pan of hot water in which the ravioli were boiled, but be sure to pour off enough of the water so that the level of the water comes only three-quarters of the way up the dish. Cover the pan and leave the ravioli for 5 minutes to absorb the flavours of the butter and cheese.

FERNANDA GOSETTI
IN CUCINA CON FERNANDA GOSETTI

Ravioli Stuffing

Farce à Raviolis

For a stuffing with a rougher texture, combine the stuffing ingredients with a fork and do not sieve them.

This stuffing can be prepared equally well with leftover cooked veal, chicken or beef daube. You may need to add a tablespoon of gravy if the meats are too dry, for although this stuffing should be firm, it must also be supple.

To serve 4

150 g	lean veal, cut into small cubes	5 oz
100 g	raw ham or green bacon, diced	3½ oz
30 g	butter	1 oz
1	onion, thinly sliced	1
1	bay leaf	1
1	sprig thyme	1
15 to 20 cl	white wine, stock or water	6 fl oz
250 g	spinach, blanched in salted water, drained and finely chopped	8 oz
2	egg yolks	2
	salt and pepper	
½	cooked calf's brain (optional)	½
30 g	*foie gras* (optional)	1 oz

Brown the veal and ham or bacon in the butter; add the onion, bay leaf and thyme; moisten with the white wine, stock or water; cover and simmer for about 1 hour. The meat should be well cooked and the gravy almost completely reduced.

Turn the meat out on to a large plate to cool, discarding the bay leaf and thyme. When cool, add the calf's brain and *foie gras*, if using. Pound the meat mixture with the spinach; add the egg yolks, season, and press through a fine sieve.

J. B. REBOUL
LA CUISINIÈRE PROVENÇALE

Stuffed Pasta with Potatoes and Cheese

Pierogi z Ziemniakami i Serem

The techniques of mixing and rolling pasta dough and of filling rounds of pasta are on pages 44 and 54.

To serve 4

350 g	flour	12 oz
1	egg	1
	water	
	salt	
60 g	butter, melted	2 oz

Potato and cheese stuffing

500 g	potatoes, cooked and mashed	1 lb
125 g	curd cheese, crumbled	4 oz
½	onion, chopped	½
30 g	butter	1 oz
1 tsp	salt	1 tsp
	pepper (optional)	
1	egg (optional)	1

Place the flour on a board, add the egg and a little water and work into a dough with your fingertips. Knead the dough, adding water little by little so that the dough does not become too thin. Its final consistency should be such that it neither falls apart nor sticks to your fingers. Roll the dough out to the thickness of a knife blade and cut out rounds about 5 cm (2 inches) in diameter.

To prepare the stuffing, place the mashed potatoes and crumbled cheese in a mixing bowl. Fry the chopped onion in the butter and add it to the potatoes and cheese. Add salt, and pepper if desired. An egg may also be added at this stage to improve the taste and nutritional value of the stuffing. Mix all of these ingredients well.

Spoon the potato and cheese mixture on to the rounds of dough. Then, holding the *pierogi* lightly between your fingers, so that they remain plump and do not squash, pinch the edges together, moistening them with water to seal them. Bring a pan of salted water to the boil, throw in the *pierogi* and cook for 3 minutes. Drain the *pierogi*. Place the *pierogi* on a serving dish, pour over the melted, slightly browned butter and serve immediately.

MARIA DISSLOWA
JAK GOTOWAĆ

Ravioli with Cheese and Spinach Filling

Raviolis

Brocciu *is a Corsican cheese, made from goat's or ewe's milk. It is creamy when newly made, and becomes a grating cheese when aged. If unobtainable, substitute* ricotta *or curd cheese and a sharp, grating cheese, such as* pecorino *or Parmesan.*

To serve 4 to 6

750 g	pasta dough (*page 167*)	1½ lb
30 cl	tomato sauce (*page 166*)	½ pint
60 g	aged *brocciu*, grated	2 oz

Cheese and spinach filling		
400 g	creamy *brocciu*	14 oz
500 g	spinach, rapidly parboiled, squeezed, and finely chopped	1 lb
300 g	lamb's lettuce, finely chopped	10 oz
1	bulb fennel, parboiled for 10 minutes and finely chopped	1
5 to 10	fresh mint leaves, finely chopped	5 to 10
5 to 10	fresh sage leaves, finely chopped	5 to 10
	salt	

Mash the creamy *brocciu*, mix it thoroughly with the spinach, lettuce and fennel, and season with salt.

Roll out the dough as thinly as possible, and cut it into rectangles about 3 by 4 cm (1¼ by 1½ inches). Place a little of the stuffing mixture on each rectangle, then fold the rectangle over and pinch the edges together securely.

Poach the ravioli in boiling salted water for about 5 minutes. Drain the ravioli, and serve with the tomato sauce and the grated cheese on top.

CHRISTIANE SCHAPIRA
LA CUISINE CORSE

Chinese Ravioli

Won Ton

To serve 4		
300 g	flour, sifted	10 oz
1 tsp	salt	1 tsp
2	eggs, lightly beaten	2
	water	

Pork and shrimp filling		
500 g	cooked pork, finely chopped	1 lb
150 g	bamboo shoots, finely chopped	5 oz
40 g	mushrooms, chopped	1½ oz
125 g	shrimps, cooked and chopped	4 oz
60 g	water chestnuts, finely chopped	2 oz
1 tbsp	peanut oil	1 tbsp
2 tbsp	sesame seeds, browned without fat in a frying pan over a medium heat	2 tbsp
3 tbsp	soy sauce	3 tbsp
	salt	

To make the pasta dough, combine the flour and the salt, add the beaten eggs and just enough water to make a stiff dough. Roll out the dough until it is very thin on a lightly floured board. Cut into 10 cm (4 inch) squares.

Combine all the filling ingredients in a frying pan, and cook over a medium heat until the mixture is dry. Remove from the heat and set aside to cool.

To fill the pasta squares, place 1 teaspoon of the mixture on one corner of each square. Fold the filled portion over two or three times. Pinch together the two opposite free corners of the wrapper, leaving the fourth corner free.

Steam until the dough is cooked—about 30 minutes—or fry in deep hot oil until golden-brown. Drain the ravioli on absorbent paper and serve.

ALICE MILLER MITCHELL (EDITOR)
ORIENTAL COOKBOOK

Tortellini with Cream Sauce

Tortellini alla Panna

The square shapes referred to as tortellini *in this recipe are more commonly known as ravioli; the technique of making them is demonstrated on page 53.*

To serve 6		
500 g	pasta dough (*page 167*)	1 lb
30 g	butter	1 oz
15 g	Parmesan cheese, grated	½ oz
½ litre	double cream	16 fl oz
Curd cheese and spinach stuffing		
250 g	spinach, parboiled, drained and chopped	8 oz
250 g	*ricotta* or fresh curd cheese	8 oz
100 g	Parmesan cheese, grated	3½ oz
2	eggs, beaten	2
	ground allspice	
	salt and freshly ground black pepper	

Mix together the spinach, *ricotta* or curd cheese, 100 g (3½ oz) of the grated Parmesan, the eggs and a pinch of allspice, and season with a little salt and pepper.

On a floured board roll out the pasta dough into one thin sheet. Put small teaspoonfuls of the spinach and cheese mixture in straight lines about 5 cm (2 inches) apart on half of the sheet. Fold the remaining half of the pasta over and press, quite firmly, between the mounds of stuffing. Cut the *tortellini* with a pastry wheel and let them stand for a short while. Cook in boiling, salted water for 5 minutes, or until tender.

Remove the pasta with a perforated spoon and place in a serving dish. Cover the *tortellini* with a cream sauce made by swirling and thickening the butter, the remaining grated Parmesan and the cream over a medium heat. Serve very hot and pass more grated Parmesan and pepper at table.

FRANCO LAGATTOLLA
THE RECIPES THAT MADE A MILLION

Persian Ravioli Soup

Gushe Barreh

The techniques of mixing and rolling pasta dough are demonstrated on page 44.

To serve 5 or 6

150 g	flour	5 oz
$\frac{1}{4}$ tsp	salt	$\frac{1}{4}$ tsp
1.25 litres	water	2 pints
$\frac{1}{4}$ tsp	ground cinnamon	$\frac{1}{4}$ tsp
1 tsp	dried mint	1 tsp
4 to 5 tbsp	chopped parsley	4 to 5 tbsp
About 2 tbsp	vinegar	About 2 tbsp
	yogurt (optional)	

Meat filling

250 g	very lean lamb or beef, minced	8 oz
1	small onion, grated	1
1 tsp	salt	1 tsp
$\frac{1}{4}$ tsp	pepper	$\frac{1}{4}$ tsp
$\frac{1}{4}$ tsp	ground cinnamon	$\frac{1}{4}$ tsp

To make the dough, sift the flour and salt into a bowl. Make a hollow in the centre of the flour. Gradually add about 8 cl (3 fl oz) water and mix well with a fork or your hands. Turn the dough on to a lightly floured board and knead well until it is smooth. Put the dough in the bowl, cover with a tea towel and let the dough rest for 10 minutes.

To make the filling, put the beef or lamb in a bowl, add the grated onion, salt, pepper and cinnamon, and mix well.

Divide the dough into 3 workable parts. On a floured board, roll out one part of the dough into a rough circle about 30 to 35 cm (12 to 14 inches) in diameter. Cut the dough into 4 cm (1$\frac{1}{2}$ inch) squares. Put half a teaspoonful of the meat mixture in the centre of each square and place another square on top (like a sandwich). Pinch the four edges of these ravioli squares together well with your fingers or a fork. Repeat until all of the dough is used up.

Lightly salt the remaining water, bring to the boil and add the ravioli squares. Let them boil until done. Mix the cinnamon with the mint. Add this and the parsley to the pan just before removing it from the heat. Season the soup with vinegar to taste. Some people like to eat this soup with yogurt.

MAIDEH MAZDA
IN A PERSIAN KITCHEN

Vareniki with Cabbage and Mushrooms

Vareniki are filled pasta shapes, generally triangular. The techniques of mixing and rolling pasta dough are demonstrated on page 44.

To serve 6

500 g	flour	1 lb
17.5 cl	cold water	6 fl oz
2	eggs	2
$\frac{1}{2}$ tsp	salt	$\frac{1}{2}$ tsp
	Cabbage and mushroom filling	
900 g	sauerkraut, squeezed dry, or 1 kg (2 to 2$\frac{1}{2}$ lb) fresh cabbage, cored and finely shredded	1$\frac{3}{4}$ lb
90 g	butter	3 oz
100 g	dried mushrooms, soaked until tender and parboiled in lightly salted water, water reserved, mushrooms chopped	3$\frac{1}{2}$ oz
2	onions, finely chopped	2
	salt and freshly ground black pepper	

To make the *vareniki* dough, mix the flour, water, eggs and salt together. The dough must be smooth so that it rolls out easily and the edges stay together to hold in the filling. Roll out the dough very thinly and cut it into 5 cm (2 inch) squares.

To make the filling, add one-third of the butter and the reserved mushroom cooking liquid to the sauerkraut or cabbage and simmer until tender. Meanwhile, sauté the onions and mushrooms in another third of the butter for 4 to 5 minutes. Add them to the sauerkraut or cabbage. Season with salt and pepper to taste and mix well.

Place 1 teaspoon of the filling in the centre of each square of *vareniki* dough. Fold the square into a triangle and firmly press together the edges of each *vareniki*.

To cook, drop the *vareniki* into a large saucepan containing plenty of boiling water, and simmer for 5 or 6 minutes, or until the *vareniki* rise to the surface. Skim off any scum that forms during the cooking. Remove the *vareniki* with a slotted spoon and put them into a colander to drain. Transfer the *vareniki* to a warm bowl or serving dish. Melt the remaining butter and pour it over the *vareniki*. Toss lightly to prevent the *vareniki* from sticking together, and serve.

N. I. GEORGIEVSKY, M. E. MELMAN, E. A. SHADURA, A. S. SHEMJAKINSKY
UKRAINIAN CUISINE

Green Roll

Rotolo Verde

The technique of making a pasta roll is shown on page 64. In this recipe, the mixture is divided in two to make two rolls.

Instead of using *ricotta* cheese in the filling, you can substitute about 150 g (5 oz) of sausage-meat, browned with the spinach. Add a handful of chopped parsley and a minced garlic clove to the meat mixture. The roll is served accompanied by tomato sauce.

To serve 4		
250 g	flour	8 oz
2	eggs	2
1 tbsp	water	1 tbsp
100g	butter	3½oz
5 tbsp	grated Parmesan cheese	5 tbsp
Spinach and ricotta cheese filling		
1 kg	spinach, washed	2 to 2½ lb
40 g	butter	1½ oz
250 g	*ricotta* cheese, sieved	8 oz
3 tbsp	grated Parmesan cheese	3 tbsp
	salt and pepper	

For the filling, cook the spinach in the water remaining on the leaves after washing. Drain the spinach, squeeze it dry, and then chop it. In a frying pan, brown the butter, add the spinach and stir over a low heat for about 5 minutes. Remove the spinach from the heat, add the *ricotta*, the grated Parmesan cheese, salt and pepper. Mix well and leave to cool.

For the dough, sieve the flour on to a board, make a well in the flour, and break in the eggs. Add the water, and knead the flour and eggs for about 10 minutes until the pasta dough is firm. Divide the mixture in half. Put one half in a plastic bag to prevent it drying out, and roll out the other half into a strip about 25 cm wide by 50 cm long (10 by 20 inches), or to fit the length of the dish or fish kettle in which it is to be cooked.

Spread half of the spinach mixture evenly over the rolled pasta, using a spatula. Then, starting from one of the short sides, roll up the pasta, enclosing the spinach filling. Wrap the roll in a piece of muslin. Tie the cloth at both ends and in the middle. Repeat the process with the other piece of pasta.

Fill a deep, oval dish or fish kettle with salted water; when the water boils, add the pasta rolls and cook for 40 minutes to 1 hour. The rolls must remain immersed in the water throughout the cooking. Add more boiling water if necessary.

Melt the butter over a low heat. Take one roll from the water, remove the cloth and slice the roll into 1 cm (½ inch) slices with a sharp knife; put each slice into a casserole. When you have made one layer, sprinkle with a little of the melted butter and grated Parmesan. Add a second layer, and so on, repeating the process until both rolls have been used up.

Stand the casserole in a bain-marie. Make sure no water gets into the dish. Cover and simmer for a few minutes for the pasta to absorb the flavour of the butter and cheese. The dish may be kept warm for up to 30 minutes in this manner.

FERNANDA GOSETTI
IN CUCINA CON FERNANDA GOSETTI

Stuffed Pasta with Fresh Peas and Beans

Tortelle di Piselli e di Faggioli Freschi

Bartolomeo Scappi was a 16th-century chef reputed to have worked for Pope Pius V. His Opera dell'Arte del Cucinare, *published in Venice in 1610, is the best known and most complete book on Italian Renaissance cuisine. It is also notable for its illustrations, including the first known picture of a fork.*

The technique of making pasta dough is shown on page 44; the technique of filling tortellini *is shown on page 54.*

To serve 4		
350 g	pasta dough (*page 167*)	12 oz
2 tbsp	grated Parmesan cheese	2 tbsp
1 tbsp	sugar	1 tbsp
1 tsp	ground cinnamon	1 tsp
Pea and bean filling		
250 g	fresh peas, shelled	8 oz
250 g	fresh green beans, shelled	8 oz
1.75 litres	meat stock (*page 165*)	3 pints
6	spring onions, chopped	6
30 g	butter	1 oz
2	egg yolks	2
½ tsp	ground cinnamon	½ tsp
¼ tsp	ground cloves	¼ tsp
½ tsp	grated nutmeg	½ tsp
1 tbsp	sugar	1 tbsp
	pepper	
30 g	Parmesan cheese, grated	1 oz
60 g	fresh *ricotta* or *provatura* cheese	2 oz

Boil the peas and beans in the meat stock for 15 minutes. Reserve the stock. Grind the peas and beans in a mortar and pass them through a sieve. Lightly fry the spring onions in a little butter, then mix them into the sieved peas and beans. Add the egg yolks, cinnamon, cloves, nutmeg and sugar. Season with a little pepper, then add the cheeses and mix well. Use this mixture to fill the *tortellini*. Cook them in the reserved stock for 5 minutes and serve them sprinkled with the Parmesan cheese, sugar and cinnamon.

BARTOLOMEO SCAPPI
OPERA DELL'ARTE DEL CUCINARE

Dumplings

Pumpkin Gnocchi

Gnocchi di Zucca alla Versiliese

This is a traditional recipe from the Versilia district of Tuscany, Italy, and is still used by families in and around the main town, Pietrasanta.

The gnocchi may be served with a good meat sauce, but taste better with butter and Parmesan cheese, as here.

To serve 6 to 8

350 g	pumpkin, cut into cubes about the size of a walnut	12 oz
4 tbsp	water	4 tbsp
	salt	
2	eggs	2
500 g	flour	1 lb
60 g	butter	2 oz
45 g	Parmesan cheese, grated	1½ oz

Put the cubed pumpkin into a deep saucepan, add the water and season with a pinch of salt. Cook slowly, stirring from time to time, for about 20 minutes or until the pumpkin cubes have disintegrated. Pass the pumpkin through a sieve. Allow the purée to cool, then add the eggs and flour and mix well, until a fairly thick paste is obtained which does not slide off the spoon. Throw small spoonfuls of the mixture into salted boiling water and cook until they rise to the surface. Remove from the water with a skimmer and serve the *gnocchi* tossed in butter and Parmesan cheese.

MARIÙ SALVATORI DE ZULIANI
LA CUCINA DI VERSILIA E GARFAGNANA

Boiled Beef with Hodgils

Hodgil is an old word for "border", given to these oatmeal dumplings, no doubt because they are served as "trimmings" for the boiled beef.

To serve 6

1.5 to 2 kg	salt beef, soaked overnight	3 to 4 lb
1	bay leaf	1
750 g	carrots, peeled and quartered	1½ lb
500 g	onions, chopped	1 lb
350 g	parsnips or swede, peeled and cut into chunks	12 oz

Hodgils

250 g	oatmeal	8 oz
1 tbsp	finely cut chives	1 tbsp
	salt and pepper	

Weigh the beef before putting it into a large pan with the bay leaf. Cover the meat with cold water and slowly bring it to the boil. Cover the pan, lower the heat and simmer. Calculate the cooking time at 25 minutes to the pound of meat plus 25 minutes. Add the vegetables 1½ hours before the beef is ready.

To make the hodgils, mix the oatmeal with the chives and plenty of seasoning. Skim fat from the top of the beef cooking liquid to bind the oatmeal mixture together, then roll it into balls, making about 10 in all. Leave the hodgils to stand for 20 minutes, then cook them with the meat for 15 minutes.

Serve the meat with the vegetables and hodgils. Use the cooking liquid as gravy, adjusting the seasoning if necessary.

JANET WARREN
A FEAST OF SCOTLAND

Cheese and Spinach Dumplings

Les Caillettes

Brousse *is fresh, unsalted sheep's milk cheese—the Provençal equivalent of* ricotta, *which may be substituted. The dumplings may be flattened into patty shapes and browned in oil.*

To serve 6

500 g	*brousse* cheese	1 lb
500 g	spinach, stems removed, washed, dried and chopped	1 lb
1 tbsp	finely chopped parsley	1 tbsp
1	garlic clove, finely chopped	1
30 g	butter	1 oz
250 g	flour	8 oz
	salt	
3	eggs	3

Sauté the chopped spinach in the butter until it is soft and the liquid has evaporated. Leave to cool.

Mix together the cheese, half of the flour, the spinach, parsley, garlic and a pinch of salt. Add the eggs and work the mixture well, adding more flour gradually until you have a firm but malleable dough. Divide the mixture into 12 to 15 pieces; form each piece into a thick, short sausage shape.

Roll the dumplings lightly in the remaining flour and toss them into a pan of boiling water. Cover and simmer the dumplings for 15 minutes, then drain and serve them.

C. CHANOT-BULLIER
VIEILLES RECETTES DE CUISINE PROVENÇALE

Vegetable Dumplings

Gnocchi à la Niçarde

To serve 6 to 8

200 g	spinach, stems removed, finely chopped	7 oz
200 g	chard, stems removed, finely chopped	7 oz
200 g	lettuce, finely chopped	7 oz
	salt	
1 kg	flour	2 to 2½ lb
1 tbsp	olive oil	1 tbsp
2	eggs	2
50 g	Parmesan cheese, grated	2 oz
30 g	butter, melted	1 oz

Salt the spinach, chard and lettuce and leave to stand for 30 minutes. Squeeze out any excess water.

Mix thoroughly together the flour, a pinch of salt, the olive oil, the eggs, the squeezed greens and two-thirds of the Parmesan, adding a little water if necessary to form a malleable dough. Leave to stand for 30 minutes.

Keeping your hands floured, form the dough into small dumplings, rolling them between your palms. Poach the dumplings for about 20 minutes in a covered pan containing a large quantity of boiling salted water.

Drain the dumplings, place them on a hot serving dish and sprinkle over the foaming butter and remaining Parmesan cheese. Alternatively, serve the dumplings in the juice from a Provençal beef daube and sprinkle the cheese over them.

C. CHANOT-BULLIER
VIEILLES RECETTES DE CUISINE PROVENÇALE

Lithuanian Meat Dumplings

Kołduny Litewskie

If fresh kidney fat is not available, use suet. The technique of stuffing pasta rounds is shown on page 54.

The *kołduny*, or small meat dumplings, should be made small enough to be put into the mouth whole, as the juice runs out of them if they are cut. The best meat to use is fillet of beef, which should be juicy and soft.

To serve 4

250 g	flour	8 oz
2	eggs	2
4 tbsp	water	4 tbsp
	salt	
1 litre	meat stock (*page 166*)	1¾ pints

Stuffing

250 g	raw meat, finely chopped	8 oz
250 g	ox kidney fat, trimmed and chopped	8 oz
	salt and pepper	
	marjoram	
1	onion, grated	1

Place the flour on a board, add the eggs and a little water and work into a dough with your fingertips. Continue to knead the dough, adding the remaining water little by little. Roll it out thinly and cut out rounds 5 cm (2 inches) in diameter.

To prepare the stuffing, put the meat and fat into a bowl and mix thoroughly. Add salt, pepper and marjoram to taste. Scald the grated onion in a little of the stock, lift it out with a perforated skimmer and add to the meat.

Top each dough circle with meat mixture, fold it over, moisten the edges and stick them together. Bring the stock to the boil again, put in the dumplings and boil them and then serve straight from the pan at the table. There is no need to add butter or sauce as the *kołduny* are sufficiently moist.

MARIA DISSLOWA
JAK GOTOWAĆ

Cornmeal Dumplings

To serve 6

40 g	cornmeal	1½ oz
90 g	flour	3 oz
1½ tsp	baking powder	1½ tsp
½ tsp	salt	½ tsp
5 tbsp	milk	5 tbsp
1	egg	1
2 tbsp	bacon dripping or 30 g (1 oz) butter, just melted	2 tbsp

Mix the cornmeal, flour, baking powder and salt in a bowl. Beat in the milk, egg and bacon dripping or butter. Drop the dumplings by tablespoonfuls on to boiling greens or meat. There should be a generous amount of liquid and enough vegetables or meat to prevent the dumplings from sinking to the bottom of the saucepan. Cover tightly and poach at a simmer for 15 minutes. Serve the dumplings with greens or meat and some of the pan liquid.

JEANNE A. VOLTZ
THE FLAVOR OF THE SOUTH

Dumpling with Salt Pork
La Mique

This filling peasant dish is typical of the Sarladais district of Perigord in south-western France.

To serve 6

750 g	salt pork, cut into 6 portions and soaked for 12 hours in several changes of water	1½ lb
250 g	stale bread, with crusts, cubed	8 oz
100 g	fresh pork fat, diced	3½ oz
About 8 cl	warm milk, meat stock (*page 165*) or water	About 3 fl oz
	salt and pepper	
1 tsp	baking powder	1 tsp
3	eggs	3
1 tbsp	rendered pork or goose fat, or oil	1 tbsp
150 g	flour	5 oz
125 g	cabbage, coarsely chopped	4 oz
1	onion, quartered	1
1	white turnip, peeled and coarsely chopped	1
1	leek, coarsely chopped	1
125 g	Swiss chard, ribs discarded, coarsely chopped	4 oz
2	celery sticks, coarsely chopped	2
1 tsp	ground cloves	1 tsp

Fill a bowl with the cubes of bread, and add the diced pork fat. Moisten with enough of the warm milk, stock or water to dampen the bread without softening it. Season, and mix in the baking powder. Beat the eggs lightly as for an omelette, and stir in the goose or pork fat, or oil. Mix the egg mixture with the bread and pork fat. Sprinkle the flour over this, and bind into a firm but pliable mass. This should be done by holding the bowl in both hands and tossing the contents slowly and lightly. Do not touch the mixture with hands or spoon. When the mixture comes away from the sides of the dish in a mass, form it into an elongated dumpling the shape of a rugby ball. Dust it with flour and cover it with a tea towel.

Cook the salt pork and vegetables for 1½ hours, in plenty of water. Half way through the cooking time, add the dumpling. Turn it over with a skimming ladle after about 20 minutes. When cooked, it should have doubled in volume. To serve, slice the dumpling in half crosswise and put it on a serving dish surrounded by the vegetables and topped with the pork.

ZETTE GUINAUDEAU-FRANC
LES SECRETS DES FERMES EN PÉRIGORD NOIR

Potato Dumplings
Strapachka

To serve 4

600 g	potatoes, peeled and grated	1¼ lb
300 g	wholemeal flour	10 oz
1	egg	1
	salt	
90 g	lard	3 oz
100 g	streaky bacon, diced	3½ oz
150 g	curd cheese	5 oz

Make a dough of the potatoes, flour, egg, ½ teaspoon salt and the lard. Knead well, then form the dough into dumplings the size of eggs. Cook the dumplings in a large pan of boiling, salted water for about 20 minutes or until they are fluffy-textured and cooked through. Drain them in a colander and keep them warm while you cook the bacon.

Fry the bacon until crisp. Remove the bacon cracklings from the pan, add the dumplings to the fat and mix well until coated with bacon fat. Serve the dumplings with the cracklings and the cheese on top.

JOZSEF VENESZ
HUNGARIAN CUISINE

Cabbage Dumplings

To serve 4

4	bread rolls	4
500 g	cabbage, core removed, shredded	1 lb
325 g	butter	11 oz
60 cl	milk	1 pint
2	eggs	2
4	egg yolks	4
100 g	flour	3½ oz
1 tsp	salt	1 tsp
60 g	lard	2 oz
100 g	Gruyère cheese, grated	3½ oz

Dice two of the rolls and fry them in 60 g (2 oz) of the butter until they are golden-brown. Crumble the other two rolls and soak them in the milk.

Cream 200 g (7 oz) of the butter and mix it with the whole eggs and the egg yolks, the flour and the salt. Stew the cabbage gently in the lard for about 10 minutes or until it loses its crispness, then combine it with the egg mixture. Remove the rolls from the milk, sieve them, then add them to the cabbage mixture with the fried, diced bread rolls. Mix well and form the mixture into dumplings about the size of eggs. Cook the dumplings in a pan of boiling water for about 15 minutes, or until they are cooked through but still firm.

Melt the remaining butter, strain the dumplings and serve them with the melted butter over them and the cheese on top.

JOZSEF VENESZ
HUNGARIAN CUISINE

Cottage Cheese Dumplings

If the cottage cheese is rather dry, use a little less semolina.

	To serve 4 to 6	
750 g	cottage cheese, sieved	1½ lb
4	eggs	4
150 g	semolina	5 oz
	salt	
60 g	lard	2 oz
140 g	fresh white breadcrumbs	4½ oz
20 cl	soured cream	7 fl oz

Mix the cottage cheese with the eggs, the semolina and a little salt. Let the mixture stand for about 1 hour for the semolina to become soft. Then, with wet hands, shape the mixture into about 20 dumplings, each about the size of an egg. Cook the dumplings in boiling, salted water for about 15 minutes or until they are firm and cooked through.

Meanwhile, melt the lard and fry the breadcrumbs in it until they are crisp and golden. Roll the dumplings in the crumbs and serve with soured cream.

JOZSEF VENESZ
HUNGARIAN CUISINE

Potato Dumplings with Cheese

Zemiakové Halušky s Bryndzou

Bryndze *is soft sheep cheese, similar to* feta *and drier and sharper than* ricotta. *It may be replaced by 300 g (10 oz) of cream cheese or 20 cl (7 fl oz) of soured cream. Butter may be used instead of smoked bacon.*

	To serve 6 to 8	
1 kg	new potatoes, grated	2 to 2½ lb
	salt	
300 g	flour	10 oz
100 g	smoked bacon, chopped into small pieces	3½ oz
250 g	bryndze, crumbled	8 oz
	chives or dill, finely chopped	

Place the grated potato in a large mixing bowl, add salt and the flour and mix well. The dough, when ready, should not stick to the sides of the bowl. Place the dough on a wooden board, cut into small pieces and throw these small dumplings into a pan of boiling water. When they rise to the surface, take them out with a slotted spoon and place them on a serving dish. Meanwhile fry the bacon. Sprinkle the dumplings with the crumbled cheese (or dot them with the cream cheese or spoon over the soured cream) and the chives or dill. Pour over the pieces of bacon with their fat and serve immediately.

VOJTECH SPANKO (EDITOR)
SLOVENSKÁ KUCHÁRKA

Leek Dumplings

Nioques aux Poireaux

	To serve 4 to 6	
500 g	leeks, cleaned and cut into 2 to 3 mm (⅛ inch) thick slices	1 lb
3 litres	water	5 pints
	salt	
250 g	potatoes	8 oz
3	eggs	3
	pepper	
100 g	flour	3½ oz
250 g	Gruyère cheese, grated	8 oz
50 g	butter, melted or 4 tbsp double cream	2 oz

Bring the water to the boil in a large saucepan. Salt the water lightly, add the leeks and cook them for 15 minutes. With a slotted spoon, remove the leeks; reserve the cooking liquid. Place the leeks in a cloth and twist it to squeeze out excess liquid, then chop the leeks finely. Place the leeks in a bowl.

Cook the potatoes in the leeks' cooking liquid for 20 to 25 minutes. Drain the potatoes, reserving the liquid again, and purée them through a sieve. Mix the purée with the leeks, and stir in the eggs, one by one. Taste for salt, and season with pepper. Add the flour, a spoonful at a time, kneading the mixture until it forms a firm, elastic dough.

On a floured pastry board, shape the mixture into long rolls the thickness of your little finger. Cut the rolls into 3 cm (1¼ inch) lengths. Roll each piece between your hands until it is pointed at both ends. Bring the reserved cooking liquid to the boil and plunge the dumplings into it. Adjust the heat to maintain a light boil. The dumplings will float to the surface when they are ready. Remove the dumplings with a slotted spoon and drain them on a cloth.

Arrange them in a buttered ovenproof dish, sprinkling each layer of dumplings with a handful of grated Gruyère cheese. Pour over the top a little melted butter or double cream, according to taste. Bake on the top shelf of an oven preheated to 240°C (475°F or Mark 9) for 15 minutes, or until golden-brown. Serve hot.

PIERRE ANDROUET
LA CUISINE AU FROMAGE

Whole Pulses

Haricot Beans

Weisse Bohnen

Some beans need pre-cooking to destroy toxins: see page 78.

In Westphalia, Germany, it is customary to mix the haricot beans with apples or pears, which are cooked separately in a little water and butter.

To serve 6 to 8

500 g	dried haricot beans, soaked overnight and drained	1 lb
1 litre	water	1¾ pints
2	bay leaves	2
1	bunch soup vegetables (carrot, leek, celery and parsley, tied together)	1
125 g	smoked streaky bacon, diced	4 oz
2	onions, finely chopped	2
1	garlic clove, chopped	1
	salt and pepper	
	marjoram or thyme	
1 tbsp	wine or cider vinegar (optional)	1 tbsp

Put the beans in a pan, add the cold water, bay leaves and soup vegetables and simmer for about 1 to 1¼ hours or until the beans are soft. In a second pan, fry the diced bacon; add the chopped onion and garlic and fry until golden. Remove the soup vegetables and bay leaves from the beans. Add the beans and their cooking liquid to the bacon mixture. Season with salt, pepper, marjoram and the vinegar, if desired. Simmer for a few minutes. If you prefer the beans puréed, pass them through a sieve before adding them to the bacon mixture.

GRETE WILLINSKY
KOCHBUCH DER BÜCHERGILDE

Haricot Beans in Sauce

Haricots Blancs en Sauce

Some beans need pre-cooking to destroy toxins: see page 78.

To serve 10

600 g	dried haricot beans, soaked overnight and drained	1¼ lb
5	onions, 2 chopped and 3 thinly sliced	5
¼ tsp	powdered saffron	¼ tsp
200 g	butter	7 oz
1 tsp	pepper	1 tsp
	salt	
6 tbsp	chopped parsley	6 tbsp

Put the beans in a casserole with the chopped onions, a pinch of saffron dissolved in 2 tablespoons of water, and the butter. Cover with water, bring to the boil and simmer, covered, for about 2 hours until the beans are almost tender. Add the sliced onions, the pepper, salt to taste, and the parsley. As soon as the onions are soft, remove the casserole from the heat. If the sauce is too thick, add a little more water. Serve very hot in a deep serving dish.

AHMED LAASRI
240 RECETTES DE CUISINE MAROCAINE

Spiced Haricot Beans

La Loubia

Some beans need boiling to destroy toxins: see page 78.

To serve 6

1 kg	dried haricot beans, soaked in water overnight and drained	2 to 2½ lb
4	garlic cloves	4
	ground cumin	
1 tsp	paprika	1 tsp
2	cloves	2
	salt	
1	small red chili pepper	1
1 tbsp	olive oil	1 tbsp

Simmer the beans in unsalted water for 1½ hours. Pound the garlic, a good pinch of cumin, the paprika, cloves, a little salt and the chili pepper in a mortar; add the olive oil and mix with the beans. Cook the beans and their sauce for a further 20 minutes or until the beans are tender.

LÉON ISNARD
LA CUISINE FRANÇAISE ET AFRICAINE

White Beans

Bohnenkerne

	To serve 4	
500 g	dried haricot beans, soaked overnight and drained	1 lb
1	bay leaf	1
	salt	
50 g	butter	2 oz
50 g	smoked streaky bacon, diced	2 oz
1	onion, sliced	1
500 g	tomatoes, sliced	1 lb
50 g	Gruyère cheese, grated	2 oz

Put the beans and the bay leaf in a saucepan with water to cover. Simmer, covered, for 2 hours or until the beans are tender. Salt the beans to taste towards the end of cooking.

Melt half of the butter and in it fry the bacon and onion until lightly browned.

Fill a greased fireproof dish with alternate layers of the beans, tomatoes, and bacon and onions. Dot with the remaining butter, sprinkle with grated cheese, and bake in an oven preheated to 180°C (350°F or Mark 4) for 1 hour or until the surface is crisp and browned.

ELIZABETH SCHULER
MEIN KOCHBUCH

Meat Casserole with Haricot Beans

Mon Favori

	To serve 4	
250 g	dried haricot beans, soaked overnight, drained and cooked for 30 minutes in boiling water	8 oz
300 g	lean pork, cut into pieces	10 oz
300 g	veal, cut into pieces	10 oz
250 g	turkey or chicken gizzards, hearts, necks and wing tips	8 oz
4	small smoked cooking sausages	4
30 g	butter	1 oz
2	tomatoes, puréed through a sieve	2
	salt	

Heat the butter in a heavy pot. Add the pork and sauté lightly, then add the veal, giblets and sausages, and sauté until all the meat is golden. Add the partially cooked haricot beans,

together with their cooking liquid: there should be enough liquid to cover all of the ingredients. Finally add the puréed tomato. Cover and simmer over a low heat for 3 hours. Add salt to taste before serving.

EDOUARD NIGNON (EDITOR)
LE LIVRE DE CUISINE DE L'OUEST-ÉCLAIR

Haricot Beans in Spiced Pumpkin Sauce

In this recipe, the beans are cooked in very little water because more liquid is obtained from the pumpkin and, towards the end of cooking, from the juices of the tomatoes. The beans may be served with whole wheat pasta.

	To serve 4	
250 g	haricot beans, soaked overnight and drained	8 oz
1 kg	pumpkin, peeled, seeded and chopped	2 to 2½ lb
1	large onion, finely chopped	1
1	garlic clove, finely chopped	1
1 tbsp	chopped savory	1 tbsp
2 tbsp	tomato purée	2 tbsp
250 g	tomatoes, scalded, skinned and halved	8 oz

Put the beans in 60 cl (1 pint) water, and boil for 15 minutes. Mix in the chopped pumpkin, onion, garlic, savory and tomato purée. Cover and simmer gently for 1½ hours.

Squeeze the tomato seeds into a sieve placed over a bowl and rub them with a wooden spoon to extract the juices. Add the juices to the beans and cook for a further 30 minutes, still covered. Slice the tomato shells and add them to the pan just before serving, so they heat through but stay firm.

GAIL DUFF
GAIL DUFF'S VEGETARIAN COOKBOOK

Egyptian Brown Beans

Ful Medames

The hamine eggs mentioned in this recipe are eggs hard-boiled very slowly with onion skins. Use the skins of several onions and simmer on the gentlest possible heat for at least 6 hours. Pour a thin layer of oil over the water to stop it evaporating too quickly during cooking. Dried field beans have tough, bitter skins and should be peeled after soaking or cooking.

Ful Medames is pre-Ottoman and pre-Islamic, claimed by the Copts and probably as old as the Pharaohs. According to an old Arab saying: "Beans have satisfied even the Pharaohs".

To serve 6

1 kg	dried field beans, soaked overnight and drained	2 to 2½ lb
2 to 4	garlic cloves, crushed (optional)	2 to 4
6	*hamine* eggs or hard-boiled eggs	6
8 tbsp	chopped parsley	8 tbsp
	olive oil	
3	lemons, quartered	3
	salt and freshly ground black pepper	

Boil the beans in a fresh portion of unsalted water in a large saucepan until tender, about 2 hours. Care must be taken not to overcook the beans. When the beans are soft, drain them, season with salt and add crushed garlic to taste, or pass some of the garlic round with the other garnishes for people to take as much as they want.

Serve the beans in soup bowls. Put an egg in each bowl on top of the beans, and sprinkle with chopped parsley. Pass round olive oil, quartered lemons, salt and black pepper for each person to add to the beans as they wish. Most people like to break the egg up with a fork and crush the pieces together with the beans to allow the seasonings to penetrate.

CLAUDIA RODEN
A BOOK OF MIDDLE EASTERN FOOD

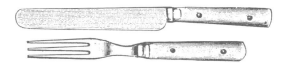

Haricot Beans with Pork Rinds

Haricots aux Couennes

Some dried beans need pre-cooking to destroy toxins: see page 78. Fresh haricot beans can be used in this recipe instead of dried. If using fresh beans, there is no need to soak the beans overnight. They should be put into boiling, unsalted water and cooked for 1 to 2 hours or until tender.

This peasant dish comes from Perigord in south-western France. The dish can be dressed with a tablespoonful of groundnut oil and a few drops of wine vinegar, or served with a salad of dandelion leaves or endives seasoned with groundnut oil, wine vinegar, slices of onion, salt and pepper.

To serve 4

250 g	dried haricot beans, soaked overnight and drained	8 oz
125 g	fresh pork rinds	4 oz
2	onions, chopped	2
2	carrots, chopped	2
1	garlic clove, chopped	1
2 tbsp	chopped parsley	2 tbsp
30 g	fresh pork fat	1 oz
	salt and pepper	
2	tomatoes, skinned, seeded and chopped	2

Put the beans and pork rinds into fresh, cold water to cover and bring to the boil. Add the onions and carrots, cover, and simmer for about 2 hours or until the beans and rinds are tender. Half an hour before the end of the cooking time, add the garlic, parsley, pork fat and seasoning to taste. Add the tomatoes just before serving.

ZETTE GUINAUDEAU-FRANC
LES SECRETS DES FERMES EN PÉRIGORD NOIR

T-Dart Pinto Beans

This recipe comes from the T-Dart Ranch in Arizona. Some beans need pre-cooking to destroy toxins: see page 78.

To serve 8

1 kg	pinto beans, soaked for 12 hours and drained	2 to 2½ lb
1 kg	minced beef	2 to 2½ lb
200 g	onion, chopped	7 oz
1	garlic clove, crushed	1
2 tsp	salt	2 tsp
	oregano	
1	dried red chili pepper, finely crushed	1
50 g	bacon fat	2 oz

Add fresh cold water to cover the beans and bring to the boil. Reduce the heat, bringing the beans to a slow simmer. Mix the meat with the onion, garlic, 1 teaspoon of the salt, a pinch of oregano and the chili pepper. Melt the bacon fat in a frying pan. Add the meat mixture and fry until golden-brown. Add to the pan containing the beans and simmer, partially covered, for 4 hours. Add more salt to taste.

CLEMENTINE PADDLEFORD
THE BEST IN AMERICAN COOKING

Chile con Carne

Some beans need pre-cooking to destroy toxins: see page 78.
The chili powder used here is American (see recipe, right).

	To serve 8	
500 g	dried beans (red kidney, pinto or similar) soaked overnight and drained	1 lb
1 kg	lean stewing beef, cut into cubes	2 lb
2	bay leaves	2
2	large onions, sliced	2
1	garlic clove, minced	1
2 tbsp	oil	2 tbsp
5	tomatoes, skinned and puréed	5
2 tsp	salt	2 tsp
1 tbsp	cornflour or 2 tbsp fine cornmeal	1 tbsp
1½ tsp	black pepper	1½ tsp
¼ tsp each	dried oregano and sage, and powdered cumin	¼ tsp each
1 tbsp	chili powder	1 tbsp

Put the beans and meat in enough water to cover and bring them to the boil. Add the bay leaves, onion and garlic.

When the beans are tender (in about 2 hours), heat a frying pan then add the oil. Stir in the tomato purée, salt, cornflour or cornmeal, herbs and seasonings. Mix them thoroughly and simmer for 5 minutes. Add the mixture to the beans, and simmer for 1 more hour.

GEORGE C. BOOTH
THE FOOD AND DRINK OF MEXICO

Red Kidney Beans

Haricots Rouges

	To serve 6	
750 g	red kidney beans, soaked in water overnight and drained	1½ lb
	salt and pepper	
200 g	streaky bacon, rind removed, cut into 2.5 by 1 cm (1 by ½ inch) pieces	7 oz
1 tbsp	oil or butter	1 tbsp
15 g	flour	½ oz
30 cl	red wine	½ pint
20 cl	water	7 fl oz
30 g	butter, cut into small pieces	1 oz

Put the beans in a pan with water and boil for 10 minutes, then simmer, covered, for 2 hours or until tender. Salt to taste.

Meanwhile, blanch the bacon for 5 minutes. Drain the bacon, place it in a heavy 2 litre (3½ to 4 pint) saucepan with the oil and sauté gently until lightly coloured on all sides. Add the flour and stir with a wooden spoon for 3 minutes over a medium heat. Add the wine, water, salt and pepper and simmer for 25 minutes. Drain the beans and add them to the saucepan. Add the butter, and shake the pan until the butter has melted. Serve at once.

JULES GOUFFÉ
LE LIVRE DE CUISINE

Cowpoke Beans

American chili powder, as called for in this recipe, is a blend of
hot and sweet peppers and is much milder than the chili
powder available here. If American chili powder is not avail-
able, use a mixture of half cayenne pepper and half paprika.

	To serve 6 to 8	
500 g	dried pinto or red kidney beans, soaked overnight and drained	1 lb
	ham bone	
1	red chili pepper (optional)	1
2 tsp	salt	2 tsp
125 g	suet, chopped	4 oz
1	large onion, chopped	1
1	garlic clove, chopped	1
4	ripe tomatoes, skinned, seeded and chopped	4
6 tbsp	chopped parsley	6 tbsp
½ tsp	ground cumin	½ tsp
½ tsp	dried marjoram	½ tsp
1½ tbsp	chili powder	1½ tbsp

Put the beans in a saucepan and cover with cold water. Add the ham bone, the red chili pepper and 1 teaspoon of salt. Bring to the boil, after 10 minutes reduce the heat, cover and simmer gently for 2 to 3 hours, or until the beans are tender. Drain the beans and reserve the cooking liquid.

Heat the suet in a large skillet, stir in the onion and the garlic and cook for 5 minutes or until the onion takes on a little colour. Add the tomatoes, parsley, ¼ litre (8 fl oz) of the bean liquid, salt to taste and all the remaining ingredients. Cook over a low heat, stirring frequently, for 45 minutes. Add the beans, cover and simmer for 20 minutes.

THE EDITORS OF AMERICAN HERITAGE
THE AMERICAN HERITAGE COOKBOOK

Savoury Beans

Frijoles a la Charra

Some beans need pre-cooking to destroy toxins: see page 78.

The Mexican title of this dish means, literally, beans cooked in the way a lady *charro* would prepare them (the *charros* are the elegant horsemen of Mexico). The green chilies and coriander give the beans a unique and interesting flavour.

To serve 6

250 g	dried pink or pinto beans, soaked in water overnight and drained	8 oz
125 g	fresh pork rind, cut into small squares	4 oz
$\frac{1}{4}$	onion, sliced	$\frac{1}{4}$
2	small garlic cloves, peeled and sliced	2
1.5 litres	water	$2\frac{1}{2}$ pints
$1\frac{1}{4}$ tsp	salt	$1\frac{1}{4}$ tsp
125 g	streaky bacon, cut into small pieces	4 oz
30 g	lard or pork dripping	1 oz
350 g	tomatoes, skinned, seeded and chopped, juice strained and reserved, or canned tomatoes	12 oz
3	*chiles serranos*, finely chopped	3
2	large whole sprigs fresh coriander	2

Put the pork rind squares together with the beans, onion and garlic into a bean pot or large saucepan. Add the water and bring to the boil. Reduce the heat, cover the pot, and let the beans cook gently until they are tender—about $1\frac{1}{2}$ hours. Add the salt and cook them, uncovered, for another 15 minutes.

Cook the bacon gently in the lard or pork dripping until it is slightly browned. Add the tomatoes with their juice and the rest of the ingredients. Cook the mixture over a fairly high heat for about 10 minutes, until it is well seasoned.

Add the tomato mixture to the beans and let them cook together, uncovered, over a low heat for about 15 minutes.

Serve in small individual bowls with grilled meat, such as beef or veal, or add some more liquid and serve as a soup.

DIANA KENNEDY
CUISINES OF MEXICO

Curried Red Lentils

Masūr Dāl

To serve 4

200 g	red lentils, washed, soaked for 1 hour and drained	7 oz
1 tsp	salt	1 tsp
2 tbsp	*ghee* or clarified butter	2 tbsp
2	onions, chopped	2

Masala paste

1 tsp	cumin seeds	1 tsp
1 tsp	poppy seeds	1 tsp
1 tsp	paprika or chili powder	1 tsp
1 tsp	ground turmeric	1 tsp
2 tsp	coriander seeds	2 tsp
6	cloves	6
5 cm	stick cinnamon	2 inch
4	green cardamom pods	4
90 g	coconut, grated	3 oz
4	black peppercorns	4
4	garlic cloves	4

Cover the lentils with fresh water, add the salt, and bring to the boil. Cook over a medium heat for 30 minutes or until the lentils are soft and have absorbed all of the water. Meanwhile, grind all the ingredients for the *masala* paste. Heat the *ghee* or clarified butter and fry the onions until golden. Add the *masala* paste and fry for a few minutes. Stir this mixture into the lentils just before they are ready. Serve hot with rice.

JACK SANTA MARIA
INDIAN VEGETARIAN COOKERY

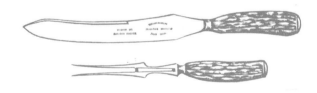

Sautéed Lentils

Lentejas Salteadas

To serve 4

350 g	beige or Puy lentils	12 oz
About 1 litre	boiling salted water	About $1\frac{1}{2}$ pints
45 g	butter	$1\frac{1}{2}$ oz
4 tbsp	chopped parsley	4 tbsp
1	lemon, juice strained	1
	black pepper	
16	triangular croûtons	16
4	eggs, hard-boiled and sliced	4
8	rashers streaky bacon, grilled until crisp	8

Boil the lentils in the salted water for 1 hour, or until tender. Drain them. Melt the butter in a heavy frying pan. Add the lentils, and cook until they begin to colour. Add the parsley, lemon juice and a pinch of black pepper and continue cooking, stirring frequently, until the lentils are browned. Serve garnished with croûtons, and the egg and bacon slices.

MANUEL M. PUGA Y PARGA
LA COCINA PRÁCTICA

Millet Lentil Loaf

To serve 4 to 6

90 g	millet, cooked	3 oz
200 g	lentils, cooked and drained	7 oz
2	spring onions, thinly sliced	2
4 tbsp	oil	4 tbsp
100 g	spinach, coarsely chopped	3½ oz
2	eggs, beaten	2
2	apples, peeled, cored and grated	2
1 tbsp	ground coriander	1 tbsp
	salt	
1 tbsp	lemon juice	1 tbsp

Preheat the oven to 180°C (350°F or Mark 4). Sauté the spring onions in oil for a minute, then add the spinach and toss lightly to steam for another minute or two. Combine the millet, lentils, sautéed vegetables and remaining ingredients. Turn into an oiled ½ litre (1 lb) loaf tin and bake in the preheated oven for 30 to 40 minutes, or until firm and golden-brown on top. Serve warm.

NANCY ALBRIGHT
RODALE'S NATURALLY GREAT FOODS COOKBOOK

Lentils with Dried Apricots

Linsen mit Backaprikosen

To serve 4

250 g	dried lentils, soaked for 3 to 4 hours, drained and cooked in fresh water for 45 minutes, then drained	8 oz
50 g	dried apricots, soaked for 15 minutes in warm water, and drained	2 oz
1	large onion, finely chopped	1
40 g	butter	1½ oz
	salt and pepper	
4	walnuts, shelled and chopped	4
2 tbsp	chopped parsley or coriander leaves	2 tbsp

Fry the apricots with the onions in the butter over a low heat until they begin to soften. Season with salt and pepper. Add this mixture and the chopped walnuts to the cooked lentils in

a saucepan. Place over a very low heat for about 10 minutes so the lentils heat through but do not dry out. Serve the lentils sprinkled with chopped parsley or coriander.

KULINARISCHE GERICHTE: ZU GAST BEI FREUNDEN

A Pot of Lentils

Cocido de Lentejas

This recipe comes from Ibiza. Butifarrón, *a Balearic and Catalan speciality, is a sausage that derives its dark colour from the cooked blood that is its main ingredient. It is lightly spiced and may contain pine-nuts, almonds, cumin seeds and cinnamon. It may be purchased in shops specializing in Spanish food, but if none is obtainable use* chorizo *sausage which is generally more readily available.*

To serve 4

350 g	lentils	12 oz
4 tbsp	olive oil	4 tbsp
2	medium-sized onions, chopped	2
6	tomatoes, skinned, seeded and chopped	6
2	garlic cloves, peeled	2
6	slices *butifarrón*	6
125 g	green beans, topped and tailed and chopped into 2.5 cm (1 inch) lengths	4 oz
	salt and pepper	
90 cl	water	1½ pints
150 g	potatoes, cut into cubes	5 oz

Cover the lentils with water, bring them to the boil and drain them. Pour the oil into a pan and fry together the onions, tomatoes, garlic, *butifarrón* sausage and green beans. Season with salt and pepper, and add the water. Add the lentils and potatoes, cover and simmer for 1¼ to 1½ hours, or until the lentils are soft and all of the liquid has been absorbed.

LUIS RIPOLL
COCINA DE LAS BALEARES

Lentils and Oxtail with Cream

Sahne-Linsen mit Ochsenschwanz

To serve 4 to 6

500 g	small whole lentils, soaked overnight and drained	1 lb
3 litres	strong meat stock (page 165)	4½ pints
2	large onions, one stuck with cloves, one sliced	2
3 tbsp	chopped ham	3 tbsp
400 g	potatoes, peeled and diced	14 oz
1	oxtail, jointed	1
2 tbsp	oil	2 tbsp
1	garlic clove, crushed	1
½	celeriac, diced	½
1	leek, cut into strips	1
2	carrots, sliced	2
2 tbsp	tomato purée	2 tbsp
1 litre	red wine	1¾ pint
¼ litre	thick soured cream	8 fl oz
	salt and pepper	

Simmer the lentils in the meat stock with the onion stuck with cloves, the chopped ham and potatoes, until the lentils are tender (about 45 minutes to 1 hour).

In a separate pan, fry the oxtail in the oil over a high heat, turning the pieces frequently. Cook for 10 minutes, then add the garlic, celeriac, leek, carrots, sliced onion and tomato purée. Reduce the heat and cook for another 5 minutes, stirring frequently. Add the wine, cover the pan and simmer for 2 hours or until the meat is tender. Remove the oxtail, bone the meat while it is still warm and cut it into cubes. Add the meat, vegetables and stock to the lentils. Pour in the soured cream and bring to the boil. Season before serving.

HANS KARL ADAM
DAS KOCHBUCH AUS SCHWABEN

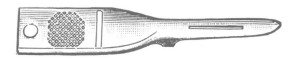

Lentils with Rishta (Noodles)

Recipes for rishta—fresh noodles—appeared in Ancient Arab manuscripts. Rishta can be made using the recipe for egg pasta dough (page 167); the dough is kneaded, rolled and cut as demonstrated on pages 44 and 48.

Use brown lentils if you want to leave them whole; red and yellow ones if you prefer a purée. Make a purée before adding the noodles by rubbing the lentils through a sieve or by puréeing them in an electric blender.

To serve 4

250 to 350 g	lentils	8 to 12 oz
350 g	rishta noodles	12 oz
	salt and pepper	
2	onions, finely chopped	2
2 tbsp	oil	2 tbsp
2 or 3	garlic cloves, crushed	2 or 3
1 tsp	ground coriander	1 tsp
30 g	butter	1 oz

Boil the lentils in salted water to cover, about 60 cl (1 pint). Cook for 30 minutes to 1½ hours, or until the lentils are soft and the water has been absorbed. Drain the cooked lentils thoroughly and put them into a large pan which will accommodate the noodles as well. Fry the onions in the oil until soft and golden. Add the garlic and coriander, and continue to fry gently for about 2 minutes, until golden. Add this mixture to the cooked lentils, and season to taste with salt and pepper. Bring a large pan of salted water to the boil, add the noodles and cook for about 5 minutes until just tender. Drain the noodles well and add them to the pan with the lentils. Stir in the butter and mix thoroughly. Serve very hot.

CLAUDIA RODEN
A BOOK OF MIDDLE EASTERN FOOD

Yellow Peas Berlin-Style

Löffelerbsen nach Berliner Art

To serve 4

500 g	dried yellow peas, soaked overnight and drained	1 lb
1	onion, chopped	1
1	leek, chopped	1
1	small celeriac, shredded	1
30 g	lard	1 oz
500 g	pig's ears and snout, scrubbed, blanched in water for 5 minutes, drained and diced	1 lb
1 tsp	thyme or marjoram	1 tsp
	salt and pepper	
2	potatoes, diced	2

Fry the onion, leek and celeriac in the lard in a large saucepan. Add the peas, cover generously with water, and bring to the boil. Add the diced meat and the herbs, season with salt and pepper, cover and simmer for 40 minutes. Add the potatoes and cook, covered, for a further 20 minutes or until the potatoes and peas are tender. Serve with fresh rolls.

ELIZABETH SCHULER
MEIN KOCHBUCH

Spiced Gram

Amti

To serve 4

250 g	yellow split peas (*channa dal*), soaked for 1 hour and drained	8 oz
2 tbsp	*ghee*	2 tbsp
½ tsp	mustard seeds	½ tsp
3	green chili peppers, seeds removed, chopped (optional)	3
1	onion, finely chopped	1
½ tsp	ground turmeric	½ tsp
½ tsp	paprika or chili powder	½ tsp
12	black peppercorns	12
2.5 cm	stick cinnamon, broken into pieces	1 inch
4	cloves	4
2	green cardamom pods	2
1 tbsp	lemon juice	1 tbsp
1 tsp	salt	1 tsp

Boil the split peas in 60 cl (1 pint) of water for 40 minutes until soft and all the water is absorbed. Heat the *ghee* and fry the mustard seeds till they sputter. Add the green chili peppers and onion and fry till golden. Stir in the turmeric and paprika or chili powder. Crush the peppercorns, cinnamon, cloves and cardamom in a mortar and add these to the pan. Fry for 2 minutes. Stir this mixture into the dal. Add the lemon juice and salt, mix well and simmer for a few minutes. Serve hot.

JACK SANTA MARIA
INDIAN VEGETARIAN COOKERY

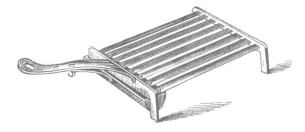

Hopping John

This unusually named dish, said to be named after a lame waiter, is from the American Deep South and is supposed to bring good luck if eaten on New Year's Day before noon.

To serve 6

250 g	black-eyed peas, soaked overnight, or brought to the boil and left to stand for 2 hours, and drained	8 oz
1	ham hock, split	1
1	onion, chopped	1
½ tsp	crushed dried red chili pepper, or more to taste	½ tsp
200 g	rice	7 oz
1 tsp	salt	1 tsp

Place the ham hock, onion, red chili pepper and water to cover in a saucepan. Bring to the boil and simmer, covered, for 30 minutes. Add the ham hock mixture with its liquid to the drained peas. Add more water if needed to cover the peas. Cover and simmer for 45 minutes, or until the peas are tender. Add more boiling water as needed to keep the peas moistened. Add the rice and salt, stir lightly, cover and simmer for 20 minutes, or until the rice is tender. Add more boiling water if needed during cooking. Serve hot.

JEANNE A. VOLTZ
THE FLAVOR OF THE SOUTH

Mung Beans with Capers and Lemon

To serve 4

250 g	mung beans, soaked for 1 hour and drained	8 oz
60 cl	water	1 pint
4 tbsp	olive oil	4 tbsp
2	medium-sized onions, finely chopped	2
1	garlic clove, chopped	1
2 tbsp	chopped capers	2 tbsp
1	large lemon, rind grated, juice strained	1
4 tbsp	chopped parsley	4 tbsp

In a covered pot simmer the beans in fresh water for 40 minutes and drain them if necessary. Heat the oil in a saucepan over a low heat. Mix in the onions and garlic and cook them until they are soft. Stir in the beans, capers and the rind and juice of the lemon. Cover and simmer for 2 minutes. Mix in the parsley just before serving.

GAIL DUFF
GAIL DUFF'S VEGETARIAN COOKBOOK

Mung Beans with Pork and Shrimps

Gulay Na Mongo

To serve 4

200 g	mung beans, soaked in water for 1 hour and drained	7 oz
150 g	pork shoulder, cut into small pieces	5 oz
150 g	large shrimps or prawns, shelled and black veins removed, halved lengthwise and then crosswise	5 oz
1 litre	water	1¾ pints
2	garlic cloves, chopped	2
30 g	lard	1 oz
1	small onion, chopped	1
4 tbsp	tomato juice	4 tbsp
	salt	

Boil the beans in the water for 40 to 60 minutes or until tender. Drain and keep them hot. Sauté the garlic in the lard and add the onion, stirring until it is transparent. Then add the pork and cover the pan. Stir occasionally until the pork is well done, about 30 minutes. Pour in the tomato juice. Add the shrimps or prawns. Cook, covered, for 10 minutes and then add the hot mung beans. Stir thoroughly and add salt to taste.

ALICE MILLER MITCHELL (EDITOR)
ORIENTAL COOKBOOK

Aubergines with Chick Peas

Aubergines aux Pois Chiches Moronia

To serve 6 to 8

1.5 kg	aubergines, cut into 2 cm (¾ inch) thick rounds, soaked in salted water for 30 minutes, drained and dried	3 lb
250 g	chick peas, soaked overnight and drained	8 oz
1 kg	beef short ribs or chuck steak	2 to 2½ lb
1 tsp	paprika	1 tsp
4	garlic cloves	4
About 2 litres	cold water	About 3½ pints
15 cl	oil	¼ pint
	salt and pepper	

Put the beef, chick peas, paprika and garlic in a saucepan and pour over the water to cover. Bring to the boil, skim, then lower the heat, partially cover and simmer for 2 hours. Add boiling water, if necessary.

Fry the aubergine slices in the hot oil and drain them on absorbent paper; lay the aubergines on top of the chick peas and the meat. Season with salt and pepper and cook uncovered for a further hour, by which time there should be about a ladleful of sauce left.

IRÈNE AND LUCIENNE KARSENTY
LA CUISINE PIED-NOIR

Chick Peas with Green Peppers and Chilies

If green chili peppers are not available, substitute ½ teaspoon of Tabasco sauce, adding it with the lemon juice.

To serve 4

250 g	chick peas, soaked overnight and drained	8 oz
2	medium-sized sweet green peppers, ribs removed, seeded and diced	2
4	green chili peppers, cored, seeded and finely chopped	4
3 tbsp	olive oil	3 tbsp
1	large garlic clove, finely chopped	1
1	lemon, juice strained	1

In a covered pan, simmer the chick peas in fresh water for up to 3 hours or until tender. Drain them if necessary.

Heat the oil in a frying pan over a low heat. Stir in the sweet peppers, chili peppers and garlic, and cook them for 5 minutes. Add the chick peas and cook them until they are just showing signs of browning. Pour in the lemon juice and let it bubble. Serve the chick peas as soon as you can.

GAIL DUFF
GAIL DUFF'S VEGETARIAN COOKBOOK

Chick Pea Fritters

Panisses

To serve 4

250 g	chick pea flour	8 oz
1 litre	salted water	1¾ pints
2 tbsp	olive oil	2 tbsp
	oil for deep frying	
	freshly ground pepper	

Bring the salted water to the boil. Add the olive oil to the water and sprinkle the chick pea flour into it. Stir the mixture briskly with a wooden spoon and cook over a very low heat for approximately 20 minutes, stirring constantly. When the mixture is very thick, pour it into four lightly oiled saucers. Leave it until cool, turn out of the saucers and cut the rounds into slices two fingers thick.

Fry the slices in very hot oil for 3 minutes. When they turn a golden colour, they are ready. Serve them with a dash of freshly ground pepper.

BENOIT MASCARELLI
LA TABLE EN PROVENCE

Chick Peas Majorcan-Style

Garabanzos

To serve 6 to 8

500 g	chick peas, soaked overnight and drained	1 lb
250 g	pumpkin in one piece, weighed after removing shell and pith	8 oz
3	garlic cloves, chopped	3
4 tbsp	olive oil	4 tbsp
250 g	tomatoes, skinned, seeded and chopped	8 oz
1	egg, hard-boiled and finely chopped	1
	salt and black pepper	
4 tbsp	finely chopped parsley	4 tbsp

Place the chick peas in a pan with 2½ litres (4 pints) of cold water, together with the slice of pumpkin. Cook, covered, over a low heat for about 2 to 3 hours or until the chick peas are soft. When they are cooked, drain off the liquid. Fry the garlic in the olive oil in a glazed earthenware pot. When the garlic is lightly browned, add the tomatoes. Pass the pumpkin through a colander. When the tomatoes are soft, add the pumpkin and the hard-boiled egg to the pot. Season with salt and black pepper, add the chopped parsley and finally the chick peas. Mix everything together well and serve.

COLOMA ABRINAS VIDAL
COCINA SELECTA MALLORQUINA

Friday Chick Peas

Les Pois Chiches du Vendredi

Traditionally, chick peas were served on a Friday with **brand-ade** of salt cod and puréed potatoes, as a sign of "penitence". Never cook less than 500 g (1 lb) of chick peas at a time. This will be slightly too much for four people, but the leftovers may be used as the base for a soup, in a salad, or in a paella or couscous. The bean stock is good on its own as a soup and is excellent for the digestion.

To serve 4

500 g	chick peas, soaked overnight and drained	1 lb
2	large carrots	2
1	large onion, stuck with 1 clove	1
3	garlic cloves	3
4 tbsp	olive oil	4 tbsp
	salt	
About 1 tbsp	white wine vinegar	About 1 tbsp
	freshly ground black pepper	

Rinse the chick peas thoroughly and place them in a large, deep saucepan. Pour in enough water to cover the chick peas well. The pan should be big enough for the water to reach no more than two-thirds of the way up the sides. Add the carrots, onion, garlic and 3 tablespoons of the olive oil. Bring the water quickly to the boil and then reduce to a simmer. Cover the pan and simmer for 2 hours, taking care that the water does not boil over or the correct combination of water, oil and vegetable juices will be lost. Add a little salt, cover the pan again and cook for another hour.

Drain the chick peas. Reserve the cooking liquid and remove the carrot, onion and garlic. Serve the chick peas hot with a little of the cooking liquid, a dash of wine vinegar, the remaining olive oil and a little freshly ground pepper.

ALBIN MARTY
FOURMIGUETTO: SOUVENIRS, CONTES ET RECETTES DU LANGUEDOC

Mixed Beans with Pumpkin

T bikha à la Courge Rouge

Dried broad beans have tough, bitter skins and should be peeled after soaking, as here, or if cooked on their own, after cooking. The technique of making harissa *is on page 39.*

To serve 4		
100 g	chick peas, soaked overnight and drained	3½ oz
100 g	dried broad beans, soaked overnight drained and peeled	3½ oz
500 g	pumpkin, peeled, seeded and diced	1 lb
2	onions, cut into pieces	2
20 cl	olive oil	7 fl oz
250 g	tomatoes skinned, seeded and flesh puréed	8 oz
1½ tsp	*harissa*	1½ tsp
1½ tsp	cayenne pepper	1½ tsp
½ litre	water	16 fl oz
150 g	sweet red pepper, seeded and chopped	5 oz
1	bunch parsley	1
	salt	

Fry the onions gently in the olive oil in a deep casserole. Add the puréed tomatoes, *harissa*, cayenne pepper, the chick peas and broad beans. Add the water, cover the pan, and cook over a medium heat for 2 to 3 hours. Add the pumpkin and the sweet pepper, together with the parsley. Season with salt and cook over a gentle heat for a further 30 minutes or until the pumpkin pieces are soft but still whole. Arrange on a serving dish and serve very hot.

AHMED LAASRI
240 RECETTES DE CUISINE MAROCAINE

Puréed Pulses

Well-Fried Beans with Totopos

Frijoles Refritos

Some beans need pre-cooking to destroy toxins: see page 78. The technique of making frijoles refritos *is demonstrated on page 80. The* totopos *used to garnish the beans are triangular pieces of tortilla fried in lard until golden-brown. Tortillas are maize-flour flatbreads; they can be bought at speciality shops. To cut a radish into a "rose", make two slits to form a cross in the top of the radish, then another diagonally. Plunge the radish into very cold water for 15 minutes.*

To serve 6		
250 g	black, pink, red kidney or pinto beans, soaked overnight and drained	8 oz
12	*totopos*	12
About 1 litre	water	About 1¾ pints
½	onion, finely chopped	½
125 g	lard or pork dripping	4 oz
	salt	
60 g	fresh curd cheese, crumbled	2 oz
	cos lettuce leaves	
6	radishes, cut into roses	6

Put the beans into a pan and cover them with cold water. Add half the onion and 30 g (1 oz) of the lard and bring to the boil. Cover and simmer the beans—2 hours for black beans, 1½ hours for other varieties, or until tender but firm. Do not stir during this time. Add a large pinch of salt and simmer for another 30 minutes. Set aside, preferably until the next day. There should be about 90 cl (1½ pints) of bean cooking liquid.

To make the well-fried beans, heat the remaining lard in a frying pan and fry the rest of the onion until it is soft but not browned. Add ¼ litre (8 fl oz) of beans in their cooking liquid to the pan and mash them well over a very high heat. Add the rest of the beans gradually, mashing them all the time, until you have a coarse purée. When the purée begins to dry out and sizzle at the edges, it will start to come away from the surface of the pan. As you let it continue cooking, tip the pan from side to side. The purée will form itself into a loose roll. This process will take from 15 to 20 minutes.

Tip the roll, rather as if folding an omelette, on to the serving dish, garnish with the cheese and spike it with the *totopos*. Garnish the dish with the lettuce and radishes.

DIANA KENNEDY
CUISINES OF MEXICO

Pease Pudding

To serve 6

500 g	split peas soaked for 1 hour and drained, or dried whole peas, soaked overnight and drained	1 lb
60 g	butter, cut into small pieces	2 oz
1	large egg	1
	salt and pepper	

Put the peas in a pan, cover them with plenty of fresh water and simmer until tender. Split peas will take from 45 to 60 minutes, whole dried peas will need at least 2 hours. Drain off the liquid—keep it for soup—and put the beans through a food processor to make a purée which is not too smooth. Mix in the butter, then add the egg and season well with salt and pepper. Put the mixture into a buttered 1.25 litre (2 pint) pudding basin, cover the basin with foil or a cloth and steam for 1 hour in a saucepan of boiling water. Turn out the pudding and serve it with boiled salt pork.

JANE GRIGSON
ENGLISH FOOD

Yellow Pea Purée

Erbsenpüree

Served with sauerkraut and pork knuckles, this is a traditional Berlin dish and a great favourite in northern Germany generally. In place of the meat stock, you may cook the peas with smoked or salted pork knuckles or ribs, cut into neat pieces and added to the peas with ½ litre (16 fl oz) of water. The meat may be served with the puréed peas.

To serve 6

500 g	dried whole yellow peas, soaked overnight and drained	1 lb
1.25 litres	water	2 pints
½ litre	meat stock (*page 165*)	16 fl oz
	salt and pepper	
	marjoram	
60 g	butter	2 oz
2	onions, finely chopped	2

Put the peas in a saucepan with the water. Cook until most of the water has been absorbed and the peas are swollen but still whole. Add the stock and continue to cook until the peas are tender. Drain the peas; pass them through a sieve, and season the purée with salt, pepper and marjoram. Stir in half of the butter. Keep the purée warm. Brown the onions in the remaining butter and pour them over the pea purée.

GRETE WILLINSKY
KOCHBUCH DER BÜCHERGILDE

Chick Pea Polenta

La Socca

To serve 4

About 125 g	chick pea flour	About 4 oz
About 30 cl	salted water	About ½ pint
2 tbsp	olive oil	2 tbsp
	freshly ground pepper	

Put the chick pea flour into a saucepan and stir the salted water gradually into the flour, taking care not to form lumps. Cook over a low heat, stirring and adding more water if necessary until the mixture has a slightly thickened consistency. Pour it on to a large, round, oiled iron baking sheet and spread it out thinly. Sprinkle with oil and bake in an oven preheated to 220°C (425°F or Mark 7) for 5 to 10 minutes. When it is golden-brown it is ready. Serve hot sprinkled with freshly ground pepper.

C. CHANOT-BULLIER
VIEILLES RECETTES DE CUISINE PROVENÇALE

Falafel

Falafel *is a dish common to Egypt and Israel, and it is also eaten throughout the Middle East. Street vendors sell these fried chick pea balls, which are eaten with salad and* tahini *(sesame-seed paste) inside the pocket-shaped Arab pita bread. Falafel is also served as an appetizer on a small plate of* hummus *(ground chick pea paste), garnished with quartered hard-boiled eggs and sprinkled with chopped parsley, cayenne pepper,* tahini *and a few drops of rich green olive oil.*

To serve 4

500 g	chick peas, soaked overnight, drained, then finely ground in a blender	1 lb
1 tsp	ground coriander	1 tsp
1	garlic clove, chopped	1
1 tsp	ground cumin	1 tsp
½ tsp	cayenne pepper	½ tsp
	salt	
30 g	flour	1 oz
	oil for deep frying	

Mix the ground chick peas with the coriander, garlic, cumin, cayenne pepper and salt. Add the flour and mix thoroughly. From the dough form small balls each one about 3 cm (1¼ inches) in diameter. Deep fry the balls in very hot oil until golden-brown, about 2 to 3 minutes.

NAOMI AND SHIMON TZABAR
YEMENITE AND SABRA COOKERY

Pea, Bean and Lentil Stews

Stew with Chick Peas

T'fina aux Pois Chiches

You may substitute dried haricot beans for the chick peas.

	To serve 6	
300 g	chick peas, soaked overnight and drained	10 oz
1 kg	fresh brisket of beef, boned and rolled	2 to 2½ lb
1	calf's foot	1
10 to 12	potatoes, peeled and soaked in salted water for several hours	10 to 12
6	eggs	6
1	garlic head	1
1 tsp	honey	1 tsp
1 tsp	paprika	1 tsp
1 tbsp	olive oil	1 tbsp
	salt and pepper	
About 2 litres	water	About 3½ pints

	Meat ball	
300 g	minced beef	10 oz
100 g	bread, with crusts removed, soaked in water, squeezed	3½ oz
	freshly grated nutmeg	
	mace	
	mixed spice	
	salt and pepper	
1 tbsp	chopped parsley	1 tbsp
1	garlic clove, chopped	1
1	egg	1

To make the meat ball, mix together the minced beef, bread, nutmeg, mace, mixed spice, salt, pepper, parsley and garlic clove, and bind it with the egg. Put it aside.

In a thick-bottomed casserole, put the brisket, the calf's foot, chick peas, potatoes and the six eggs, still in their shells. Add the garlic head to the pan with the honey, paprika, olive oil, salt and pepper. Pour the water over, bring to the boil, add the meat ball, cover and simmer for 4 hours.

Preheat the oven to 130°C (250°F or Mark ½), and cook the stew uncovered for 1 hour or more—there should be very little liquid remaining in the pot.

Shell the eggs before serving. Put the chick peas, potatoes and shelled eggs in a deep serving dish; arrange the meats on a separate platter.

IRÈNE AND LUCIENNE KARSENTY
LA CUISINE PIED-NOIR

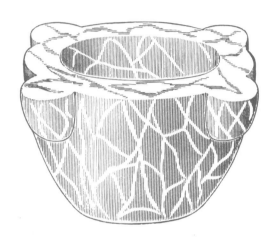

Guernsey Bean Jar

Some beans need pre-cooking to destroy toxins: see page 78.

Until the 1920s Guernsey Bean Jar was the usual Guernsey breakfast. A few still so indulge. It is preferable to season to taste when the dish is cooked.

	To serve 4	
500 g	dried haricot beans, soaked overnight and drained	1 lb
1	pig's trotter	1
1	beef shin bone (optional)	1
300 g	tripe (optional)	10 oz
500 g	small onions	1 lb
500 g	carrots	1 lb
1	bouquet of thyme, sage and parsley	1

Place all of the ingredients in a large earthenware jar or casserole, using plenty of herbs, and cover with water. Bring to the boil and then simmer, covered, for 8 hours, adding more water when necessary during cooking.

J. STEVENS COX (EDITOR)
GUERNSEY DISHES OF BYGONE DAYS

Lamb and Haricot Beans
Haricot de Mouton

To serve 6

750 g	dried haricot beans, soaked overnight and drained, then cooked in water until tender and drained	1½ lb
500 g each	neck, breast and boned shoulder of lamb, cut into pieces	1 lb each
60 g	butter	2 oz
2	turnips, thinly sliced	2
4	garlic cloves, crushed	4
30 g	flour	1 oz
1 litre	water	1¾ pints
	salt and freshly ground pepper	
1	bouquet garni	1
3	tomatoes, skinned, seeded and roughly chopped	3
200 g	green bacon cut into lardons, blanched and sautéed in butter	7 oz
250 g	baby onions, sautéed in butter until golden	8 oz

Heat the butter in a pan, add the meat and turnips and cook over a medium heat until golden. Add the garlic and the flour, and cook for 5 minutes. Pour in the water, season with salt and pepper, and add the bouquet garni and the tomatoes. Cover and cook over a low heat for 50 minutes.

Pour the contents of the pan into a large sieve placed over a bowl. Transfer the meat to a casserole, scatter the bacon lardons and onions over the meat, and place the beans on top. Degrease the strained sauce, and pour it over the contents of the casserole. Bring to the boil, then cover and cook in an oven preheated to 170°C (325°F or Mark 3) for 1 hour.

EDOUARD NIGNON (EDITOR)
LE LIVRE DE CUISINE DE L'OUEST-ÉCLAIR

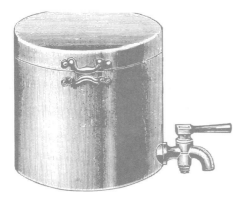

Cassoulet Castelnaudary-Style
Le Cassoulet de Castelnaudary

To serve 8

800 g	dried haricot beans, soaked overnight and drained	1 lb 10 oz
300 g	green bacon	10 oz
200 g	fresh pork rinds tied in bundles	7 oz
1	carrot	1
1	onion, stuck with 2 cloves	1
2	bouquets garnis	2
5	garlic cloves	5
	salt	
750 g	boned pork spare-rib	1½ lb
500 g	boned shoulder of lamb	1 lb
About 10 cl	rendered goose fat	About 3½ fl oz
	pepper	
200 g	onion, chopped	7 oz
30 cl	meat stock (*page 165*)	½ pint
10 cl	puréed tomato	3½ fl oz
100 g	garlic boiling sausage	3½ oz
100 g	dried sausage	3½ oz
	breadcrumbs	

Cook the beans, with the bacon, pork rinds, carrot, onion, one bouquet garni and three garlic cloves, well covered with the water, over a very low heat for about 2 hours.

Sauté the pork and the lamb in 2 tablespoons of goose fat. Add salt and pepper. When the meat is browned, add to the pan the chopped onion, the other bouquet garni and the remaining two garlic cloves. Moisten with a little stock and the puréed tomato. Cover the pan, simmer for 30 minutes, moistening the meat from time to time with a little more stock. When the beans are just tender, salt them and remove the flavouring vegetables and the bouquet garni. Add the meat and sausages to the beans, along with their braising liquid. Simmer for 1 hour, covered. Take the pork, lamb and sausages from the pan and drain them. Cut the pork and lamb into slices. Skin the two sausages and slice them. Drain the beans, reserving the cooking liquid.

In a 2 litre (3½ pint) casserole, layer the meats and beans, finishing with a layer of beans, and add enough cooking liquid to fill the spaces but not cover the top layer of beans. Sprinkle with breadcrumbs and dot with goose fat. Cook, uncovered, in an oven preheated to 140°C (275°F or Mark 1) for 1½ hours. During this time, the crust should be broken at least three times (the traditional number is seven) and partially submerged, and the casserole basted with the rest of the cooking liquid. The aim is a thick, rich, gratin crust.

HISTORIA HORS SERIE, NO. 42: LES FRANÇAIS À TABLE

Cassoulet

To serve 6 to 8

1 kg	goose (breast or leg)	2 to 2½ lb
	mixed herbs	
	salt	
	goose fat from inside the bird	

Bean stew

1 kg	dried haricot beans, soaked overnight and drained	2 to 2½ lb
175 g	fresh pork rinds, rolled and tied with a string	6 oz
250 g	lean green bacon	8 oz
1	pig's trotter	1
2	carrots, cut into pieces	2
1	large onion stuck with 2 cloves	1
2	garlic cloves	2
1	bouquet garni	1
1	*cervelas* or other garlic boiling sausage, pricked with a fork	1
	salt	

Lamb stew

About 1.5 kg	lamb shoulder, surface fat removed, cut into large pieces but not boned	About 3 lb
2	medium-sized carrots, cut into 2 cm (¾ inch) pieces	2
2	medium-sized onions, coarsely chopped	2
	salt and freshly ground pepper	
2 tbsp	flour	2 tbsp
30 cl	dry white wine	½ pint
5	garlic cloves	5
1	bouquet garni	1
3 or 4	tomatoes, skinned, seeded and chopped	3 or 4
	white breadcrumbs	

Reduce a large pinch of mixed herbs to a powder in a mortar, sprinkle the goose with the herbs and a pinch of salt and leave it overnight. Then wipe the goose dry. Melt the goose fat with about 6 tablespoons of water over a low heat. When nothing solid is left but the cracklings, strain off the pure fat. Cook the goose gently, well bathed in this fat for 1 to 1½ hours, turning it after about 15 minutes. Reserve the fat.

Put the pork rind, green bacon and pig's trotter into a saucepan and cover them with cold water. Bring them to the boil, simmer them for a few minutes, then drain and rinse them in cold water. Put the drained beans into a heavy pan along with the vegetables, garlic, bouquet garni, pork rind, bacon, pig's trotter and sausage. Pour in enough water to cover everything by about 5 cm (2 inches), bring the water slowly to the boil and adjust the heat so that, covered, the barest simmer is maintained. Do not salt. The sausage should be removed and reserved after about 40 minutes of cooking time, and the bacon taken out when it is tender but still firm, after about 1 hour. The trotter and rind should remain with the beans until done, about 2 hours in all. Put the rind and trotter aside with the sausage and bacon. Discard the onion and bouquet garni. Salt the cooking liquid to taste.

For the lamb stew, in a heavy sauté pan big enough to hold the pieces of meat placed side by side, stew the carrots and onions in 2 tablespoons of the reserved goose fat. Cook the vegetables for about 15 minutes, stirring regularly, until lightly browned. Remove the onions and carrots, making certain to leave no fragment of onion behind. Increase the heat and colour the pieces of lamb in the same fat. Salt them just before turning them; when they are browned all over, sprinkle them with flour. Turn the pieces of meat over again, and return the vegetables to the pan. When the flour is lightly cooked, about 4 to 5 minutes, add the wine, three of the garlic cloves and the bouquet garni. Scrape and stir the contents of the pan with a wooden spoon to loosen and dissolve frying adherents. Add the tomatoes and enough of the bean cooking liquid to cover, and put a lid on the pan. Simmer very slowly for 1½ hours, skimming off the surface fat two or three times during this period. Carefully remove the pieces of meat and carrot and reserve them, discard the bouquet garni, and press the rest of the mixture through a sieve. Return this sauce to the pan, bring it to the boil and then set the pan half way off the heat, so that the sauce's cooking is regulated to a bubble. Cook it uncovered, skimming frequently, for 15 minutes.

Rub the bottom and sides of a 2 litre (3½ pint), medium-deep earthenware casserole with the two garlic cloves, until they are completely absorbed. Untie the pork rind, cut it into small rectangles about 1 cm (½ inch) by 5 cm (2 inches) and distribute the rectangles regularly over the bottom of the dish. Cut the goose into two pieces, place them on the bed of rind. Drain the beans, reserving their cooking liquid. Distribute about one third of the beans over and around the pieces of goose.

Split the trotter, remove and discard the largest bones, cut each half into three or four pieces and arrange them, along with the pieces of lamb and carrot (both those from the lamb stew and from the beans) evenly over the surface. Sprinkle generously with pepper and cover with half the remaining beans. Slice the sausage into rounds two fingers thick; distribute it throughout the casserole. Slice the bacon into 2.5 cm (1 inch) lengths and scatter it on top of the beans. Add a good pinch of pepper, and cover with the remaining beans.

Generously sprinkle the top with breadcrumbs and carefully, so as to moisten the breadcrumbs without displacing them, ladle over them the sauce from the lamb stew. Continue until the liquid has risen just to the surface of the beans. Dust again lightly with breadcrumbs, sprinkle several tablespoons of melted goose fat over the surface and put the dish into an oven preheated to 220°C (425°F or Mark 7) until it is heated through and the surface begins to bubble. Turn the oven down to 150°C (300°F or Mark 2) so that a gentle bubbling is maintained.

After about 20 minutes, begin to baste the surface, first with the remaining lamb sauce and, when that is used up, with the bean cooking liquid. Continue to do this every 20 minutes or so, and when a golden, crisp gratin has formed on the surface, break it regularly all over with a spoon so that part becomes submerged and the rest is moistened with the sauce. The cassoulet should remain at least 2 hours in a slow oven, and the gratin should be broken a minimum of three times but if the basting liquid runs short before this time, it is better to stop the gratinéing process, than to risk the dish becoming too dry.

RICHARD OLNEY
THE FRENCH MENU COOKBOOK

Cassoulet from Toulouse
Le Cassoulet de Toulouse

To serve 4

500 g	dried haricot beans, soaked overnight and drained	1 lb
100 g	fresh pork rinds, tied in a bundle, blanched for 5 minutes	3½ oz
1	boiling sausage, pricked	1
1	bouquet garni	1
2	carrots, sliced	2
5	garlic cloves, 2 crushed	5
¼	goose, cut into 2 serving pieces	¼
4 tbsp	rendered goose fat	4 tbsp
2	tomatoes, skinned, seeded and chopped	2
100 g	dried sausage, thinly sliced	3½ oz

Cook the beans in boiling salted water for 1 hour. Drain them. Cover them again with boiling water, adding the pork rinds, boiling sausage, bouquet garni, carrots and three of the garlic cloves. Cover and simmer for 1 hour. Slice the boiling sausage and return it to the beans.

Sauté the goose in the goose fat with the remaining two crushed garlic cloves and the tomatoes. When the goose is well coloured, add the contents of the pan to the beans and cook the mixture for another 2 hours. Drain the beans, reserving the cooking liquid, and layer them with the boiling sausage, the dried sausage and the goose in an earthenware casserole. Top the casserole with a layer of beans. Pour in enough of the bean cooking liquid almost to cover the top layer of beans. Reserve the rest of the liquid.

Stew the dish, uncovered, in an oven preheated to 130°C (250°F or Mark ½) for 1½ to 2 hours. Allow a crust to form; break it about eight times during the cooking and baste it with more bean cooking liquid. Serve in the dish.

HISTORIA HORS SERIE, NO. 42: LES FRANÇAIS À TABLE

Baked Bean Pot
Frackh

Frackh is a traditional Saturday midday meal among Moroccan Jews. No fire may be lit on the sabbath, so the oven is lit on Friday at dusk and the bean stew left to simmer all night and part of the next day, to be ready when the men come home from morning service at the synagogue. For cooking in the oven, a pot big enough to hold 7.5 to 10 litres (6 to 8 quarts) water is needed. The ingredients are placed in it and the lid is sealed with a flour and water paste.

To serve 8 to 10

2	calf's feet, including foot, ankle and lower shank, hair singed, washed, bones cracked	2
200 g	dried beans (haricot beans, flageolets or butter beans, for example), soaked overnight and drained	7 oz
200 g	chick peas, soaked overnight and drained	7 oz
60 g	parsley, finely chopped	2 oz
4	garlic heads, separated into cloves, unpeeled	6
6	medium-sized potatoes	6
8 to 10	eggs in the shell	8 to 10
1 tbsp	salt	1 tbsp
1 tbsp	ground cumin seed	1 tbsp
½ tsp	chopped red chili peppers	½ tsp
2 tbsp	paprika	2 tbsp
¼ litre	olive oil, heated	8 fl oz

Place all the ingredients in a deep pot, but do not mix them. Pour in 1.25 litres (2 pints) water. Cover the pot tightly and cook over medium-high heat or in an oven preheated to 130°C (250°F or gas Mark ½). An hour later add ¾ litre (1¼ pints) of water, then the same an hour afterwards. More water should not be necessary, if the lid is on tight, but check towards the end of the cooking time to make sure the dish is not drying up. Add a little more water if necessary. A total cooking time of 4 hours produces a good dish, but the longer cooked, the better. The consistency will be much like that of other baked bean stews—slightly moist although not sloppy—but the taste lent by the bones and spices is special.

IRENE F. DAY
KITCHEN IN THE KASBAH

Lamb Neck and Bean Casserole

This dish takes a long time to make, but it can be assembled in stages or made completely in advance and reheated.

To serve 6

500 g	pink or pinto beans or dried haricot beans, soaked overnight, drained and simmered in fresh water for 2 hours	1 lb
750 g	neck of lamb, cut into small pieces	1½ lb
4 tbsp	oil	4 tbsp
	salt and pepper	
2	medium-sized onions, sliced	2
2	garlic cloves, finely chopped	2
350 g	tomatoes, skinned and chopped, or drained canned tomatoes, chopped	12 oz
½ tsp	dried thyme	½ tsp
1	bay leaf	1
½ tsp	crushed dried red chili pepper (optional)	½ tsp
¼ litre	dry red wine	8 fl oz

Dry the lamb pieces with paper towels. Heat the oil in a heavy frying pan. Toss in the lamb and brown the pieces over a medium heat. Transfer the lamb to an ovenproof casserole, and salt and pepper lightly. Sauté the onions and garlic over low heat in the same frying pan, stirring to scrape up the browned bits and juices of the lamb. Add the tomatoes, herbs and wine and bring to the boil, stirring constantly. Simmer the sauce for a few minutes.

Drain the beans and reserve their cooking liquid. Gently mix them into the lamb, taking care not to mash the beans. Pour the hot tomato and wine sauce over the contents of the casserole; if the sauce does not cover the lamb and beans completely, add enough bean liquid to take care of that. Put a lid on the casserole, or make one out of a double thickness of aluminium foil, sealing it tightly at the edges. Put the casserole in an oven preheated to 170°C (325°F or Mark 3) for about 1 hour. In this time, the beans should absorb most of the liquid; if the mixture seems too juicy (it shouldn't be too dry either), remove the lid, turn up the heat to 190°C (375°F or Mark 5) and bake until the excess moisture evaporates.

MIRIAM UNGERER
GOOD CHEAP FOOD

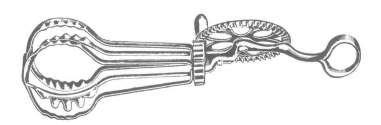

Red-Hot Bean Casserole

If you cannot buy red chili peppers, use either fresh green ones or ¼ teaspoon cayenne pepper. Savoury brown rice is almost essential with this dish.

To serve 4

250 g	red kidney beans, soaked overnight and drained	8 oz
500 g	tomatoes, scalded, skinned, seeded and sliced	1 lb
2	medium-sized onions, thinly sliced	2
1	large garlic clove, finely chopped	1
2	large sweet red peppers, ribs removed, seeded and cut into matchstick strips	2
2	fresh red chili peppers, seeded and finely chopped	2
2 tsp	paprika	2 tsp

In a covered pot, simmer the beans in about 60cl (1 pint) water for 1 hour. Drain them if necessary.

Put half of the tomatoes in the bottom of a casserole. Add half the onions and garlic, half the sweet peppers, half the chopped chili peppers and one teaspoon of the paprika.

Put in all of the kidney beans and follow with the other layers in reverse order, topping with the onion and, finally, the tomatoes. Cover the casserole and put it into an oven preheated to 170°C (325°F or Mark 3) for 1½ hours. Mix everything together before serving.

GAIL DUFF
GAIL DUFF'S VEGETARIAN COOKBOOK

Baked Tuscan Beans

Fagioli al Forno

If pancetta *is not available, substitute green streaky bacon.*

To serve 6

600 g	dried cannellini beans, soaked overnight in 1.5 litres (2½ pints) water	1¼ lb
125 g	*pancetta* cut into small pieces	4 oz
2	large garlic cloves, peeled	2
6 or 7	fresh sage leaves	6 or 7
4 tbsp	olive oil	4 tbsp
125 g	canned tomatoes	4 oz
	water	
	salt and freshly ground black pepper	

Drain the beans and place them in a casserole. Preheat the oven to 190°C (375°F or Mark 5). Add the *pancetta* to the casserole along with the garlic, sage, olive oil and tomatoes.

Pour in enough cold water—about ¾ litre or 1¼ pints—to cover the beans completely, then sprinkle with salt and pepper.

Cover the casserole and place it in the preheated oven for 3½ to 4½ hours. (Cooking time of beans varies because older beans are drier and must cook longer). Check the beans every half hour, and stir gently. Remove the casserole from the oven and allow the beans to cool, still covered, for 15 minutes. Serve the beans from the same casserole.

GIULIANO BUGIALLI
THE FINE ART OF ITALIAN COOKING

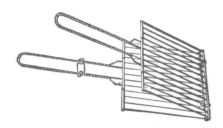

Meat Balls with Courgettes and Chick Peas
Karyaprak

To serve 4

250 g	chick peas, soaked overnight, drained and partially cooked (about 1 hour)	8 oz
500 g	slightly fatty beef, finely chopped	1 lb
1 kg	courgettes, cut into thick rounds	2 to 2½ lb
100 g	bread, crusts removed, soaked in water, squeezed	3½ oz
4	garlic cloves, chopped	4
2 tbsp	chopped parsley	2 tbsp
	salt and pepper	
½ tsp	mixed spice	½ tsp
½ tsp	grated nutmeg	½ tsp
2	eggs	2
4 tbsp	flour	4 tbsp
20 cl	oil	7 fl oz
3	onions, chopped	3
4	tomatoes, skinned, seeded and chopped	4
½ litre	hot water	16 fl oz

To make the meat balls, mix together the beef, bread, garlic and parsley. Season with salt, pepper, mixed spice and nutmeg. Incorporate one egg and mix well. Form the mixture into four meat balls the size of tangerines.

Beat the remaining egg. Roll the meat balls in the flour, then dip them in the beaten egg and fry them for 15 minutes in hot oil. Take the meat balls from the pan and, in the same oil, gently cook the chopped onions and tomatoes for 20 minutes.

Season them with salt and pepper to taste and add the hot water. Simmer for a few minutes, and put this mixture through a sieve. Set the resulting sauce aside.

Lay the chick peas in the bottom of an earthenware dish, cover them with the courgettes and put the meat balls on top. Pour the sauce over all, cover the dish with a piece of aluminium foil in which several slits have been made and cook in an oven preheated to 180°C (350°F or Mark 4) for 2 hours.

IRÈNE AND LUCIENNE KARSENTY
LA CUISINE PIED-NOIR

Black-Eyed Peas with Bacon

To serve 4 to 6

350 g	black-eyed peas, washed, picked over, soaked overnight and drained	12 oz
	salt	
60 g	lean bacon, cut into matchsticks	2 oz
1	large onion, chopped	1
1	small hot red chili pepper, finely chopped, or 1 dried chili pepper, chopped and soaked in a few tablespoons of water for 30 minutes	1
6	thick rashers lean bacon	6
400 g	cooked rice	14 oz
2 tbsp	wine or cider vinegar	2 tbsp
	black pepper (optional)	
2 tbsp	chopped parsley	2 tbsp

Cover the peas with fresh water, add salt, and simmer until tender, about 45 minutes to 1 hour. Fry the bacon matchsticks in their own fat, until they begin to brown, starting them off in a cold frying pan. Drain them on paper towels.

In the same frying pan, sauté the onion in the bacon fat until tender and very lightly browned. Add the chopped, fresh chili pepper or the soaked, dry chili pepper together with its soaking liquid. Grill the bacon rashers and cook the rice while the peas are cooking.

When the black-eyed peas are tender, drain them, reserving 10 cl (3½ fl oz) of the cooking liquor. Mix together the peas, bacon matchsticks, onion mixture, rice and vinegar—this should be done with a delicate touch to avoid mashing the peas—use a chopstick or the handle of a wooden spoon. Add salt and black pepper, if necessary. Butter a casserole and turn the mixture into it. Dribble over it the reserved cooking liquor, lay the grilled bacon slices on top, and bake in an oven preheated to 180°C (350°F or Mark 4) for about 20 minutes. Sprinkle with parsley and serve with a green salad.

MIRIAM UNGERER
GOOD CHEAP FOOD

Boston Baked Beans

To serve 6 to 8

600 g	dried haricot or kidney beans, soaked overnight and drained	1¼ lb
75 g	brown sugar	2½ oz
12.5 cl	molasses	4 fl oz
2 tsp	dry mustard	2 tsp
2 tsp	salt	2 tsp
1	medium-sized onion	1
175 g	salt pork or green bacon, cut into 3 pieces	6 oz

Put the beans in a saucepan with cold water to cover. Bring quickly to the boil. Drain the water from the beans, saving the liquid. Put the beans in a 1.5 litre (2½ pint) bean pot or deep casserole. Stir in the brown sugar, molasses, mustard and salt. Poke the onion down into the centre. Stick two pieces of the pork down into the beans and place the third piece on top. Add enough of the reserved liquid to cover the beans. Bake, covered, all day, usually 7 to 8 hours, at 140°C (275°F or Mark 1). Check occasionally to be sure the beans are still moist, adding more of the reserved liquid if necessary. Uncover the pot for the last hour of cooking. Remove the onion before serving the beans.

CHARLOTTE TURGEON AND FREDERIC A. BIRMINGHAM
THE SATURDAY EVENING POST ALL AMERICAN COOKBOOK

Brazilian Black Bean Stew

Feijoada Completa

Some beans need pre-cooking to destroy toxins: see page 78.

Brazil is the biggest producer of beans in the world. The *feijão* or black bean is the main ingredient in the national dish, *feijoada completa*. Jerked beef, also known as *carne seca* and *charqui*, is sun-dried salted beef and should be used if possible; otherwise, use salt beef. Manioc flour (*farinha*) is tradi-

tionally served on the side with this dish so each diner can sprinkle his helping with it. Plain boiled or Spanish rice is usually served as an accompaniment.

To serve 8 to 10

500 g	black beans, soaked overnight and drained	1 lb
350 g	jerked beef, soaked overnight and drained, parboiled for 5 minutes, drained again and cooled	12 oz
250 g	smoked boiling sausage	8 oz
250 g	smoked pork	8 oz
125 g	smoked tongue	4 oz
125 g	lean bacon	4 oz
1	pig's trotter, blanched and scraped	1
1	pig's ear	1
1	pig's tail	1
	Chili sauce	
2 to 3	small red chili peppers, seeded and chopped or ½ teaspoon cayenne pepper	2 to 3
2 tbsp	oil	2 tbsp
1	onion, chopped	1
1	spring onion, chopped	1
60 g	sausage-meat	2 oz
1	garlic clove, finely chopped	1

Put all of the meat into a pan, cover with tepid water and bring slowly to boiling point. Simmer for about 1½ hours until nearly tender. Put the beans into a separate pan, cover with water and bring to the boil. Cover and simmer for about 1½ hours, until tender. Then put the meat and beans together and cook for a further 45 minutes, or until the meat is very tender and the beans soft enough to mash easily.

Half an hour before the end of the cooking time heat the oil in a frying pan and make the chili sauce, slowly fry the onion and spring onion with the sausage-meat until they begin to brown. Then add the garlic and chili peppers or cayenne pepper. Stir and let the mixture brown thoroughly. Then add 150 g (5 oz) of beans from the pot and partially mash them with a wooden spoon. Add about 30 cl (½ pint) of the bean and meat cooking liquid and stir and simmer until the mixture is reduced to a sauce. Add this sauce to the meat and beans and simmer until everything is well blended.

To serve, remove the meats from the pot, slice them and arrange them on a large dish. Traditionally, the tongue should be in the centre. Moisten the meats with some of the beans and liquid from the pot. The rest of the beans and liquid are served on the side.

CORA, ROSE AND BOB BROWN
THE SOUTH AMERICAN COOK BOOK

Standard Preparations

Meat Stock

This general-purpose strong stock will keep for up to a week if refrigerated and brought to the boil every two days.

To make about 3 litres (5 pints) stock		
1 kg	shin or leg of beef	2 lb
1 kg	shin of veal, including meaty veal knuckle	2 lb
1 kg	chicken backs, necks, feet and wing tips	2 lb
About 5 litres	water	About 9 pints
1	bouquet garni, including leek and celery	1
1	garlic head	1
2	medium-sized onions, 1 stuck with 2 cloves	2
4	large carrots	4
	salt	

Place a round metal pastry cutter or trivet in the bottom of a large stock-pot to prevent the ingredients from sticking. Fit all the meat, bones and chicken pieces into the pot and add water to cover by about 5 cm (2 inches). Bring slowly to the boil and, with a slotted spoon, skim off the scum that rises. Keep skimming, occasionally adding a glass of cold water, until no more scum rises—after about 10 to 15 minutes. Add the bouquet garni, garlic, onions, carrots and salt, and skim once more as the liquid returns to the boil. Reduce the heat to very low, cover the pot with the lid ajar and simmer for 4 to 5 hours, skimming at intervals. If the meat is to be eaten, remove the veal after 1½ hours, the beef after 3 hours.

Ladle the stock into a colander lined with dampened muslin placed over a large bowl. Leave the strained stock to cool completely, then remove the last traces of fat from the surface with a skimmer and a paper towel; if the stock has been refrigerated to cool, lift off the solidified fat with a knife.

Veal stock: Omit the beef, beef bones and chicken pieces and substitute about 2 kg (4 lb) of meaty veal trimmings (neck, shank or rib tips). For a richer, more gelatinous stock, you can add a calf's foot, cleaned, split and blanched for 5 minutes in boiling water.

Beef stock: Substitute 2 kg (4 lb) of beef tail, shank or chuck for the shin of veal and the chicken pieces, and simmer the stock for about 5 hours. A veal knuckle or calf's foot can be added to the pot if a more gelatinous stock is desired.

Chicken stock: Old hens and roosters yield the richest stock. Use about 2.5 kg (5 lb) of carcasses, necks, feet, wings, gizzards and hearts, and simmer for 2 hours.

Mutton stock: Use about 3 kg (6 to 7 lb) of mutton bones and shank and neck or scrag end, and simmer for 7 to 8 hours.

Basic White Sauce

This recipe can be used whenever béchamel sauce is called for. If the sauce is to be used to form the basis of a soufflé, omit the double cream, use half as much milk, double the quantity of flour and cook the sauce for only a few minutes after the milk has come to the boil.

To make about 45 cl (¾ pint) sauce		
30 g	butter	1 oz
2 tbsp	flour	2 tbsp
60 cl	milk	1 pint
	salt	
	pepper (optional)	
	freshly grated nutmeg (optional)	
	double cream (optional)	

Melt the butter in a heavy saucepan over a low heat. Stir in the flour to make a roux and cook gently, stirring, for 2 to 3 minutes. Pour the milk in all at once, whisking constantly to blend the mixture smoothly. Increase the heat and continue whisking while the sauce comes to the boil. Reduce the heat to very low and simmer, uncovered, for about 40 minutes, stirring occasionally to prevent the sauce from forming a skin or sticking to the bottom of the pan. Season to taste with salt and, if desired, white pepper and a pinch of nutmeg. Whisk again until the sauce is perfectly smooth. Add a little double cream if you prefer a richer sauce.

Tomato Sauce

When fresh, ripe summer tomatoes are not available, use drained canned Italian tomatoes.

An alternative method of making the sauce, without using a sieve, is to skin and seed the tomatoes before cooking them. Immerse the tomatoes in boiling water for 30 seconds; remove and skin them. Halve each tomato horizontally and scoop out the seeds. Lightly sauté a finely chopped onion and a chopped garlic clove in a little oil and butter. Add the tomatoes and cook over a brisk heat, stirring occasionally, for 10 minutes or until the tomatoes are reduced to a pulp. Season and add herbs to taste. About 30 g (1 oz) butter can be added at the end of the cooking to enrich the sauce.

To make about 30 cl (½ pint) sauce

750 g	very ripe tomatoes, quartered	1½ lb
1	bay leaf	1
1	large sprig dried thyme	1
	coarse salt	
1	onion, sliced, or 1 garlic clove, crushed (optional)	1
About 30 g	butter (optional)	About 1 oz
	freshly ground pepper	
1 to 2 tsp	sugar (optional)	1 to 2 tsp
1 tbsp	finely chopped parsley	1 tbsp
1 tbsp	basil leaves, torn into small pieces	1 tbsp

Place the tomatoes in a tinned copper or stainless steel saucepan with the bay leaf, thyme and a pinch of coarse salt. Add the onion or garlic if desired. Bring to the boil, crushing the tomatoes lightly with a wooden spoon and cook, uncovered, over a fairly brisk heat for 10 minutes or until the tomatoes have disintegrated into a thick pulp. Remove the bay leaf and thyme. Tip the tomatoes into a plastic or stainless steel sieve placed over a bowl and, using a wooden pestle, push them through the sieve. Discard the skins and seeds and return the sieved tomato pulp to the pan. Cook, uncovered, over a low heat until the sauce is reduced to the required consistency. If you like, whisk in a little butter to enrich the sauce. Taste for seasoning and sweeten with the sugar if using canned tomatoes. Sprinkle with parsley and basil.

Meat Sauce

This sauce is sometimes called a Bolognese sauce. It can be varied by the addition of such ingredients as garlic, carrots, parsley, lemon rind and stock.

To make about 60 cl (1 pint) meat sauce

250 g	leftover meat, cut into small pieces, minced beef or fresh chopped meat	8 oz
3 tbsp	olive oil	3 tbsp
1	onion, chopped	1
	salt	
1	bouquet garni or mixed herbs and bay leaf	1
20 cl	wine or water	7 fl oz
1 kg	tomatoes, skinned, seeded and chopped or puréed tomato or canned tomatoes	2 to 2½ lb

Lightly brown the meat in the oil. Add the onion and cook, stirring occasionally, until soft. Then season with salt and add the herbs. Increase the heat to high, pour in the wine or water, while stirring with a wooden spoon, and cook, stirring constantly, until the liquid has almost completely evaporated, about 3 to 4 minutes. Then add the tomatoes.

Cover the pan and simmer the sauce gently for 1 hour or so. If necessary, remove the lid towards the end of the cooking time to reduce the liquid and thicken the sauce, until the required consistency is obtained.

Pastry

This is a butter shortcrust pastry. For a softer pastry with a distinctive taste (*page 72*), substitute about 12.5 cl (4 fl oz) of olive oil for the butter and one or two eggs for some of the water. Combine all of the ingredients in a bowl and blend thoroughly with a fork until the mixture is loosely bound. Knead the dough with your knuckles, sprinkling in more flour if the dough becomes too sticky. Gather the dough into a ball, cover with a cloth and place it in the refrigerator for about 1 hour before rolling out.

To make about 750 g (1½ lb) pastry dough

400 g	flour	14 oz
2 tsp	salt	2 tsp
350 g	cold, hard butter, cut into small pieces	12 oz
About 12.5 cl	water	About 4 fl oz

Sift the flour and salt into a bowl. Add the butter. Rub the butter into the flour with your fingers (or cut the butter into the flour with two knives), until the mixture has a coarse, pebbly texture with large fragments of butter visible. Stirring lightly with a fork, add just enough water to allow you to gather the dough into a firm ball. Wrap the dough in plastic film, greaseproof paper or aluminium foil, and chill it in the refrigerator for at least 30 minutes before rolling out.

Standard Pasta Dough

Strong flour, used for bread-making, or extra-fine semolina are best to use for hand-made pasta dough although any type of wheat flour can be used. The exact proportion of flour to eggs depends on the type of flour and the size of the eggs used, but 100 g (3½ oz) flour to one egg is a good mean ratio. If preparing a smaller amount of dough, combine the ingredients in a mixing bowl.

To make 750 g (1½ lb) pasta dough

500 g	flour	1 lb
5 or 6	eggs	5 or 6
	salt	
2 to 3 tbsp	olive oil	2 to 3 tbsp

Mound the flour on a smooth work surface. Make a well in the centre of the flour and break the eggs into it. Add a generous pinch of salt and the olive oil. With one hand, gradually incorporate the flour from around the edge of the well into the eggs, stirring with your fingers to form a batter. Use the other hand to support the edge of the flour well and prevent the eggs from flowing out. Continue incorporating the flour until the batter becomes a fairly stiff but malleable paste. Gather the dough into a ball, and place it on a lightly floured surface.

Knead the dough, pressing it flat with the heel of your hand, folding it double and pressing again. If cutting pasta by hand, knead for 5 to 10 minutes or until the dough is silky and elastic; if using a pasta machine, knead by hand briefly to combine the ingredients; the machine will knead the dough thoroughly. When you have finished kneading, cover the dough with a cloth and leave it to rest for 1 hour.

Divide the dough into fist-sized portions. Roll out each portion on a lightly floured surface until you have a thin circle. The dough can now be cut into the required shapes.

Coloured Pasta Dough

The suggested amount of each colouring ingredient is given for the standard pasta dough quantities listed above. If you wish to prepare two or three different pasta colours, divide the dough and colouring ingredient quantities accordingly.

It is simpler to amalgamate the ingredients for coloured pasta dough in a mixing bowl rather than on a flat surface, particularly if using small quantities. To compensate for extra moistness when colouring with vegetables (especially spinach), you will need to add extra flour to the dough when kneading and rolling out. The technique of kneading and rolling with a pasta machine is demonstrated on page 46.

Green pasta: Parboil 250 g (8 oz) of spinach for about 2 minutes or chard for 5 minutes. Drain, rinse in cold water and squeeze the leaves as dry as possible. Purée the spinach or chard through a sieve or just chop it finely if a pasta machine is to be used. With a fork, combine the spinach or chard with the pasta dough ingredients. Knead and roll out.

Speckled green pasta: Trim, wash, pat dry and finely chop about 6 tablespoons of mixed fresh herbs—parsley, sorrel, thyme, one or two sage leaves, tarragon, lovage, marjoram, basil, dandelion, rocket, hyssop and tender savory shoots are all suitable. However, the strong herbs—thyme, sage, savory, majoram and tarragon—do not marry well with some others, so choose your herb mixture carefully. Stir the herbs into the pasta dough ingredients with a fork. Knead and roll out.

Red pasta: Boil two small, unpeeled beetroots in salted water for 40 minutes to 1 hour, or until tender. Peel and chop the beetroots, then purée them. Stir the purée into the pasta dough ingredients. Knead and roll out.

Orange pasta: Stir about 4 to 6 tablespoons of well-reduced tomato sauce (*page 166*) or puréed preserved tomatoes into the pasta dough ingredients. Knead and roll out.

Yellow pasta: Add a pinch of powdered saffron to the flour and salt for the pasta dough. Mix well. Stir in the eggs and oil. Knead and roll out.

Stiff Pasta Dough

This dough, suitable for grating or shredding, is prepared in the same way as a standard pasta dough (above), but 125 g (4 oz) extra flour for every 500 g of flour in the standard dough must be incorporated during the kneading. Continue kneading, constantly working in more flour, until you obtain a smooth dough that is as stiff as it can possibly be without crumbling. To facilitate grating, wrap the prepared dough in plastic film and place in the freezer for at least 30 minutes. Remove the dough and coarsely grate it on to a sheet of greaseproof paper. If not using the shreds immediately, flour them generously to prevent them from sticking together.

Recipe Index

English recipe titles are listed by categories such as "Barley", "Haricot Bean", "Lasagne" and "Sauce", and within those categories alphabetically. Foreign recipe titles are listed alphabetically without regard to category.

General Index/Glossary

Included in this index are definitions of many of the culinary terms used in this book: definitions are in italics. The recipes in the Anthology are listed in the Recipe Index on page 168.

Aduki beans, 13; soaking and cooking times, 78
Al dente: *Italian, literally translated as "to the tooth". Used to describe the texture of cooked pasta or vegetables, when they are firm to the bite, not too soft on the outside, and barely cooked through;* 58
Ali-Bab, 6
Allspice: *the dried berry—used whole or ground—of a member of the myrtle family. Called allspice because it has something of the aroma of clove, cinnamon and nutmeg combined;* 52
Almonds, 27
Anchovies, in seafood sauce, 57
Aromatic vegetables, 14, 21, 78, 81
Aromatics: *all substances—such as vegetables (q.v.), herbs and spices—that add aroma and flavour to food when used in cooking.*
Artichoke hearts, in paella, 28-31; in pasta pie, 72
Aubergines, 57, 71
Bacon, with beans, 82; green, with baked beans, 86; in cassoulet, 82-85; with leftover rice, 32-33
Baking, beans, 86; cassoulet, 82, 84-85; pasta dishes, 57, 62-63, 65, 71, 74-75; pastry case, 72-73; sauces for, 14
Bamboo shoots: *ivory-coloured, conical-shaped shoots of tropical bamboo; available in cans from Oriental food shops.*
Barley, 5, 6, 9; cooking, 18-19; see also Pearl barley, Pot barley
Basil, 15, 51, 59
Batter, 71; noodles, 60-61
Bay leaves, 27, 29, 52, 78, 82, 83
Bean pots, 76, 86
Beans, 5, 7, 12-13; flour, for pasta, 6; soaking and cooking, 78-79; see also individual beans
Beef, fillet, with leftover rice, 32-33; marrow, in risotto, 22-23; meat sauce, 14-15, 57; stock, 21; in stuffing, 52
Beehive dish, 57, 68-70
Beer, 6,7
Beetroot, pasta colouring, 43, 50-51
Bicarbonate of soda, 78
Biscuit cutter, 54
Black beans, 13; soaking and cooking times, 78
Black-eyed peas, 12, 13; soaking and cooking times, 78-79
Blanch: *to plunge food into boiling water for a short period. Done for a number of reasons: to remove strong flavours, such as the excess saltiness of some bacon; to soften vegetables before further cooking; to facilitate the removal of skins or shells. Another meaning is "to whiten".*
Blanched almonds: *almonds that have been peeled by blanching (q.v.).*
Boiling, pasta, 52, 58; pulses, 78-79; rice, 18-19
Borlotti beans, 13; soaking and cooking times, 78
Bouquet garni: *bunch of mixed herbs—the classic three being parsley, thyme and bay leaf—used for flavouring sauces and stews;* 78, 83
Braising, lamb for cassoulet, 82-83; meat for stuffings, 52; sweetbreads for timbale, 69
Breadcrumbs, 34-35; in cassoulet, 82, 84-85; as dressing for pasta, 57, 60-61
Broad beans, 12, 13; fresh, 7, 24-25; peeling, 13, 24; soaking and cooking times, 78
Brown rice, 8, 9; cooking, 18-19

Brown sugar, 76, 86
Buckwheat, 5, 9; cooking, 19; noodles, 10; roasted groats, 9
Burghul, 6, 8
Butter, 58, 72; in baked pasta dishes, 62-63; in couscous, 39; in lentil purée, 80-81; in pasta dough, 6, 44; in pilaff, 20-21; in polo, 24; in potato dumplings, 6; with pulses, 77, 80; in risotto, 22; in roux, 14, 68; for sautéing, 23, 27, 57, 60-61
Butter beans, 13; soaking and cooking times, 78
Butterflies, pasta shape, 11, 43, 49
Cabbage, in polenta, 40-41
Calf's lung, in soufflé, 74-75
Cannellini beans, 13; soaking and cooking times, 78
Cannelloni, 11, 65
Capelli d'angeli, 10
Caraway seeds, 39
Cardamom, 26-27
Carrots, 23, 36, 69, 78; in cassoulet, 82-85; in sauces, 14; in stock, 21
Casings, aubergines, 71; courgettes, 71; macaroni timbale, 10, 68-70; for pasta pie, 72-73
Casserole, 20, 86; earthenware, for cassoulet, 82, 84
Cassoulet, 7, 77, 82-85
Celery, 14, 21, 78
Cellophane noodles, 10
Ceps, 15
Chard, 50, 52
Cheese, 7, 17, 34-35, 56, 57, 60, 61, 62-63, 71, 74, 81; see also individual cheeses
Chelo, 24
Chick peas, 7, 12, 13, 36; soaking and cooking times, 78
Chicken, 28; baked pasta and aubergine mould, 71; in couscous, 17, 36; liver, 57, 68, 71; in mousseline forcemeat, 68, 69; stock, 21
Chiles serranos: *pickled chili peppers (q.v.), available in cans from delicatessens and speciality food stores.*
Chili peppers: *numerous varieties of small, finger-shaped hot peppers, native to tropical America and the West Indies;* 39
Chilling, pasta dough, 44-45
Chinese-style cooking, leftover rice, 32
Chinese egg noodles, 10, 66
Cinnamon, 26-27, 37
Clams, 28-31, 57
Clarified butter: *butter from which the water, milk solids and salt have been removed.*
Cloves, 26, 27, 78, 83
Cod, salt, see Salt cod
Colouring, pasta, 43, 50-51
Conchiglie, 11
Copper bowl, for beating egg whites, 74, 75
Coriander leaves, 32-33, 36-37
Corn, see Maize
Cornflour, 32
Cornmeal, 9; dumplings, 60; polenta, 40-41
Courgettes, 57; casing, 71; in couscous, 38; in pasta pie, 72
Couscous, 6, 7, 8, 36-39
Couscoussier, 36-38
Crab, with fried noodles, 66-67
Cracked wheat, 8; pilaff, 20
Cream, 14, 56, 57, 72; in marinade, 26-27; in meat sauce, 57; in mousseline forcemeat, 68-69; see also Soured cream
Croquettes, 34-35
Croûtons: *small cubes of bread fried in butter and used as garnish.*
Crust, on cassoulet, 7, 77, 82, 84-85; rice, 17, 24-25
Curd cheese, pasta filling, 43, 52, 53, 54; see also Cheese
Curry powder, 26
Deep frying, 34
Deglazing, 83-84
Diet, balanced, 7
Dill, 24-25
Doughs, 6, 43; for general purpose pasta, 44-45; grating, 44-45, 74; mixing, kneading and rolling, 44-45, 72-73; for pasta machine, 42-43, 46-47; pastry, 72-73; rolling for stuffed pasta, 53; shaping, 48-49, 53, 54-55; see also Pasta
Dried mushrooms, 14-15
Drying, boiled rice, 19
Duck, 77
Dumplings, 6, 60-61; Sardinian, 11
Durum wheat, 6, 8, 10; flour for pasta, 6, 44

Dutch brown beans, 13; soaking and cooking times, 78
Eel, 26
Egg whites, in baked pasta dishes, 62-63; in mousseline forcemeat, 68, 69; in soufflé, 74-75
Egg yolks, 52; in baked pasta dishes, 62-63, 65; in pasta dough, 6, 43; in soufflé, 74, 75
Eggs, 24, 52; in batter noodles, 60; in bean pudding, 80; binder for minced lung, 74; binder for rice, 32-33, 34-35; and flour batter, 71; hard-boiled, 71; in pasta dough, 6, 43, 44-45, 46; pasta fillings, 52, 65, 71; in pastry dough, 72; see also Egg whites, Egg yolks
Electric food processor, 50-51, 55, 69
Escoffier, Auguste, 6
Farfalle, 11
Fennel, 25, 26, 51
Field beans, 12, 13; soaking and cooking times, 78
Figures-of-eight, pasta shape, 43, 49
Filling, cannelloni, 65; pasta pie, 73; pasta roll, 64-65; pasta shapes, 53, 54, 55; ravioli, 53; rice croquettes, 34-35; for timbale, 68-70; see also Stuffings
Fines herbes: *mixture of finely chopped fresh herbs that always incorporates parsley plus one or more other herbs, such as chives, tarragon and chervil.*
Fish, 17, 28, 32, 40; in macaroni timbale, 68; pasta stuffing, 43, 52; in seafood sauce, 57; see also individual fish
Fish kettle, 64
Flageolet beans, 13; soaking and cooking times, 78
Flavouring, pasta, 43, 50-51
Flour, 6, 8; in batter noodles, 60; bean, 6, 77; in dumplings, 60; and egg batter, 71; in pasta dough, 6, 43, 44, 46, 58; in pastry dough, 72-73; in roux, 14, 68
Folding, pasta dough, 47, 48
Fontina: *hard, cooked, Italian cheese with a sweet, nutty flavour and smooth texture;* 34
Food mill, 80, 81
Forcemeat, mousseline, 57, 68-70
Foul medames, 13
French beans, 28, 30, 58-59
Frying and steaming, rice, 24-25; see also Deep frying
Fusilli, 11
Game, 7, 17, 77
Garam masala: *mixture of ground spices, usually equal parts of cinnamon, cloves, cardamoms, black cumin seeds, nutmeg and mace, and sometimes also coriander seeds and bay leaves. Available from Indian grocers.*
Garlic, 15, 28-30, 32, 39, 55, 59, 78, 79, 83-84; sausages, in cassoulet, 82-85
Gelatine, pork, 77, 82
Ghee: *Indian cooking fat; either clarified butter or made from vegetable fats. It can be bought from Indian grocers and will keep for up to one year if refrigerated.*
Ginger root, 32-33
Gluten, 44
Glutinous rice, 9
Gnocchi sardi, 11
Goose, in cassoulet, 7, 77, 82-85; preserved, 7, 82; salting, 82
Grains, 5, 7; cooking, 18-19; flour, for pasta, 6; see also individual grains
Grated pasta, 44, 45, 57; soufflé, 74-75
Gratin, 77
Grating, pasta, 44-45, 74
Greaseproof paper, 26-27, 45, 72
Green bacon: *unsmoked bacon;* with baked beans, 86; in cassoulet, 82-85
Green peas, 12, 13
Grits, 8
Groats, 8, 9
Hake, in forcemeat, 68
Ham, 7, 34-35, 52, 56; in baked pasta dishes, 62-63; with leftovers, 32-33; in pasta pie, 72; in risotto, 22-23; in soufflé, 74-75; see also Prosciutto
Haricot beans, 13, 77, 86; in cassoulet, 7, 77, 82-85; fresh, 7; soaking and cooking times, 78
Harissa sauce, 36, 37, 39
Herbs, for colouring and flavouring pasta, 43, 50-51, 57; see also individual herbs
Home-made pasta, 6, 42-51, 64; cooking time, 58; shaping, 48-49
Hominy, 9

Recipe Credits

The sources for the recipes in this volume are shown below. Page references in brackets indicate where the recipes appear in the Anthology.

Adam, Hans Karl, *Das Kochbuch aus Schwaben*. © Copyright 1976 by Verlagsteam Wolfgang Hölker. Published by Verlag Wolfgang Hölker, Münster. Translated by permission of Verlag Wolfgang Hölker (*pages 121, 152*).
Alberini, Massimo, *Cento Ricette Storiche*. Copyright Sansoni Editore, Firenze. Published by Sansoni Editore, Florence, 1974. Translated by permission of G. C. Sansoni Editore Nuova S.p.A. (*pages 126, 135*).
Albright, Nancy, *Rodale's Naturally Great Foods Cookbook*. Copyright © 1977 by Rodale Press, Inc. Published by Rodale Press, Inc., Emmaus, P.A. 18049. By permission of Rodale Press, Inc. (*page 151*).
Alston, Beth, *The Best of Natural Eating Around the World*. Copyright © 1973 by Elizabeth Alston. Published by the David McKay Company, Inc., New York. By permission of the David McKay Company, Inc. (*page 110*).
American Heritage, The Editors of, *The American Heritage Cookbook*. © 1964 American Heritage Publishing Co., Inc., New York. Published by American Heritage Publishing Co., Inc. By permission of American Heritage Publishing Co., Inc. (*page 149*).
Anderson, Beth, *Wild Rice for All Seasons Cookbook*. © 1977 Minnehaha Publishing. Published by Minnehaha Publishing, Minnesota. By permission of Beth Anderson and Minnehaha Publishing (*pages 104, 105*).
Androuet, Pierre, *La Cuisine au Fromage*. © 1978, Éditions Stock. Published by Éditions Stock, Paris. Translated by permission of Éditions Stock (*page 145*).

Artusi, Pellegrino, *La Scienza in Cucina e l'Arte di Mangiar Bene*. Copyright © 1970 Giulio Einaudi Editore S.p.A., Torino. Published by Giulio Einaudi Editore S.p.A. (*page 92*).
Aureden, Lilo, *Was Männern so Gut Schmeckt*. Copyright 1954 Paul List Verlag, München. Published by Paul List Verlag, Munich. Translated by permission of Paul List Verlag (*pages 92, 101*).
Ayrton, Elisabeth, *The Cookery of England*. Copyright © Elisabeth Ayrton, 1974. Published in 1977 by Penguin Books Ltd., London. By permission of Penguin Books Ltd. (*page 102*).
Beard, James A., *James Beard's American Cookery*. Copyright © 1972 by James A. Beard. First published by Little, Brown and Company, Boston. Published in 1974 by Hart-Davis MacGibbon Ltd., Granada Publishing Ltd., Hertfordshire. By permission of Granada Publishing Ltd. (*page 107*).
Booth, George C., *The Food and Drink of Mexico*. Copyright © 1964 by George C. Booth. Published in 1976 by Dover Publications, Inc., New York. By permission of Dover Publications, Inc. (*page 149*).
Borer, Eva Maria, *Tante Heidi's Swiss Kitchen*. English text Copyright © 1965 by Nicholas Kaye Ltd. Published by Kaye & Ward Ltd., London. Originally published as "Die Echte Schweizer Küche" by Mary Hahns Kochbuchverlag, Berlin W., 1963. By permission of Kaye & Ward Ltd. (*page 114*).
Bozzi, Ottorina Perna, *Vecchia Milano in Cucina*. © 1975 by Aldo Martello Giunti Editore S.p.A. Published by Aldo Martello Giunti Editore S.p.A. Translated by permission of Aldo Martello Giunti Editore S.p.A., Florence (*page 100*).
Brown, Cora, Rose and Bob, *The South American Cook Book*. Originally published by Doubleday, Doran & Company, Inc., in 1939. Republished by Dover Publications Inc., New York in 1971 (*page 164*).
Bugialli, Giuliano, *The Fine Art of Italian Cooking*. Copyright © 1977 by Giuliano Bugialli. Published by Times Books, a Division of Quadrangle/The New York Times Book Co., Inc., New York. By permission of Times Books, a Division of Quadrangle/The New York Times Book Co., Inc. (*pages 134, 162*).
Buonassisi, Vincenzo, *The Classic Book of Pasta*. English

translation © 1976 Macdonald and Jane's Publishers Limited. Published by Macdonald and Jane's Publishers Limited, London. Originally published as "Il Codice della Pasta" in 1973 by Rizzoli Editore, Milan. © 1973, Rizzoli Editore Milano. By permission of Macdonald and Jane's Publishers Limited (*pages 122 and 134*).
Buonassisi, Vincenzo, *Il Codice della Pasta*. © 1973, Rizzoli Editore Milano. Translated by permission of Rizzoli Editore, Milan (*page 127*).
Carnacina, Luigi and Buonassisi, Vincenzo, *Il Libro della Polenta*. © di Aldo Martello Editore, Milano. Published by Aldo Martello Editore, Milan, 1967. Translated by permission of Aldo Martello Giunti Editore S.p.A., Florence (*pages 111, 112 and 113*).
Carreras, Marie-Thérèse and Lafforgue, Georges, *Les Bonnes Recettes du Pays Catalan*. © Presses de la Renaissance, 1979. Published by Presses de la Renaissance, Paris. Translated by permission of Presses de la Renaissance (*page 93*).
Cavalcanti, Ippolito, Duca di Buonvicino, *Cucina Teorico-Pratica*. Sixth Edition. November 1849, Naples (*page 129*).
Chamberlain, Narcisse and Narcissa G., *The Chamberlain Sampler of American Cooking*. Copyright © 1961 by Hastings House, Publishers, Inc. Published by Hastings House, Publishers, Inc., New York. By permission of Hastings House, Publishers, Inc. (*page 110*).
Chanot-Bullier, C., *Vieilles Recettes de Cuisine Provençale*. Published by Tacussel, Éditeur, Marseilles. Translated by permission of Tacussel, Éditeur (*pages 142, 143 and 157*).
Chantiles, Vilma Liacouras, *The Food of Greece*. Copyright © 1975 by Vilma Liacouras Chantiles. Published by Atheneum, New York in 1975. By permission of Vilma Liacouras Chantiles (*pages 97, 103*).
Cheng, S. K. (Editor), *Shanghai Restaurant Chinese Cookery Book*. Published in 1936 by the Proprietors of The Shanghai Restaurant, London (*page 123*).
Correnti, Pino, *Il Libro d'Oro della Cucina e dei Vini di Sicilia*. © Copyright 1976 Ugo Mursia Editore. Published by Ugo

Mursia Editore, Milan. Translated by permission of Ugo Mursia Editore (*pages 119, 120 and 128*).
Cox, J., Stevens (Editor), *Guernsey Dishes of Bygone Days.* © James and Gregory Stevens Cox, The Toucan Press, Guernsey, 1974. Published by The Toucan Press, Guernsey. By permission of Gregory Stevens Cox, The Toucan Press (*page 158*).
Crossley, Rosemary, *The Dole Cookbook.* Copyright © 1978 by Rosemary Crossley and Prudence Borthwick. Published by Outback Press, Melbourne. By permission of Outback Press (*page 115*).
David, Elizabeth, *Italian Food.* Copyright © Elizabeth David 1954, 1963, 1969. Published by Penguin Books Ltd., London. By permission of Penguin Books Ltd. (*pages 94, 99*).
Davidson, Alan, *Mediterranean Seafood.* Copyright © Alan Davidson, 1972. Published by Penguin Books Ltd., London. By permission of Penguin Books Ltd. (*page 130*).
Davidson, Alan, *North Atlantic Seafood.* Copyright © Alan Davidson, 1979. Published by Macmillan London Ltd. and Penguin Books Ltd., London. By permission of Penguin Books Ltd. (*page 102*).
Davidson, Alan, *Seafood of South-East Asia.* © Alan Davidson 1976. First published by the author in 1976 at World's End, Chelsea, London. Also published by Macmillan London Ltd. in 1978. By permission of Alan Davidson (*page 99*).
Day, Irene, F., *Kitchen in the Kasbah.* Copyright © 1975 by Irene F. Day. Published in 1976 by André Deutsch Limited, London. By permission of André Deutsch Limited (*pages 106, 161*).
Devi, E., Maheswari, *Handy Rice Recipes.* © Copyright MPH Publications Sdn Bhd 1971. Published by MPH Publications Sdn Bhd, Singapore, 1971. By permission of MPH Publications Sdn Bhd (*page 90*).
Disslowa, Maria, *Jak Gotowac.* Published by Instytut Gospodarstwa Domowego, Wydawnictwo Rybitwa. Translated by permission of Agencja Autorska, Warsaw, for the author (*pages 127, 138 and 143*).
Donati, Stella, *Le Famose Economiche Ricette di Petronilla.* © Casa Editrice Sonzogno 1974. Published by Casa Editrice Sonzogno S.p.A., Milan, 1974. Translated by permission of Casa Editrice Sonzogno S.p.A. (*page 93*).
Dubois, Urbain, *École des Cuisinières.* Sixth edition. Published by E. Dentu, Paris, 1887 (*page 133*).
Duff, Gail, *Gail Duff's Vegetarian Cookbook.* © Gail Duff 1978. Published in 1978 by Macmillan London Limited. By permission of Macmillan, London and Basingstoke (*pages 147, 153, 154 and 162*).
Engle, Fannie and Blair, Gertrude, *The Jewish Festival Cookbook.* Copyright 1954 by Fannie Engle and Gertrude Blair. Published by the David McKay Company, Inc., New York. By permission of the David McKay Company, Inc. (*pages 110, 116*).
Eren, Neşet, *The Art of Turkish Cooking.* Copyright © 1969 by Neşet Eren. Published by Doubleday & Company, Inc., Garden City, New York. By permission of Neşet Eren (*page 108*).
Feng, Doreen Yen Hung, *The Joy of Chinese Cooking.* First published by Faber and Faber Limited, London in 1952. By permission of Faber and Faber Limited (*page 100*).
Francesconi, Jeanne Caròla, *La Cucina Napoletana.* Copyright 1965 by Casa Editrice Fausto Fiorentino, Napoli. Published by Casa Editrice Fausto Fiorentino, Naples, 1965. Translated by permission of Jeanne Caròla Francesconi (*pages 118, 119*).
Georgievsky, N. I., Melman, M. E., Shadura, E. A., Shemjakinsky, A. S., *Ukrainian Cuisine.* © English translation, Technika Publishers, 1975. Published by Technika Publishers, Kiev, 1975. By permission of VAAP, The Copyright Agency of the USSR, Moscow (*pages 108, 140*).
Gosetti, Fernanda, *In Cucina con Fernanda Gosetti.* © 1978 Fabbri Editori S.p.A., Milano. Published by Fabbri Editori S.p.A., Milan. Translated by permission of Fabbri Editori S.p.A. (*pages 117, 131, 137 and 140*).
Gouffé, Jules, *Le Livre de Cuisine.* Published by Librairie Hachette, Paris, 1867 (*page 149*).
Green, Karen, *The Great International Noodle Experience.* Copyright © 1977 by Karen Green. Published by Atheneum Publishers, New York, 1977. By permission of Jane Jordan Browne, agent for the author (*page 131*).
Grigson, Jane, *English Food.* Copyright © Jane Grigson, 1974. First published by Macmillan 1974. Published by Penguin Books 1977. By permission of Macmillan, London and Basingstoke (*page 157*).
Guasch, Juan Castelló, *Bon Profit! El Libro de la Cocina Ibicenca.* Published in 1967 by Imprenta Alfa, Palma, Majorca. Translated by permission of Juan Castelló Guasch (*page 97*).
Guinaudeau-Franc, Zette, *Les Secrets des Fermes en Périgord Noir.* © 1978, Éditions Serg, Paris. Published by Éditions Serg, Paris. Translated by permission of Madame Guinaudeau (*pages 144, 148*).
Hawliczkowa, Helena, *Kuchnia Polska.* (Editor: Maria Librowska.) Published by Panstwowe Wydawnictwo Ekonomiczne, Warsaw, 1976. Translated by permission of Agencja Autorska, for the author (*pages 107, 109*).
Hazelton, Nika, *The Regional Italian Kitchen.* Copyright © 1978 by Nika Hazelton. Published by M. Evans and Company, Inc., New York. By permission of Curtis Brown Ltd., New York (*page 104*).
Historia Hors Série, No. 42: Les Français à Table (bi-monthly review). © Librairie Jules Tallandier, 1975. Published by Librairie Jules Tallandier, Paris. Translated by permission of Librairie Jules Tallandier (*pages 159, 161*).
Holkar, Shivaji Rao and Shalini Devi, *Cooking of the Maharajas.* Copyright © 1975 by Shivaji Rao Holkar and Shalini Devi Holkar. First published in 1975 by The Viking Press, Inc., New York. By permission of Shivaji Rao Holkar (*page 106*).
Iny, Daisy, *The Best of Baghdad Cooking.* Copyright © 1976 by Daisy Iny. Published by Saturday Review Press/E. P. Dutton & Co., Inc., New York. By permission of Manuscripts Unlimited, New York for the author (*page 98*).
Isnard, Léon, *La Cuisine Française et Africaine.* © Albin Michel, 1949. Published by Éditions Albin Michel, Paris. Translated by permission of Éditions Albin Michel (*page 146*).
Jarratt, Enrica and Vernon, *The Complete Book of Pasta.* © 1969 by Enrica and Vernon Jarratt. Published by Michael Joseph Ltd., London, 1975. English translation © 1975 by Vernon Jarratt. By permission of Michael Joseph Ltd. (*page 122*).
Junior League of New Orleans, The, *The Plantation Cookbook.* Copyright © 1972 by The Junior League of New Orleans, Inc. Published by Doubleday & Company, Inc., Garden City, New York. By permission of Doubleday & Company, Inc. (*page 92*).
Kagawa, Aya, *Japanese Cookbook.* © 1967 by Japan Travel Bureau, Inc. Published by Japan Travel Bureau, Inc., Publishing Division, Tokyo. By permission of Japan Travel Bureau, Inc. (*page 88*).
Karsenty, Irène and Lucienne, *La Cuisine Pied-Noir.* (Cuisines du Terroir.) © 1974, by Éditions Denoël, Paris. Published by Éditions Denoël. Translated by permission of Éditions Denoël (*pages 154, 158 and 163*).
Kennedy, Diana, *Cuisines of Mexico.* Copyright © 1972 by Diana Kennedy. Published by Harper & Row, Publishers, Inc., New York. By permission of Harper & Row, Publishers, Inc. (*pages 150, 156*).
Khayat, Marie Karam and Keatinge, Margaret Clark, *Food from the Arab World.* © Marie Karam Khayat and Margaret Clark Keatinge 1959. Published in 1959, 1961, 1965 by Khayats, Beirut. By permission of S.A. Les Éditions Khayat (EDIK), Paris (*page 109*).
Kouki, M., *Poissons Méditerranéens.* © by Mohamed Kouki. Published in collaboration with L'Office National des Pêches, Tunis, 1970. Translated by permission of Mohamed Kouki (*page 91*).
Kouki, Mohamed, *La Cuisine Tunisienne d' "Ommok Sannafa".* © by Mohamed Kouki. Published in collaboration with L'Office National des Pêches, Tunis, 1974. Translated by permission of Mohamed Kouki (*page 115*).
Kulinarische Gerichte: Zu Gast bei Freunden, Copyright Verlag für die Frau DDR, Leipzig. Published by Verlag für die Frau, Leipzig and Verlag MIR, Moscow, 1977. Translated by permission of VAAP, The Copyright Agency of the USSR, Moscow (*page 151*).
Kürtz, Jutta, *Das Kochbuch aus Schleswig-Holstein.* © Copyright, 1976 by Verlagsteam Wolfgang Hölker. Published by Verlag Wolfgang Hölker, Münster. Translated by permission of Verlag Wolfgang Hölker (*page 107*).
Laasri, Ahmed, *240 Recettes de Cuisine Marocaine.* © 1978, Jacques Grancher, Éditeur. Published by Jacques Grancher, Éditeur, Paris. Translated by permission of Jacques Grancher, Éditeur (*pages 100, 146 and 156*).
Lagattolla, Franco, *The Recipes that Made a Million.* © Franco Lagattolla 1978. Published by Orbis Publishing Limited, London. By permission of Orbis Publishing Limited (*pages 128, 139*).
Lang, George, *The Cuisine of Hungary.* Copyright © 1971 by George Lang. Published by Atheneum Publishers, Inc., New York. By permission of Atheneum Publishers, Inc. (*page 133*).
Lecourt, H., *La Cuisine Chinoise.* © 1968 by Éditions Robert Laffont. Published by Éditions Robert Laffont, Paris. Translated by permission of Éditions Robert Laffont (*page 124*).
Lin, Florence, *Florence Lin's Chinese Vegetarian Cookbook.* Copyright © 1976 Florence Lin. Published by Hawthorn Books, Inc., New York. By permission of John Schaffner, Literary Agent, New York (*page 123*).
Lopez, Candido, *El Libro de Oro de la Gastronomia.* © 1979 by Candido Lopez. Published by Plaza & Janes S.A., Barcelona. Translated by permission of Plaza & Janes S.A. (*page 90*).
Manual de Cocina. Published by Editorial Almena, Instituto del Bienestar, Ministerio de Cultura, Madrid, 1965. Translated by permission of Editorial Almena, Instituto del Bienestar, Ministerio de Cultura (*page 103*).
Maria, Jack Santa, *Indian Vegetarian Cookery.* © Jack Santa Maria 1973. Published by Rider and Company, an imprint of the Hutchinson Publishing Group, London. By permission of the Hutchinson Publishing Group (*pages 88, 89, 150 and 153*).
Martini, Ann (Editor), *Pasta & Pizza.* English translation Copyright © 1977 by Mondadori, Milan. Published by St. Martin's Press, New York, 1977. Originally published in Italian under the title "Pasta & Pizza" Copyright © 1974 Arnoldo Mondadori Editore. By permission of Angus and Robertson (UK.) Ltd., London (*pages 116, 124, 126 and 136*).
Marty, Albin, *Fourmiguetto: Souvenirs, Contes et Recettes du Languedoc.* Published by Éditions CREER, Nonette, 1978. Translated by permission of Éditions CREER (*pages 129, 155*).
Mascarelli, Benoît, *La Table en Provence & sur la Côte d'Azur.* Published by Jacques Haumont, Paris, 1947 (*page 155*).
Mazda, Maideh, *In a Persian Kitchen.* Copyright in Japan, 1960 by Charles E. Tuttle Co., Inc. Published by Charles E. Tuttle Co., Inc., Tokyo, 1960, 1975. By permission of Charles E. Tuttle Co., Inc. (*page 140*).
Mitchell, Alice Miller (Editor), *Oriental Cookbook.* Copyright, 1954, by Alice Miller Mitchell. Published by Rand McNally & Company, New York. By permission of Rand McNally & Company (*pages 138, 154*).
Mondo in Cucina, Il: Minestre, Zuppe, Riso. Copyright © 1969, 1971 by Time Inc. Jointly published by Sansoni/Time-Life (*page 101*).
Nignon, M. Édouard (Editor), *Le Livre de Cuisine de L'Ouest-Éclair.* Published in 1941 by l'Ouest-Éclair, Rennes. Translated by permission of Société d'Éditions Ouest-France, Rennes (*pages 147, 159*).
Olney, Richard, *The French Menu Cookbook.* Copyright © 1970 by Richard Olney. Published by Simon and Schuster, New York. By permission of John Schaffner, Literary Agent, New York (*pages 132, 160*).
Olney, Richard, *Simple French Food.* Copyright © 1974 by Richard Olney. Published by Atheneum Publishers, New York. By permission of Jill Norman Ltd., London (*page 118*).
Paddleford, Clementine, *The Best in American Cooking.* Copyright © 1960 Clementine Paddleford. Copyright © 1970 Chase Manhattan Bank, Executors of the Estate of Clementine Paddleford. Published by Charles Scribner's Sons, New York. By permission of Charles Scribner's Sons (*page 148*).
Paradissis, Chrissa, *The Best Book of Greek Cookery.* Copyright © 1976 P. Efstathiadis & Sons. Published by Efstathiadis Group, Athens, 1976. By permission of Efstathiadis Group (*page 130*).
Petrov, Dr. L., Djelepov, Dr. N., Iordanov, Dr. E., Uzunova, S., *Bulgarska Nazionalna Kuchniya.* Copyright © by the authors, 1978, c/o Jusautor, Sofia. Published by Zemizdat, Sofia, 1978. Translated by permission of Jusautor Copyright Agency (*pages 113, 121*).
Picture Cook Book. Copyright © 1958, 1968 by Time Inc. Published by Time-Life Books, Alexandria (*pages 108, 109*).
Puga Y Parga, Manuel M. (Picadillo), *La Cocina Práctica.* Fifth edition. Privately published in La Coruña (*page 150*).

Raris, F. and T., *Les Champignons, Connaissance et Gastronomie.* © Librairie Larousse, 1974, for French language rights. Published by Librairie Larousse, Paris. Originally published by Fratelli Fabbri Editori, Milan as ''I Funghi, Cercarli, Conoscerli, Cucinarli''. © 1973 Fratelli Fabbri Editori, Milano. Translated by permission of Fratelli Fabbri Editori (*page 94*).

Reboul J. B., *La Cuisinière Provençale.* First published by Tacussel, Éditeur, Marseilles. Translated by permission of Tacussel, Éditeur (*page 138*).

Ripoll, Luis, *Cocina de las Baleares.* © by Luis Ripoll. Published in Majorca, 1974. Translated by permission of Luis Ripoll (*page 151*).

Roden, Claudia, *A Book of Middle Eastern Food.* Copyright © Claudia Roden, 1968. First published by Thomas Nelson 1968. Published by Penguin Books 1970. By permission of Claudia Roden (*pages 148, 152*).

Rossi, Emanuele, *La Vera Cuciniera Genovese.* Published by Casa Editrice Bietti, Milan, 1973. Translated by permission of Casa Editrice Bietti, Rome (*page 136*).

Scappi, Bartolomeo, *Opera dell'Arte del Cucinare.* Published in Venice, 1610 by Presso Alessandro Vecchi (*page 141*).

Schapira, Christiane, *La Cuisine Corse.* © Solar, 1979. Published by Solar, Paris. Translated by permission of Solar (*pages 114, 139*).

Schrecker, Ellen and John, *Mrs. Chiang's Szechwan Cookbook.* Copyright © 1976 by Chiang Jung-Feng and Ellen Schrecker. Published by Harper & Row, Publishers, Inc., New York. By permission of Deborah Rogers Ltd., Literary Agency, London (*page 125*).

Schuler, Elizabeth, *Mein Kochbuch.* © Copyright 1948 by Schuler-Verlag, Stuttgart-N, Lenzhalde 28. Published by Schuler Verlagsgesellschaft. Translated by permission of Schuler Verlagsgesellschaft (*pages 147, 152*).

Serra, Victoria, *Tia Victoria's Spanish Kitchen.* English text copyright © Elizabeth Gili, 1963. Published by Kaye & Ward Ltd., London, 1963. Translated by Elizabeth Gili from the original Spanish entitled ''Sabores: Cocina del Hogar'' by Victoria Serra Suñol. By permission of Kaye & Ward Ltd. (*pages 91, 124*).

Singh, Dharamjit, *Indian Cookery.* Copyright © Dharamjit Singh, 1970. Published by Penguin Books Ltd., London. By permission of Penguin Books Ltd. (*page 89*).

Smires, Latifa Bennani, *La Cuisine Marocaine.* © Les Éditions Alpha G.E.A.M., Casablanca. Published by Les Éditions Alpha G.E.A.M. 1974. Translated by permission of Société d'Édition et de Diffusion AL MADARISS, Casablanca (*page 114*).

Spanko, Vojtech, *Slovenská Kuchárka.* © Obzor, Bratislava 1968. Published by Obzor, 1968. Translated by permission of LITA, Slovak Literary Agency, Prague (*pages 116, 145*).

Stan, Anisoara, *The Romanian Cookbook.* Copyright © 1951 by Anisoara Stan. Published by Citadel Press, Inc., New York, 1969. By permission of Citadel Press, Inc., Secaucus, N.J. (*page 111*).

Tiano, Myrette, *Pâtes et Riz.* © Solar 1978. Published by Solar, Paris. Translated by permission of Solar (*pages 95, 117, 119*).

Turgeon, Charlotte and Birmingham, Frederic A., *The Saturday Evening Post All American Cookbook.* Copyright © 1976 by The Curtis Publishing Company, U.S.A. First published in Great Britain in 1977 by Elm Tree Books Ltd., Hamish Hamilton Ltd., London. By permission of Hamish Hamilton Ltd. (*page 164*).

Tzabar, Naomi and Shimon, *Yemenite & Sabra Cookery.* Copyright © 1963, 1966, 1974 by SADAN Publishing House Ltd. Published by SADAN Publishing House Ltd., Tel-Aviv. By permission of SADAN Publishing House Ltd. (*page 157*).

Ungerer, Miriam, *Good Cheap Food.* Copyright © 1973 by Miriam Ungerer. First published by The Viking Press, Inc., New York, 1973. By permission of John Schaffner, Literary Agent, New York (*pages 162, 163*).

Valente, Maria Odette Cortes, *Cozinha Regional Portuguesa.* Published by Livraria Almedina, Coimbra, 1973. Translated by permission of Livraria Almedina (*page 93*).

Venesz, József, *Hungarian Cuisine.* © by Mrs József Venesz. Published by Corvina Press, Budapest. By permission of Artis-jus Literary Agency, Budapest, for Mrs József Venesz (*pages 144, 145*).

Vidal, Coloma Abrinas, *Cocina Selecta Mallorquina.* Published in 1975 by Imprenta Roig, Campos, Majorca (*page 155*).

Volpicelli, Luigi and Freda, Secondino, *L'Antiartusi: 1,000 Ricette.* © 1978 Pan Editrice, Milano. Published by Pan Editrice, Milan. Translated by permission of Pan Editrice (*pages 95, 102, 120 and 125*).

Voltz, Jeanne A., *The Flavor of the South.* Copyright © 1977 by Jeanne A. Voltz. Published by Doubleday & Company, Inc., Garden City, New York, 1977. By permission of Doubleday & Company, Inc. (*pages 110, 143 and 153*).

Warren, Janet, *A Feast of Scotland.* Copyright © 1979 by Janet Warren. Published by Hodder & Stoughton Ltd., London. By permission of Hodder & Stoughton Ltd. (*page 142*).

White, Florence (Editor), *Good Things in England.* Published by arrangement with Jonathan Cape Ltd., 1968 by The Cookery Book Club, London. By permission of Jonathan Cape Ltd. (*page 108*).

Willinsky, Grete, *Kochbuch der Büchergilde.* © Büchergilde Gutenberg, Frankfurt am Main 1958. Published by Büchergilde Gutenberg, 1967. Translated by permission of Büchergilde Gutenberg (*pages 126, 146 and 157*).

Wilson, José (Editor), *House and Garden's New Cookbook.* Copyright © 1967 by The Condé Nast Publications Inc. Published by The Condé Nast Publications Inc., New York. By permission of The Condé Nast Publications Inc. (*pages 105, 129*).

Wilson, José (Editor), *House and Garden's Party Menu Cookbook.* Copyright © 1973 by The Condé Nast Publications Inc. Published by The Condé Nast Publications Inc., New York. By permission of The Condé Nast Publications Inc. (*pages 88, 98 and 105*).

Zuliani, Mariù Salvatori de, *La Cucina di Versilia e Garfagnana.* Copyright © by Franco Angeli Editore, Milano. Published in 1969 by Franco Angeli Editore, Milan. Translated by permission of Franco Angeli Editore (*pages 96, 122 and 142*).

Acknowledgements and Picture Credits

The Editors of this book are particularly indebted to Gail Duff, Maidstone, Kent; and Ann O'Sullivan, Mallorca.

They also wish to thank the following: Caroline Baum, York; Eliott Burgess, Mallorca; Josephine Christian, Bath; Emma Codrington, Richmond, Surrey; Clare Coope, London; Nona Coxhead, London; Jennifer Davidson, London; Fiona Duncan, London; Mimi Errington, London; Geoffrey Grigson, Swindon; Maggie Heinz, London; Marion Hunter, Sutton, Surrey; Brenda Jayes, London; Maria Johnson, Hatfield; Alison Kerr, Cambridgeshire; Rosemary Klein, London; John Lamb, London; Lina Stores, Brewer Street, London; Dr. Alan Long, The Vegetarian Society, London; Pippa Millard, London; Mrs. Miller, Royal Horticultural Society, Wisley; Michael Moulds, London; Dilys Naylor, Kingston-upon-Thames, Surrey; Jo Oxley, Morden, Surrey; G. Parmigiani, United Preservers Ltd., Park Royal, London; Craig Sams, Harmony Foods, London; Michael Schwab, London; Anne Stephenson, London; Fiona Tillett, London; Pat Tookey, London.

Photographs by Tom Belshaw: 18, 19—top, bottom left and centre, 20—bottom, 21—bottom left and centre, 24, 25, 26—bottom, 27, 28—top, 32 to 35, 42, 44, 45—top right, bottom, 46, 47, 48—top, 49—top left and right, bottom centre and right, 52, 53, 54—top, 59—top left, 60—bottom, 61—bottom, 63—top, 65—top right, middle right, bottom right, 76, 80, 81—bottom, 82 to 85, 86—bottom.

Other photographs (alphabetically): John Cook: 14—top, 28—bottom, 29 to 31, 48—bottom, 49—top centre and bottom left, 55—bottom, 58—top, 59—top centre, 60—top, 61—top. David Davies: 15—top, 40, 41, 58—bottom, 59—top right and bottom. Alan Duns: cover, 4, 12, 13, 19—bottom right, 45—top left and centre, 50, 51, 54—top, 55—top, 56, 64, 65—top left and centre and bottom left, 66, 67, 72 to 74, 75—bottom, 78, 79, 81—top. John Elliott: 8 to 11, 14—bottom, 15—bottom, 16, 20—top, 21—top and bottom right, 22, 23, 26—top, 62, 63—bottom, 68 to 71, 75—top, 86—top and left. Edmund Goldspink: 36 to 39. Louis Klein: 2.

All line cuts from Mary Evans Picture Library and private sources.

Colour separations by Gilchrist Ltd.—Leeds, England
Typesetting by Camden Typesetters—London, England
Printed and bound by Brepols S.A.—Turnhout, Belgium.